Steeped in BLOOD

The *Life* *and* *Times* *of* *a* FORENSIC SCIENTIST

DAVID KLATZOW

As told to SYLVIA WALKER

Published by Zebra Press
an imprint of Random House Struik (Pty) Ltd
Company Reg. No. 1966/003153/07
Wembley Square, First Floor, Solan Road, Gardens, Cape Town, 8001
PO Box 1144, Cape Town, 8000, South Africa

www.zebrapress.co.za

First published 2010
Reprinted in 2010 (three times), 2011 (twice) and 2012

7 9 10 8

PUBLISHER: Marlene Fryer
MANAGING EDITOR: Ronel Richter-Herbert
EDITOR: Beth Housdon
PROOFREADER: Ronel Richter-Herbert
COVER DESIGNER: Michiel Botha
TEXT DESIGNER: Sean Robertson
TYPESETTER: Monique van den Berg
PRODUCTION MANAGER: Valerie Kömmer

Set in 11.75 pt on 15.5 pt Granjon

Printed and bound by Interpak Books, Pietermaritzburg

ISBN 978 1 86872 922 7 (print)
ISBN 978 1 77022 106 2 (ePub)
ISBN 978 1 77022 107 9 (PDF)

www.imagesofafrica.co.za

IMAGES OF AFRICA
PHOTO LIBRARY

Over 50 000 unique African images available to purchase
from our image bank at www.imagesofafrica.co.za

This book is dedicated to my wife, Shelona, whose hand on the rudder of my life has resulted in a calmer course, and whose assistance throughout my professional life has enabled my success; and to my children, James and Cathryn, who are the light of my life and the joy of my existence.

CONTENTS

Foreword vii

Preface x

Author's Note xii

Abbreviations xiv

1 Setting Sail on My Voyage of Discovery 1

2 A Scholar and a Gentleman 17

3 Alcohol Is a Good Friend, Just Don't Overdo the Friendship   34

4 The 'Hired Guns' of the Insurance Industry 47

5 The Expert Who Never Was 58

6 Queensberry Rules 64

7 Kinross: A Black Day in South Africa's History 77

8 It's Sad When the State Goes Bad 84

9 A Place Called Vlakplaas 94

10 The Murder of Ashley Kriel 104

11 The Trojan Horse Massacre: Not My Finest Hour 113

12 Orders to Eliminate, Not Illuminate 119

13 The Devil Is in the Detail 128

14 Never Send the Fox to Investigate Crimes in the Hen House   134

15 Death, Drugs and Dirty Tricks 144

16 Post-Mortems: The Good, the Bad and the Totally Inept 157

17 The Mystery of Flight 295, the *Helderberg* 165

18 The Naked Truth 197

19 Till Death Us Do Part 205

20 Bent Coppers?: The Murder of Inge Lotz 216

21 Smoke and Mirrors: The Death of Brett Kebble 228

22 The Dynamic Investment That Shrank 240

23 Too Good to Be True 250

24 Creativity Knows No Bounds 258

25 Opinions, Lies and Simple Truth 264

26 Condemned to Repeat History 272

Appendices 279

Bibliography 305

Index 308

Here's freedom to him who would speak,
Here's freedom to him who would write;
For there's none ever feared that the truth should be heard,
Save him whom the truth would indict!

– ROBERT BURNS

Nullius addictus iurare in verba magistri.
Quo me cunque rapit tempestas, deferor hospes
I am not bound to swear allegiance to the words of
any master. Where the storm carries me, I go ashore
and make myself at home.   – HORACE

FOREWORD

Justice often needs scientists to help her resolve vexed questions that arise when the truth has to be established. The mathematician, physicist, pathologist, chemist and other forensic experts in their disciplines are essential witnesses in proving where the truth lies. Often they are able to disprove the exculpatory versions put up by wrongdoers. Their evidence may lead to the conviction or the acquittal of an accused or the upholding or dismissing of a claim by a plaintiff in civil proceedings. Often the cause of an unnatural death has to be established.

Dr David Klatzow is pre-eminent among our few forensic experts. His academic qualifications and his experience of more than twenty-five years are evident in his numerous appearances as a witness in many cases, and as an advisor to both plaintiffs and defendants.

David and the late Dr Jonathan Gluckman, the country's leading pathologist, were readily available to us in the Legal Resources Centre during the apartheid years and to the legal profession as a whole. Their evidence was vital to rebut the fairy tales made up by interrogators who tortured detainees, the policemen who shot dead peaceful demonstrators and the district surgeons who distorted their findings in post-mortem reports in order to avoid responsibility for the unnatural deaths.

On one occasion, five policemen testified that a teenager was shot with fine birdshot whilst he was part of a riotous assembly. The teenager denied it and maintained that he was standing with a friend at his grandmother's gate. The shooting had rendered him a quadriplegic. David Klatzow provided expert evidence to disprove the state case, as a result of which the judge disbelieved the policemen. The youth was awarded a high amount of damages, which would not have happened if the expert evidence had not been led.

Judge H.C. Nicholas had been a teacher of English before he became an advocate and thereafter a judge. He expected a high standard from counsel. After judgment, he paid tribute to David Klatzow not only for the clear and convincing evidence he had given, but also praised his eloquent use of the English language.

Some cross-examiners tend to undervalue expert evidence. They like to tell of the one crucial question Norman Birkett KC asked in the 'Burning Car' case in the 1930s – 'What is the co-efficient of the expansion of brass?'

The expert witness conceded that he did not know. This was a devastating answer for the defence. The jury rejected the expert witness's finding that the fire may not have been a deliberate act, and as a result the accused was convicted and sentenced to death. Birkett was subsequently criticised for having put an unfair question, but the expert witness should have asked Birkett, 'Can you tell me the precise proportions of the constituents [copper and zinc] before I answer your question, Mr Birkett?' Birkett was not likely to have known, and the jury's verdict may have been different.

In this book, the author relates numerous examples of how conflicts of fact were resolved in the cases in which he testified. In most of these, his opinions were accepted. The judges complimented him on his expertise and his readiness to reconsider his opinion when new information became available during the course of a trial.

David Klatzow challenged sloppy investigation, drew attention to the lack of care in safeguarding a crime scene and exposed suspected cover-ups of serious crimes.

His scientific knowledge and investigative talents were used to good effect in investigating the tragic crash of the *Helderberg*, a case which has never been fully resolved. He courageously challenges the findings of Judge Cecil Margo and accuses the apartheid government of a cover-up.

The book contains most useful material for all who are interested in the administration of justice. No trial lawyer, senior investigating officer or potential expert witness can afford to ignore *Steeped in Blood*.

ADV GEORGE BIZOS SC
CONSTITUTIONAL LITIGATION UNIT
LEGAL RESOURCES CENTRE

PREFACE

It is difficult to tell one's life story. All too often, it can be seen as either an offensive and malicious criticism of past enemies, or an attempt to portray one's life in a more favourable light than is actually the case. My intention in this book is neither. I would like to record a story in stark relief, with the successes unadorned and the failures undiluted. Objectivity is, at best, a difficult thing to achieve. With the excesses and atrocities of the apartheid regime still so fresh in my memory, a difficult task is made doubly so – I ask for indulgence where I stray from the ideal.

For some years now, I have appeared as a guest on radio shows that have been broadcast locally and nationally. In these talks I have attempted to tell a story of what occurred during a particular period in the political and historical life of South Africa. I have recounted events from my own perspective, as I can claim no wider insight into the greater scheme of past politics in this country than anyone else. I did have the incredibly good fortune, however, of being catapulted into the maelstrom of forensic science practice in 1984, during a very turbulent period of our history. By virtue of the fact that there was no one else, I became involved in some of the most high-profile and interesting cases that have passed through our courts in the past twenty-six years.

During the radio shows mentioned above, listeners have phoned in to ask me to write the story of what had happened in those mad times. This is an attempt to place on paper my experiences and the insights that they have brought. The book has been written to entertain and to inform; it makes no claim to academic rigour. It describes some of the cases that involved the criminal activities of the state and it explains the methods that I used to investigate these cases. It also discusses many of the non-political cases on which I have worked over the past two decades, including fire investigations, murders and a wide range of other forensic analyses. In many instances, the criminals who committed the awful deeds I investigated have been brought to justice. In other cases, that process is just beginning.

I write this not to criticise and denigrate some of those who were involved, but rather to tell the tale as I saw it. I hope that the insights I have gained and my telling of them will, in a small way, inhibit the repetition of the grotesque abuse of state power that I was witness to during the terminal years of apartheid rule.

I learnt the profession of forensic science as I went along: I was fortunate in starting with a large bag of luck filled to the brim coupled with my bag of experience, which was quite empty. My great good fortune was to get a significant quantity of experience into that bag before the bag of luck emptied.

It is also my intention in this book to thank those who have guided and taught me along the way. There are many who have given unstintingly of their knowledge and wisdom and, although in some instances their earthly life is run, I must recognise and thank them for their generosity of giving. Without their input, my life would be immeasurably impoverished.

DAVID KLATZOW
JULY 2010

AUTHOR'S NOTE

How does one encapsulate over twenty years' worth of work and more than 3 000 cases in one concise book? How does one convey the genius and tenacity of a man who knows no boundaries in his quest to find answers, and possesses a unique level of honesty? It is a challenge, to put it mildly.

Working with David Klatzow has been an honour and a privilege, not only on a professional level, but also on a personal level. To be exposed to his insight, his depth of knowledge on a vast range of subjects and his humility as a human being is something not many people will experience in their lifetime.

David Klatzow is usually portrayed in the media as unsmiling and unflinching in his views, which are sometimes controversial and often unpopular – an austere man to anyone who does not know him. Yet, over the ten months that we worked on this book, spending many Saturdays and Sundays together, I believe I got to see a very different side to the public persona. He is a man who doesn't accept no for an answer and who is not scared to challenge the system, but he is also someone who genuinely cares about people and will don his boxing gloves to go the full ten rounds to help those who have been wronged.

I also witnessed a personal side to David Klatzow: he has nothing but praise for his wife and children, and his home, warm and wonderful, is in effect a farmhouse in the middle of the city. A man with many other talents, he also makes the best marmalade and home-made preserves that I have tasted in a long while!

This book has been a team effort second to none. Beth Housdon of Zebra Press provided excellent editing skills. Thank you, too, to Ronel Richter-Herbert of Zebra Press for her proofreading and collation skills. And a special thank you to David Klatzow, who demonstrated steadfast commitment and dedication to this project throughout, making my task so much easier. My hope is that, as a team, we have delivered a product that will enlighten, entertain and enthral the reader.

SYLVIA WALKER
JULY 2010

ABBREVIATIONS

ANC: African National Congress
AWB: Afrikaner Weerstandsbeweging
BEE: Black Economic Empowerment
CCB: Civil Cooperation Bureau
COSATU: Congress of South African Trade Unions
CSIR: Council for Scientific and Industrial Research
CVR: Cockpit Voice Recorder
DCA: Directorate of Civil Aviation
MADD: Mothers Against Drunken Driving
MCC: Medicines Control Council
MK: Umkhonto we Sizwe
NPA: National Prosecuting Authority
SAA: South African Airways
SAASCO: South African Air Safety Council
SABS: South African Bureau of Standards
SACC: South African Council of Churches
SADF: South African Defence Force
SAFEX: South African Futures Exchange
SAIA: South African Insurance Association
SAMJ: South African Medical Journal
SANBS: South African National Blood Transfusion Service
TRC: Truth and Reconciliation Commission
UDF: United Democratic Movement
UCT: University of Cape Town
WITS: University of the Witwatersrand

CHAPTER 1

SETTING SAIL ON MY VOYAGE OF DISCOVERY

'To thine own self be true,
And it must follow, as the night the day,
Thou canst not then be false to any man.'

– WILLIAM SHAKESPEARE,
Hamlet, Act I, scene iii, lines 78–80

There was no doubt in the police investigators' minds that Fred van der Vyver had murdered Inge Lotz. The crime scene pointed to a murderer whom she knew well – nothing was stolen and there was no sign of forced entry – and Fred knew Inge intimately. What's more, they had just had an argument. Fred had motive and perhaps some opportunity, but, most importantly, the police investigators *believed* he was guilty. All that they needed to convict him was the evidence to prove this.

So how did he get away with it, if, indeed, he did commit the crime? It's quite simple: each piece of evidence fell horribly short when subjected to scientific scrutiny. There was not a shred of evidence, scientific or other, to link Fred van der Vyver to the death of Inge Lotz. The police investigation was not about finding the truth; rather, it was so clouded by bias that reality blurred into fantasy. The ideals of forensic science were abandoned and replaced by the police's desperation to gain a conviction at any cost.

Forensic science is akin to a voyage of discovery: the scientist unravels the clues and sifts through the ashes and dust to find the gems of information that will bring him or her as close as humanly possible to the true state of events. That is the crux of the work of a forensic scientist.

In each and every case, there are many external influences at work. One of the most dangerous is personal bias, and this is where the investigation into the murder of Inge Lotz fell so terribly short. The critical difference between a scientist and a layperson is the ability to observe and analyse information in a completely unbiased way.

This lesson was brought home to me vividly in my very first chemistry practical at the University of the Witwatersrand. As first-years, we all had a little black one-rand lab book in which to record our research and results, and we arrived fresh-faced and eager, ready to conduct our first scientific experiment. With our twenty coins of the same denomination in hand, which we had been told to bring on that first day, we were sent off to the weighing room.

The task was to weigh each coin individually and note down its mass to the fourth decimal point. We then had to calculate the coins' mean and standard deviation, which is a measure of the range or dispersion of weights measured for the set of coins. No two coins ever had an identical mass, due to weighing or observation errors, or wear and tear from use.

We were then instructed to reweigh each coin and repeat the entire exercise. I discovered that the standard deviation on the second set of weighing was much smaller the second time around. Why? It was simple: the second time I weighed the coins, I subconsciously knew what the average weight was, and this influenced my later measurements. Thus, on the inaugural day of my scientific career, I was taught a fundamental lesson: as a scientist, you have to get rid of your bias. Subjective influences, knowledge you already have and misinformation can all lead to the wrong conclusions.

It is not for a scientist to pre-empt results or to seek particular findings. The scientist's task is purely to find out what nature and the laws of science have put there to be found. If the facts do not support a theory, a good scientist will discard the theory with alacrity and look past the external influences until he or she gets as close to the truth as possible. That is the craft of science, and particularly of forensic science.

External influences play a huge role not only in science, but also in the development of a child, and I was very fortunate to have some of the best influences in my early years. These moulding elements inspired my interest in and keen passion for the world of science.

Let me start at the beginning. My father's family emigrated from Russia at the turn of the century, fleeing the persecution of Jews at the time. My paternal grandparents moved independently from St Petersburg to England, where they met and married. Shortly after this, they set sail for South Africa in search of a golden future. They arrived in Durban just after the Boer War, and my father was born in Newcastle, in Natal, in November 1903. The family later moved to Bloemfontein, where they formed part of a thriving Jewish community.

I know very little about my paternal grandparents, except their names – Jonas and Leah. My father did not mention them once in all the years I was growing up, and we never had any contact with them. My father had married out of his faith – my mother was Anglican – and I suspect he was disowned for this decision. Perhaps my grandfather was never even told about the marriage.

My paternal grandparents produced four children, of which my father, Cyril, was the eldest. There were also two daughters, René and Gladys, and a younger son, Leonard.

My Aunt Gladys married a dentist in Cape Town and lived in suburbia with him for the next fifty years or so, while my father's eldest sister, René Ahrensen, became a well-known Shakespearean exponent. In fact, she started Maynardville Open Air Theatre in Wynberg, Cape Town, with Cecelia Sonnenberg. There is a plaque commemorating these two ladies on either side of the entrance to the theatre to this day. René married briefly and gave birth to one daughter, my first cousin, Noel. Growing up, I saw Aunt René only occasionally – we were not a close-knit family.

My father's youngest brother, Leonard, was by far the most interesting. He obtained a master's degree in physics from the University of the Orange Free State, and later, having been awarded a Rhodes Scholarship, furthered his studies at Oxford, where he shared lodgings with Bram Fischer. When it had become known that Leonard had applied for the scholarship, Bram, whose father was judge president of the Free State and whose grandfather had been prime minister of the Orange River Colony, approached him, generously saying, 'I see that you have applied for the Rhodes Scholarship. So have I. Because of my family connections, I will probably get it. You apply first and I will withdraw my application. I'll apply next year and see you then.'

That's exactly what happened. The two friends ended up in Oxford, where they shared a house. This was around the time when communist agents were turning Oxford students towards communism, and I am sure both Bram and Len were influenced by this. Len became chairman of the British Scientific Workers Union, and who knows what may have been in store for him had he been lured into the world of Anthony Blunt, Kim Philby, Donald Maclean, John Cairncross and others, who became communist spies after their university days in the late 1920s.

Len worked on a great many scientific projects, and had a keen interest in the effect of current passing through gases and vacuums. He was part of the team that developed the cavity magnetron, the device that generated the microwaves used in radar and became the scientific basis for microwave ovens. He also worked on the development of fluorescent coating for cameras, in the electronics world of physics, which ultimately resulted in the invention of television. His involvement in infrared bombsights eventually brought about his demise: he was killed testing a bombsight when the Wellington Bomber in which he was flying crashed. Sadly, this all happened before I was born, and I never knew him.

My mother's side of the family came from the idyllic English countryside. My grandmother was born Langsford and lived on the River Tamar, which separates Cornwall from Devon in England. The Langsfords lived at the Cotehele Mill in the late 1880s, where they enjoyed a largely self-sufficient life – they made their own butter, milk and bacon and raised their own meat; they grew their own vegetables; and salmon were caught in the nearby river.

Gran was one of thirteen children. The names of many of these children reflect the times in which they were born – one child was called Horatio and another Nelson, after the great Napoleonic Wars leader Horatio Nelson.

My maternal grandfather, James Bruno Blatchford, was born on the island of Jersey. As a young man he had trained as a fitter and turner, and he later worked in the naval dockyards in Plymouth, about fifteen miles away from the Cotehele Mill. It was at Cotehele Mill that he met my grandmother, and they eventually married.

Shortly afterwards, my grandfather contracted Malta fever, a form of brucellosis. The normal 'prescription' when a doctor didn't know how to cure an illness in those days was a long trip to a hot, dry country. This is how my grandparents arrived in South Africa.

My grandfather found employment on the mines as a fitter and turner. Eager to better himself, he decided to study at night. Eventually he wrote his mine-engineering ticket and became a mining engineer, a role he continued to perform for the rest of his life, on the far East Rand.

My grandparents' marriage was not always a bed of roses, it seems – I suspect that my grandfather had the same affinity for gambling and horse racing that my father had. Gran left him and went back to England with her first daughter when she was pregnant with her second child. My mother, Winifred Mabel, was born in Penzance shortly afterwards. A few years later, the First World War broke out, and my mother later shared with me her vivid childhood memories of seeing the Zeppelins flying over the British coast.

At about the age of eight or nine, my mother returned to South Africa with my grandmother, and my grandparents settled back down on the mines together, where they continued with their lives until my grandfather's death in about 1940. My mother's older sister, Bertha Bower, married a mine official who achieved some status as the mayor of Brakpan in the early fifties. I remember having a lot of fun driving around in the mayoral car, registration TO 1, in those days. Sadly, my aunt, who was a heavy smoker, died at the young age of forty-seven, and my mother and grandmother were the only two members of the family left. My grandmother died in 1960 when she was about eighty.

At the outbreak of the Second World War, my father signed up and went to fight. He met and married my mother towards the end of the war, and shortly afterwards, on 14 July 1944, my brother Peter was born. A few years later, on 8 December 1948, I arrived.

My father was an immensely intelligent man. He was an expert in all aspects that make a business work, and it is a great tragedy that he never formalised his knowledge or qualifications in any field. My earliest recollections are of him working at Brakpan Motors as the company secretary for a man called Syd Israel. My mother, an efficient short-hand typist, worked there as well. She had a Standard 8 education, which was considered a good qualification for a woman in those days.

From my early childhood perspective, we lived a happy, contented life in Brakpan, a small mining town on the East Rand, about fifty kilometres from Johannesburg. I was completely unaware of any sinister undercurrents in the family, or of any looming tragedy, but our reality was shattered in 1957, when I was nine years old. My father had a sustained and unjustified belief in his ability to predict which horses would win at the races. This caused considerable financial stress in the family after a particularly bad loss: my father was disgraced and ostracised by his friends and acquaintances, and found himself unemployable. Ruin was imminent, and he attempted suicide. The suicide attempt added to the stigma, as suicide was illegal in those days (as it still is today), and he was sent for psychological treatment. Through all of this trauma, we lost all our material possessions and my family was socially isolated.

Eventually, an old friend in Brakpan came to the rescue. His brother-in-law owned a glassworks in Standerton, but the business was losing money, and he offered my father a position. We moved to Standerton, and for the rest of his working life my father was beholden to Julian Berman, the man who had given him another chance. With his excellent business skills, my father managed to turn the glassworks around.

Life in Standerton for a nine-year-old was bliss. It was a rural community that made a Huckleberry Finn–type of lifestyle possible. My mother did not approve of the children who lived across the road from us, but I befriended them nonetheless. They were the children of a cabinetmaker called Alf Doubel, who was the finest wood craftsman I have ever encountered – he could make wood talk. I spent many happy hours in his workshop, and he inspired in me a love of woodworking.

Ignoring adult prejudice and blissfully unaware of any drama in my own family, I spent many happy afternoons and weekends running around barefoot, riding my bicycle, or swimming in or canoeing on the Vaal River with my new friends. A real treat was when my mother would give me ten cents and I could go to the movies and buy a cold drink. A whole afternoon's entertainment could be had for ten cents!

I was baptised an Anglican, and my mother made sure that as much religion was poured into me as possible – in fact, until my cup ran over! I suspect that the rabbi and the Anglican priest drew lots over me, and the one who lost received my soul! I was sent to an Anglican church school – St Martin's School, in Johannesburg – after we moved to Standerton, where my brother was also a pupil. He was conscientious and well behaved. The same could not be said of me. To put it mildly, I was found to be 'difficult' at school, and my school reports reflected this (two of my earlier reports are included in Appendix A).

St Martin's was one of the more liberal establishments of its day. It had begun as St Peter's, and one of its more famous pupils was Oliver Tambo. The headmaster, Michael Stern, was a man who judged no one unfairly. He had the ability to look past difficulties to see the potential in the unruly children in his care. He was passionate about the development of young minds, often overlooking broken rules if he could see that some good had resulted.

One Saturday afternoon, a friend, Donald Currie, and I were exploring a drainage canal that ran near the school into Wemmer Pan. We were strictly forbidden to go to the canal, as part of the canal was covered and obviously it was a dangerous escapade. While exploring, Currie and I found the body of a newborn black baby. We went straight to the nearest police station to report it, but this was the early 1960s and nothing could have interested the police less. I said to Currie, 'Let's go and report this to the boss (as Stern was known to us).' Currie was appalled, fearing a caning for breaking the school rules by going down to the canal. I insisted, and we timidly approached Stern in his office.

His response was electrifying. He phoned the senior officer at the police station and raised hell. The next thing, a police car with a colonel and other officers arrived at the school and I went with the police to recover the little corpse. Not a word was said about the breach of school rules, and I seem to remember that Stern gave Currie and me twenty cents each. He was that kind of man.

Michael Stern, however, committed the cardinal sin of allowing the black school cook to swim in the school's swimming pool. This was simply too liberal for South Africa at the time, as was the teachers' regular participation in protest marches and their resulting arrests. The upshot of all of this 'liberalism' was that the school board intervened, and Stern left to found Waterford School in Mbabane in Swaziland, taking some of the better teachers with him. (My brother, interestingly, went on to teach Afrikaans and Music at Waterford School the year after his matric.)

St Martin's provided a broad education. The teachers were unconventional and some were even a bit off the wall, but many of the more general lessons I was taught stood me in good stead. As Mark Twain said, 'Education is what remains after what has been taught at school has been forgotten.'

Rob Taylor taught me science in Standard 8. He must have awakened a deeply covered interest in the subject, as I went from failure marks to respectable to even good results. At that stage, I also developed an interest in biochemistry. My brother Peter was in London at the Royal College of Music at the time, and he found a second-hand bookshop in Charing Cross Road where, quite serendipitously, he bought me two books, *Biochemical Society Symposia* numbers 22 and 23, for ten shillings.

These books described the structure and functions of the membranes and surfaces of cells, and methods of separation of sub-cellular structural components, nurturing the seeds of my future academic interests. Much of the content was beyond me, but the books stimulated me to enquire more, and eventually my postgraduate studies focused on cell-surface biochemistry and culminated in a PhD in the subject. Rob Taylor encouraged this sort of enquiry, and I owe him much gratitude.

The same could not be said of the other teachers at the school. They were by and large indifferent towards me, and some did not appear to be qualified in the teaching profession. I remember Mr Yule, the maths master, who suffered from post-traumatic stress as a result of the Second World War. He was stern and strict, demanding respect from his pupils. Often, at the slightest provocation, he would fly into a blind rage, leaving us fearful and uncertain.

My English master was Jeremy Taylor, of 'Ag Pleez Daddy' fame. He left after my first year to pursue a musical career with the *Wait a Minim!* show. My brother Peter, being very musically gifted, wrote down the music of 'Ag Pleez Daddy' in note form so that Jeremy could get the copyright.

Michael de Lisle succeeded Michael Stern as headmaster at St Martin's. He was a rigid man, and I learnt some valuable lessons from him – including the fact that 'military intelligence' is a contradiction in terms! He had been a distinguished soldier during the Second World War, and we clashed from the word go, as he believed in creating and upholding rules, no matter what the consequences. Michael de Lisle and I were not destined to be happy with each other at all.

I had set my heart on studying medicine after school, but my grades were poor. The only way for me to be accepted was to put in many hours of extra work, which would mean studying in the library after prep, late into the evening. The school rules stated that we could do this two nights a week, and De Lisle was not prepared to waive them. He appeared to be totally insensitive to my motivation – rules were there to be obeyed.

I did not accept this lying down, and after ongoing tension between De Lisle and me, my mother was called in and asked to take me to a psychiatrist. De Lisle thought that I had some deep-seated personality issues that needed resolution.

The psychiatrist found me to be a reasonably normal sixteen-year-old, and I left St Martin's and returned home to Standerton.

The rest of the year was largely wasted. I attended the local Afrikaans high school to brush up on my Afrikaans, and started at Nigel High School the following year, in Standard 9 again.

I met up with Michael de Lisle recently when he attended a public lecture that I gave. He and I appear to have mellowed considerably, and he complimented me on my performance. Memories are short, and I bear him no lasting animosity – we were both products of our own experiences.

The headmaster at Nigel High School was Louis Spruyt. His wife had been at school with my mother, who had been taught by Louis in the early days of his career. He had a soft spot for me, and sometimes allowed me to use his office to study. There was none of the rigidity that I had encountered up until that point. I worked almost every evening up at the school library – I had my own key – and my results reflected the effort I put in.

Looking back, what amazes me was the short-sightedness in the education system, where teachers were often more focused on upholding rules and regulations than on recognising ambition and determination, and facilitating the development of the young minds in their care. Louis Spruyt, for me, was a breath of fresh air.

In my last two years at school at Nigel, I encountered many people who can simply be described as incredible human beings. One of these was Dr Gevers, my English master. A German by birth, he had a PhD in English and exuded wisdom and knowledge. Imposed discipline did not form part of his world: for his pupils, to disappoint Gevers was punishment in itself. We looked up to him in awe, and the many life lessons he imparted through teaching his subject still live with me today.

Gevers was Socratic in his approach to teaching, constantly questioning and engaging in debate with his students to stimulate critical thinking. I recall one such instance when we were studying William Blake's poem 'The Sick Rose':

O Rose thou art sick.
The invisible worm,
That flies in the night
In the howling storm:

Has found out thy bed
Of crimson joy:
And his dark secret love
Does thy life destroy.

The poem's bleak political overtones reflect Blake's insecurities with the changing world around him. I went to Gevers with an interpretation, and his approach was mindful. He never said that I was wrong, but questioned me on how my analysis interacted with the matrix of knowledge that I had about Blake. He did not criticise my interpretation, but pointed out in a very gentle way its inadequacy with regard to what I already knew about the poet.

These English classes taught me a number of things, one of them being the open-endedness of knowledge. I realised that you will never know everything there is to know about your subject, no matter how limited the subject matter is. There will always be others who will surpass you in knowledge – others from whom you can learn.

Another valuable lesson I was taught by Gevers is that whatever you know about a subject has to be factored into the matrix of your general understanding on that subject. Blake's poem had to fit in with whatever else Blake had done and said, with his philosophies, and with how and where he interacted in other circumstances. Any interpretation of Blake's poem had to be coherent – I could not simply create an interpretation in a vacuum.

This is true of any scientific logic, and, of course, of forensic investigation. You have to investigate everything, covering all the intersecting points and the logical flow of events. The forensic scientist has to place the actual crime scene in the context of events leading up to the incident, and needs to investigate each event carefully to ensure a coherent conclusion.

Even if you are seeing a situation for the very first time, you need to conduct research – you have to create the matrix of understanding to reach the correct conclusion. Let's say, for example, that I was to investigate the properties of a protein in the blood. I would determine the name of the protein, then research and gather all the information that is at hand about that particular protein. I would then conduct a 'what if' set of circumstances and ask how it would react under different conditions – whether it would affect coagulation, for instance. I would plot my findings and draw scientific conclusions based on results, thereby creating a picture to aid my understanding. Those conclusions would be based on scientific information and, eventually, my comprehension would become more and more coherent, reaching a final point of scientific conclusion.

Everything you do in life is like building a jigsaw puzzle. Pieces of information fit, sometimes slowly, into a greater picture, up to the point where you reach a more advanced understanding. Gevers taught me this. He also taught me never to accept anything at face value: question everything, I learnt, to find out how it fits into the matrix of your understanding.

The other English teacher who had a profound influence on me was Jean Cameron. I recall her coming to me to tell me that I was going to win the English prize. She asked me, 'Klatzow, have you read *Alice in Wonderland*?' When I replied that I had not, she said that it was high time I did. That was a huge compliment for me, as *Alice in Wonderland* is not a children's book. Lewis Carroll was a mathematical scholar, and Alice was written on multiple levels – very little of the book is accessible to children. There are many complex wordplays, and he invented words in that book that are now accepted as part of the English language – 'chortle', for instance – in order to paint a precise picture in our minds. I received a copy of *Alice in Wonderland* as a prize that year. Gevers and Cameron had a remarkable influence on me, and we corresponded and kept in touch for many years after I left school.

Through these influences, I developed an incredible love of the English language, which is one of the most amazing mediums we have at our disposal. English is the language in which some of the deepest and most noble thoughts of mankind are embedded, and is an important means of conveying concepts from one mind to another. It is not without reason that English is the lingua franca of the scientific world.

When I testify in court in my capacity as forensic scientist, I have to create a picture in the judge's mind. The more accurately and precisely I can use words to do this, the more effective I am – it's as simple as that. Everything is an image or concept in your mind, and the only way to share that with someone is through words, which paint that picture. This is true whether you are using the Queen's English or slang.

The accurate use of language enables me to give more focused and elegant explanations of my thoughts, and a case can be won or lost depending on the ability to communicate. Through the skilful use of language, you can enhance the evidence and make it accessible to the judge. In a courtroom, I teach the judge about the basics of a subject of which he or she knows nothing: the legally trained judge doesn't know how to combat a fire or measure heat or evaluate a scientific argument. My job is to lead him or her on an intellectual pathway by providing the stepping stones of thought along which he or she must tread to discover my reasoning and the conclusions that I have reached. I am not there to adjudicate the issue; I am there to tell the judge plainly what evidence I encountered and how I reached my conclusions so that he or she can make the appropriate decisions.

During my last year at St Martin's School, I spent the December holiday at Charles Johnson Memorial Hospital in a small hamlet called Nqutu in Northern Zululand run by an interesting and wonderful husband-and-wife team, Anthony and Maggie Barker, missionary doctors of great humility, kindness and skill. They ran a model hospital in the wilds of northern Natal for about thirty years before they returned to England.

The Barkers' lives were dedicated to administering medicine and treatment to the poorest of the poor. Maggie was famous for not wearing shoes, and she had thick calluses to prove it. Anthony had a huge beard that had to be swathed in a special type of operating cap during surgery. Their kindness and compassion was boundless. Anthony had the most beautiful italic script, in which he wrote even his clinical notes and prescriptions. I have included a letter he wrote to me to show something of this fine man (see Appendix B).

At Charles Johnson I was exposed to medicine in its most idealistic form. The Barkers' attitude to life can only be described as sublime. Breakfast was rough and ready but was invariably accompanied by Beethoven or any of the other great classical composers. Beethoven and Maltabella porridge will always bring memories flooding back to me of those mornings with the extraordinary couple. Sadly they were both killed in a cycling accident in Britain a few years ago. Somehow I think that is the way that they would have liked it to happen.

Another remarkable man that influenced my interest in medicine was Leon de Villiers, the district surgeon in Standerton. He became a surrogate father to me, as my own father was largely uninvolved in my life. To me, De Villiers was larger than life and my role model. He also practised as a general practitioner, pouring endless energy into treating those who could not afford private medical consultations. As district surgeon he conducted the post-mortem examinations on any unnatural deaths that occurred within the area, and I eagerly assisted him on many of these occasions. Leon would do his district rounds after the daily grind of consulting, and during my school holidays I was fortunate enough to accompany him late into the night, visiting sick folk in the district. He was a good teacher and never spoke down to the young, eager student. He was one of the many people who motivated me to aspire to great heights in the field of medical research.

Leon's wife, Thea, was also wonderful, involving me in so many of the medical activities in the Standerton area. I travelled the length and breadth of the district with her, and inoculated countless babies against smallpox, which was then in its dying days worldwide. I was also a volunteer at the local blood bank, which she managed, and spent many happy evenings taking a pint from members of the local population.

Following my dream of working in the field of medical research, I applied to the University of the Witwatersrand Medical School. To my great joy, I was accepted, and I obtained an Ernest Oppenheimer Memorial Trust Scholarship based on my matric results.

In February 1967, my mother dropped me at the residence to which I had been accepted, and I set about settling into my studies. My years of hard work were going to start paying off: I was about to climb the first rung of my ladder to success – or so I thought.

||||||||||||||||||||||||||||||||||||||||||||||||||||||||||||||

CHAPTER 2
A SCHOLAR
AND A GENTLEMAN

'Men are four:
He who knows, and knows that he knows.
He is wise, follow him.
He who knows, and knows not that he knows.
He is asleep, wake him.
He who knows not, and knows that he knows not.
He is a child, teach him.
He who knows not, and knows not that he knows not.
He is a fool, shun him.'

— ARABIAN PROVERB

Residence at Wits University in Johannesburg was awful. First-year students were 'initiated', and the hard-drinking louts who headed up the student hierarchy ensured that the treatment of first-years was crude and largely inane.

One evening – which happened to be just before an important class test in zoology – we were taken to meet Phineas, the residence mascot. We were blindfolded and led along the rocky bed of one of the tributaries of the Braamfontein Spruit. After meeting Phineas at about 1.30 a.m., we were loaded onto a bakkie, soaked to the skin and, still blindfolded, dropped off somewhere on the western side of the city.

I was wet and cold and completely lost. All I could recognise was the Brixton Tower in the distance, so I made my way towards it. Once there, I ran the few kilometres to the university and, when I arrived in my room, found that my bed had been dragged out and soaked with a firehose. Needless to say, I didn't get much sleep that night.

My mother fell ill a month or two later, and, unbeknown to me, was taken to a sanatorium in Sandringham. She had been diagnosed with depression and was receiving electroconvulsive therapy – shock treatment. She was at death's door: the 'depression' had been caused by the fact that she was really ill, having suffered a heart attack, a fact that the doctors had completely missed. The ability of her heart to pump blood had been severely affected. The anaesthetic that was being administered to her at the sanatorium as part of the therapy was causing rapid deterioration. The psychiatric oaf who administered the shock therapy had failed to note all the clinical signs of real and extreme illness, and my mother developed severe pneumonia in the sanatorium, which was also not diagnosed. She was dying.

Meanwhile, I was being subjected to the boorish rituals of initiation, and was not enjoying life in residence. I was struggling to deal with the university work, and my mother's illness was constantly on my mind. Matters came to a head one day when I forgot to do telephone duty, as I had been to see my mother. I was hauled over the coals by the residence committee chairman, who demanded that I kneel down before him and apologise in front of everybody. Something snapped inside me, and I let him have every four-letter expletive in my vocabulary (a considerable number, as I had attended a church school).

I decided to leave residence and managed to find digs near

the Park Lane Clinic in Johannesburg. It was a dingy little room at the back of a house, and my landlady spoke no English, only French – communication was difficult. After she found out that I liked kippers for breakfast, I had them every day!

The situation was really not conducive to studying. I was miserable, and decided to drop out of university, go home and start again somewhere else when I could find the strength. I went to say goodbye to a friend at varsity and, while looking for him, I bumped into a senior medical student, Beau Loots, who asked me why I was looking so down. I told him. He sat me down for an hour and, rather like Dick Whittington, turned me around. I decided not to leave and found a different flat. I have maintained a friendship with Beau ever since.

My mother, who was still extremely unwell, contacted a friend, who removed her from the sanatorium and had her admitted to Johannesburg General Hospital. Her heart condition and the lung infection were diagnosed and she was placed on appropriate medication. She then developed a persistent cough, and by June or July that year was diagnosed with bronchial carcinoma. Her health deteriorated quickly, and she died in September 1967.

My interest had always been in research and, in particular, cancer research. My mother's death was a powerful impetus to extend this interest, and my former English teacher, Dr Gevers, also encouraged me to go into research as a career. Gevers wrote a letter to me that had a huge influence on my career, and revealed much about Gevers, the man and the scholar. In this letter, which I still have to this day, he wrote:

> By now you will have gone to Johannesburg to register as a
> medical student. I wish you much luck in your endeavours.
> Some hold that the first year is the most difficult; others
> believe it's the third. In general, no doubt, it must be the first,
> but in your case there should be no trouble at all, seeing that

you have been a very independent student for some time. If you have not done any shorthand, you should begin to develop a system of your own to keep up with the lecturers. It is believed that very often the top third of a medical group, after having obtained their degrees (M.B., B.Ch.), become research men and/or Biologists, Biophysicists, Biochemists. The middle group develop into specialists, and the lowest third into medical practitioners. As you are an idealist, I take it you may become a research man.

One of the reasons I had wanted to study medicine was that I thought it would allow me to carry out research. Soon, however, I realised that medicine was not the right road to research.

Medicine is a strange set of learnings. The workings of the human body are very complex, and are based on an intimate understanding of the body's biochemistry. Its delicate balance is affected by any invasive activity, including an operation, a healing wound or medication, which affects the biochemical reactions in the body. Even something as simple as an X-ray has an impact. There is no branch of medicine that does not have an underlying biochemical basis.

Ordinary chemistry is the chemistry of elements, chemical compounds and substances, such as salts. It is about the energy needed to bond chemicals to create other compounds. Biochemistry, on the other hand, is the chemistry of living things – the study of the molecules of life – and deals with the reactions of the body to external events. A person's skin goes brown in the sun, for example, because the chemical changes that the skin undergoes are a biochemical reaction of the body to the sun's rays, producing the brown pigment, melanin. Biochemistry controls all aspects of our body, from our breathing to our heartbeat – the structure of DNA, the molecule of life, is a biochemical wonder. If a person is diseased, there is something wrong with his or her biochemistry.

I wanted to understand the biochemical pathways deep within

the cells, and I realised that medicine would give me just a smatter-ing of the knowledge I craved. Medicine would teach me how to follow a recipe, how to cut along a dotted line. I wanted to design the recipe, to establish where to place that dotted line. I needed to grasp the fundamentals; I needed an intimate understanding of chemistry.

I went to see the dean of medicine at the end of the first year, and switched from medicine to second-year chemistry and bio-chemistry. It was the golden age of biochemistry: James D. Watson and Francis Crick had just received the Nobel Prize in Medicine for their groundbreaking work on the DNA molecule, and this exciting subject seemed to me to be the answer to most of the problems confronting medicine at the time. I have not recanted from this view some forty years later.

It was not an easy year for me emotionally, with the shadow of my mother's death hanging heavily over me. My relationship with my father was also difficult. He was angry with me for dropping medicine, and when he remarried some years later, I didn't get on with his new wife at all.

Despite all of the family issues, I set about focusing on my studies. I lived in a small flat in Braamfontein that my mother had arranged for me before she died. My tuition fees were paid by the scholarship that I had been granted, and living expenses were covered by the forty rand a month my father gave me. The flat consisted of one room with a small bathroom and an alcove for cooking, which contained a two-ringed hotplate stove. The flat, which was sparsely furnished, was right next to the university in a block called Nelmay Court.

My budget was tight. The rent was twenty-eight rand per month, and electricity cost one or two rand. This left me with ten rand for food, entertainment, books, and so on. I didn't have much furniture – a fridge was a luxury I could not afford, so I would buy a half-litre of milk and drink it before it went off. I could buy a kilogram of rump steak for twenty cents and vegetables for five cents, to make myself a princely pot of food for twenty-five cents! An old family friend had given me a pressure cooker, and my hot-plate cooked many a stew, which was always tastier on the second day (it became dubious on the third day in summer, and on the fourth day in winter!).

Eating out was a luxury. A hamburger cost thirty-five cents and a mixed grill around forty cents, but this was over the top. With my home-cooked stew I could feed myself for three days on twenty-five cents! I didn't go out much, and never caught the bus or went to the movies in my entire university career. I went to my first movie since early childhood only after graduating.

My lifestyle was incredibly frugal, as there was no one to borrow money from if I ran short. It was a difficult time, and I worked during my holidays, mostly to be able to buy books. I studied, worked and lived a humble life. There was no time to cry about life being tough, and I knew no better, so I just got on with it.

Being able to afford the books I needed was one of my greatest challenges. I recall agonising over a book that cost ten rand. It was Morrison and Boyd's *Organic Chemistry*, and I had to think very carefully before I took the decision to buy it. I was fortunate to become friendly with Harry Fagan, who managed the university bookshop (who, incidentally, had worked in earlier days with Bob Edmonds, the uncle of the girl I subsequently married). Fagan gave me the little bit of help that I needed so badly: he extended credit to me, allowing me to buy the books and pay them off. He was fantastic and never pressurised me.

Another man who had a huge influence on my life was Jack Allan, a senior member of the anatomy department. I came to know him at the end of my first year, when I worked at the Electron Microscope Unit to earn some extra money. Allan was a remark-able man who had completed a vast amount of work on varicose ulcers, a condition arising when varicose veins cause the flesh to become debilitated and septic. He would come into the room and say 'Allan's ops are tops!', and it was indeed widely accepted that his knowledge of clinical anatomy was unsurpassed.

One particular incident moulded me forever: Allan entered the unit saying that he had to leave shortly to operate on a little girl to remove a glass shard, but that he was going up to the lab just to check his anatomy one more time. Despite all his knowledge and practice, he knew that it was necessary to check one more time. This valuable lesson struck me at the time, and has stayed with me all these years. We have remained friends for over forty years. When carrying out ballistics work, I would always check with Allan on the anatomical implications. I never cease to marvel at his knowledge of anatomy, and his humility in always double-checking to make sure that he is right.

In my second year of university, I had befriended a woman called Sister Faith Hermanson, who had nursed my mother in her last weeks at Johannesburg General Hospital. She told me that all leftover food from the wards is discarded at the end of each day and sent off as pig fodder, and offered to put a plate aside for me each lunch time. Every day I would walk to Ward 22 at the hospital, which was close to the university, collect my plate of food, sit behind the door and eat my lunch, wash the plate and walk back in time for my practical class in the afternoon.

I managed to find employment at a chemical company, McLaughlin and Lazar, towards the end of my third year, and was paid three rand per hour, which translated into twenty-four rand per day – a huge amount of money for me at the time. This helped enormously in paying off my debts.

In my final honours year at Wits, I worked at a shop in Braam-fontein called The Bread and Butter from 12.30 p.m. till 2 p.m., serving customers over the counter. I was paid a rand a day for the hour and a half, and I was allowed to eat one item from the menu, usually a long roll, which kept me alive in my honours year!

These times were tough, but there were some good times in between. I had very little – not even a heater or extra blankets – and spent many winter nights bitterly cold. I also did not have much in the line of clothing, and remember being hugely upset when I had saved enough money to buy a set of flannels, only to tear them on a fence the first night I wore them. Those experiences in my life may have built tenacity, but they were hard – really tough times – and I never want to go through that again.

I completed my honours year and became romantically involved with Geraldine Weatherby, who lived on the floor above me. She was about twelve years older than me and unmarried, and we grew to enjoy each other's company. Geraldine was from an old Kimberley family, and her aunt, Daphne Edmonds, was married to the then chairman of Standard Bank.

Geraldine and I tied the knot, and spent hot, dry Christmas holidays with her family in Kimberley. They were golfing people, and I felt that if I had been an accountant who played golf, I might have been more acceptable to them. Our marriage would not last, unfortunately.

Geraldine and I shared a flat opposite the university, and I taught and demonstrated in the evenings while completing my PhD. She was of immense help to me in this time. I also started giving extra lessons in maths and science, and distributed letters advertising my services.

One of the schools that I contacted was Kingsmead School for Girls. Shortly after receiving my letter, they discovered that their science mistress was pregnant – a completely unacceptable state of affairs at an all-girls school! The pleasures of carnal knowledge could not be so openly displayed, and it was causing great distress at the institution.

The headmistress, Vera Paver, was a tall, austere, angular woman. She approached me to fill the post, but was gravely suspicious of allowing a man into her school. One of her more practical problems was where would I go if I needed to use the lavatory. Caught between the devil and the deep blue sea, she was forced to hire me, and I was the only male on the premises – apart from John Male, an Anglican priest who also formed part of the school, but who was considered benign.

I taught in the mornings and worked on my PhD in the afternoons. Paver found it difficult to understand me. The girls in my class worked hard, and I would occasionally take them to The Firs, a shopping centre across the road, for coffee, to reward them. Paver never approved, and was often verbal about it. I did not change my approach, though – rules are there for the guidance of wise men and the observance of fools. Paver did not understand that sentiment or agree with it; she was rigid in her approach, a type of rigidity I had experienced all too often in my own school career. She probably wanted to dismiss me on a number of occasions, but science teachers were scarce, and having me there was less of an embarrassment than having no science teacher at all.

After two years, I left Kingsmead to accept an offer of a full-time post at the Department of Surgery at Wits Medical School. The department was headed by Professor du Plessis, a remarkable man. The students referred to him as 'God'. What he said had the effect of Holy Writ – no one ever challenged him. He either liked you or he didn't, and if you were in his good books, you could get away with a lot.

I have always believed that your results are only as good as your equipment. If you abuse your equipment – by not cleaning it properly, for example – the results will be less reliable. I started to buy my own equipment, but some pieces were costly, and I managed to get various items on loan from companies. Eventually, the value of the equipment that I had acquired on loan was substantial, and I was summoned to Du Plessis' office. Dressed the part, I waited to see him. Once inside, he read me the riot act, stating that any hired or donated equipment had to be organised through the faculty office. I had fully equipped a little lab where I could do my PhD, so I was in hot water again, but agreed to arrange things via the faculty office in the future.

I was offered a full-time research post in the surgery department at the princely salary of R400 per month, which was a fortune for me. I could focus on my passion – research – and continued to do so until Du Plessis left to take up the position as principal of Wits University and Professor Bert Myburgh took over.

One of the strange rituals in those days was the so-called 'prefects' meeting', which took place once a week at 12.30 p.m. sharp. Du Plessis would come in and we'd sit around a big boardroom table in order of decreasing rank, starting with the professors at the top, followed by the associate professors, and so on, until the bottom end of the table was reached, which was where I sat. At one of these meetings, I was asked to arrange the annual surgeon's dinner party – a challenge to say the least! In fact, it was more of an order than a request. 'Klatzow,' Du Plessis said to me, 'you have not a lot better to do, so kindly organise the surgery departmental dinner.'

The surgeons were full of demands. They didn't want chicken; they wanted lamb. They didn't want cheap wine. No disco; they wanted a live band. And they were not prepared to pay more than five rand a ticket. Venues were expensive, and I was lucky enough to secure the brand-new Bozzoli Pavilion. There were still piles of cement in places, but it was functional, and I was to organise the first event ever to be held there.

I ran around planning the menu, decor and other details, and all seemed to be on track until the evening of the dinner. I was to fill the role of MC as well. As I was supervising the last arrangements, the caterer switched on the stove and all the lights blew out: the entire building was devoid of electricity.

There was no hope of finding an electrician at 6.30 p.m. on a Saturday evening. After much panic, I found the switch-gear room at the rear of the building, and managed to break the brand-new door down so that we could get the electricity going again. The caterer had to hold a match while I worked the mechanism, but we managed to fix the problem! I raced home, had a quick bath and was back by 7.10 p.m., with no one any the wiser as to the stress we had gone through. The university tried to charge me for replacing the broken door, but Bert Myburgh, the new head of department, wouldn't allow it. The evening was a great success.

I completed my PhD amidst many difficulties with the faculty under Bert Myburgh. The heads of departments typically wanted students to work on their topics of choice. Du Plessis was the exception, but he left, shortly after I joined the Department of Surgery, to take up his position as principal of Wits University. When Bert Myburgh took over as head of department, I felt like I was being sabotaged – there seemed to be active resistance to enabling me to do my research.

The main problem was that the department was linked to transplant immunology, and I was working on cancer research. It was my passion, and I had invested many hours in my work. I felt that Myburgh was uncomfortable with my line of work, and he tried to encourage me to stop what I was doing to focus on liver immunology research. I was dead against it. In any event, transplant immunology and tumour immunology are closely linked from a scientific perspective. If you can understand the one, you will be close to understanding the other.

I also encountered unnecessary obstacles from my new supervisor, Koos Smit. One such example was that the technicians produced sterile cottons and pipettes for students to use, yet he objected to my using them – I had to make my own. As a PhD student, I should automatically have had access to these items. It became extremely difficult to work with Smit. I started working in the lab in the early mornings and evenings and spending my days in the library to avoid a confrontation with him, working around eighteen hours a day.

Matters finally came to a head when I arrived in the lab one evening at around 6 p.m. and Myburgh confronted me, asking me where I had been. I told him that I spent my days in the library, and had obtained permission from Koos Smit to do so. He claimed that I didn't have permission, and fired me there and then.

I immediately went to find Smit and challenged him. He admitted that he had been sabotaging my work, and I told him in a rage that he was to follow me to Myburgh's house and explain everything, including the fact that I had obtained his permission to work in the library.

We arrived at Myburgh's house in Sandringham at about 8.30 p.m., just as he was having supper. Smit and I waited for him until he had finished, and we sat down and spoke to him. Myburgh appeared to be very taken aback – I think he knew the truth but feigned astonishment. I was reinstated the next day, and completed my PhD based on work relating to proteins that are elevated in people suffering from cancer. It was interesting work.

The thesis was sent overseas to be marked by two external examiners. One sent back a glowing report; the other damned the thesis. Confused by this, the faculty submitted it to a third external examiner, who passed it with no difficulty. The delay took an extra year.

Researching some literature on the subject the following year, I was astonished to find a paper by the second external examiner (the same one who had held the thesis back) on exactly the same topic I had covered in my research. I am sure he did not plagiarise the material, but it certainly seemed to have been held back to give him a competitive edge. Unfortunately for him, I had already published the work in the *South African Medical Journal*. Such is science.

I met a remarkable man by the name of Gerard Vos in the early stages of my PhD, when I went to visit the Natal Blood Transfusion Service. We started talking, and he was immediately able to see the importance of the cell surface in a whole range of biological and disease processes.

Gerard had no formal qualifications other than an extraordinary ability to understand and work with blood groups, a field known as serology. He was recruited to South Africa by the Natal Blood Transfusion Service from his adopted home in Perth, Australia. He had been born in Java, Indonesia.

I learnt from other people at the time – Gerard seldom spoke of his own achievements – that he had an OBE for his work on blood groups, particularly the blood groups relating to haemolytic diseases of the newborn. He made singular and distinguished contributions to this vital field of serology. Despite his lack of formal undergraduate qualifications, the University of Natal was happy for him to complete his PhD on the work he was doing, which was of an extremely high standard. He then obtained a higher doctorate, receiving two of the highest qualifications that the university could offer.

Gerard regarded me more as a son than as a colleague, and we became very firm friends. We worked together on a number of issues and published several papers together, including an article in the serology journal *Vox Sanguinus* (the voice of blood).

It was Gerard's support during the difficult time in the surgery department at Wits, when there was severe pressure on me to abandon my chosen field of research, that saved me. His support and, above all, his belief in me were invaluable during those difficult days. Later, when I moved to Durban for a period of time, our friendship was cemented. He was a man as generous in spirit as he was erudite in the field of his choice.

In August 1977, I attended a cancer conference in Cape Town, where I met Arthur Hawtrey. Arthur was originally from Salisbury, Rhodesia. He told me that the University of Durban-Westville – which today is part of the University of KwaZulu-Natal – was looking for a lecturer in biochemistry, and I decided to apply for the position. It was a university for Indian students, forming part of the apartheid structure of separate education for separate races. At the end of 1978, I left Johannesburg, the Wits Medical School, and my wife, and moved to Durban to take up my new position in the academic world.

I rapidly discovered that the ethnic universities were a sham. The theory was that these universities should be 'separate but equal'. It was certainly separate, but definitely not equal. Many people who taught there were so lacking in ability that they could not have taught anywhere else. Some were excellent, though: Arthur Hawtrey, the head of biochemistry, for example, was probably one of the finest chemists this country has ever seen.

The university was riddled with politics, and tear gas was frequently used by the police on the campus. The students were unhappy, the staff members were unhappy, and the whole place was fraught with tension. The research facilities were very elementary, and the bureaucracy stifling.

It was as if I was starting out yet again when I moved to Durban. I had left my marriage with very little – a few rugs, a desk and my books. I had nothing else – no stove, bed, linen, fridge, or even pots and pans. One morning I went to a local furniture store and furnished my flat, using my credit card to pay. I woke up late that night in a cold sweat, realising that I had no way of paying back the enormous debt that I had just incurred.

At about 1 a.m., I took a pair of scissors and cut up my credit card, then applied my mind to making extra money. Durban has the highest median age of people living in South Africa, and women outlive men, so I concluded that there must be many elderly women who needed help with basic handyman chores. I took my last twenty rand and used this to have a sign made, which read 'Handyman. No job too small' with my telephone number. I approached a hardware store in Musgrave Centre and agreed to buy all my materials from them if they displayed my sign in their window. My phone didn't stop ringing, and I was in business!

I was lecturing during the day, and in the evenings and over weekends I would return messages, give quotes and carry out the handyman work. It was all work that I was capable of – fixing windows, hanging doors and other minor repair work.

One day I received a call to quote on fitting out a poodle parlour. The business premises were brand new and, on arrival, I realised that this was way beyond my elementary carpentry talents. I provided an outrageous quote, hoping never to hear from the owners again, but an hour later my phone rang. The chap who came to quote after me had been as drunk as a skunk, and they wanted me to do the job!

There were some men working at the university building on a new addition, and I approached the foreman to ask him if there was a carpenter on his team looking for after-hours work. Jerry Sewnarain came to work for me, and for the next two years we ran around Durban doing a wide range of handyman work. It was the only time in my life that I actually had cash in my pocket.

There was a constant demand for wooden window frames to be replaced in Durban, as the humidity meant that they used to rot quite quickly. One day we were called in to do some work at a house of a very snooty woman, whose husband was a senior anaesthetist in the city. When we arrived at her house, she served us tea in a jam tin and had the maid keep an eye on us in case we stole the spoons!

We finished fixing the window, and then she haggled over the price, but finally we were paid and we left. The story took a rather amusing twist, as I was due to be the guest speaker at an anaesthetic conference later in the month. I will remember to my dying day the look of surprise and horror on her face when she arrived at the conference with her husband, only to find the handyman sitting at the top table as the guest speaker!

I soon realised that the University of Durban-Westville was not for me, but I was not keen to be a full-time handyman, so I started looking for another position in the academic world.

An advertisement appeared for a lecturer at Wits in the Department of Biochemistry, and I applied. In 1981, three years after I had left Johannesburg, I was on my way back to work at Wits. Disillusionment was not far off. The back-biting was as bad at Wits as anywhere else, and it was particularly bad at the medical school. So much energy was being consumed just fighting battles with colleagues, and this was not where I wanted to be.

I also found that the way in which funding was provided appeared to be problematic. Universities were given grants in return for producing a certain number of papers on an annual basis. Driven by volume, not quality, some papers that were produced can only be described as rubbish. I could not be party to this, and I objected to the 'publish or perish' mentality, as, in my view, it leads to cheating and the publication of mediocre information.

I am not a conformist and wanted to publish only what I felt was worthwhile. But, coupled with my huge lecture load, I found that publishing useful, quality articles in the journals was difficult, which inevitably led to problems with the dean and the vice-chancellor of research, Professor Peter Tyson.

I also experienced petty office politics. One instance concerned the use of instruments. There was a particular instrument called an integrator. A colleague, Richard Cantril, had one in his lab, and I asked him if I could use it. He told me that I couldn't, as he was using it all the time. During tea one morning, I went to his laboratory, lifted the lid of the box it was housed in, and signed the chart paper with my name and the date. Eight weeks later, I approached him again and received the same answer – he was using it all the time. I opened the lid to see my name and date in the same place, undisturbed. I pointed this out to him, and he had no answer. The motto at Wits seemed to be that not only must one be seen to succeed, but others must be seen to fail. Teamwork and pride in the achievement of colleagues was an unknown ethos.

During my time at Wits, I organised the weekly journal club, and it was at one of these meetings that I met Hillel Shapiro, a forensic pathologist. He was accompanied by Dorothy Gill, from the Department of Health. Shapiro gave a very interesting lecture, and I realised when talking to the two of them afterwards that there were major problems in the field of forensic science in South Africa. There were no private forensic laboratories, and I saw this as a huge opportunity.

Dorothy, an analytical chemist from Britain, had been warning the authorities that there was a problem with the blood-alcohol testing procedures. After some discussion, she decided to resign from the Department of Health to start a forensic practice with me. Without much planning as to how I would start a private forensic laboratory, I decided to take the plunge and resign my post at Wits. I would seek my future outside the world of academia. A new chapter of my life was about to begin.

||||||||||||||||||||||||||||||||||||||||||||||||||||||||||||||

CHAPTER 3

ALCOHOL IS A GOOD FRIEND, JUST DON'T OVERDO THE FRIENDSHIP

*'It isn't what we don't know
that gives us trouble,
it's what we know that ain't so.'*

– WILL ROGERS,
American actor, humorist and social commentator

I waved the academic world farewell, saying goodbye to the regular pay slip. In preparation, I paid off my accommodation expenses a year in advance, so my only worry would be my living expenses for the next year.

Dorothy Gill found a position at the Jockey Club (now the National Horseracing Authority of Southern Africa). Unfortunately she would cut all ties with me after my involvement in a case against the Jockey Club, and we would not go into business together.

It is illegal to race a horse whose performance has been enhanced by certain substances, and, up until the early 1980s, blood samples had to be sent overseas to be analysed. In about 1984, the Jockey Club set up its own laboratory for testing in South Africa.

Around 1988, the first big case that came up was that of Alan Forbes, a wealthy trainer who owned and raced horses. Amidst ongoing friction between Forbes and the Jockey Club, one of his racehorses, I'm Proud, was tested, and traces of naproxen, an anti-inflammatory drug, was supposedly found in its bloodstream. Forbes was accused of enhancing his horse's performance by using drugs.

He was entitled to have his own expert cross-examine the Jockey Club expert at the hearing, and I was called in. The head of their laboratory testified at length about how he had conducted the tests and reached his conclusion that naproxen was present in the horse's bloodstream, but I managed to poke many holes in his evidence. He quoted from books, and I brought these same books with me, pointing out that his quotes were simply not there. In the end, the Jockey Club expert was disbelieved. It was a walkover, and Alan Forbes was acquitted.

I was subsequently called in to assist another trainer. This time, the Jockey Club would not allow me the privilege of cross-examining their expert – I was not permitted to attend the hearing. I flew to Durban with the trainer and suggested to him that we act in the following way: he would go into the hearing with a tape recorder and ask the first question. He would then come to me with the recording, and I would listen and give him the next question. This is what we did – by tea time we had asked only three questions!

The chairman of the inquiry was livid and said he wanted all the questions at once. I said that I couldn't do that because each question would depend on the answer to the previous question. Out of frustration, they eventually let me into the hearing, and after one or two questions, I demolished their expert again.

Animals (and people) have different levels of hormones in their systems. To prove that abnormal levels are the result of a substance being administered artificially, you have to prove it statistically, using the sample you have taken. The flaw in their case was a misunderstanding in the evaluation and analysing of this sample. The statistics were incorrect, and I even called in a statistician to show how wrong the basis of their calculation was. It was a technical error on their part, but this case was enough for them to ban me from ever being involved with the Jockey Club again. It's hardly fair, but no trainer can approach me again to assist them. I am not allowed to cross-examine their witnesses either.

Unfortunately – or maybe fortunately – Dorothy cut ties with me because of these hearings. So, I was on my own in my fledgling practice and set about finding clients. With great anticipation, I placed an advert in the South African attorneys' journal *De Rebus*, only to discover that attorneys either didn't read it or couldn't read. I watched my slender reserves of money dwindle at an alarming rate.

In order to feed myself, I had re-established my handyman business in Johannesburg, and was doing handyman work in and around the city. One of my suppliers was a glazing business called MUG Glaziers. I became friendly with the owners, and they asked me one day if I would be interested in running their shop in Greenside, a suburb of Johannesburg. I thought about it and realised that my resources were good for another two months at the most, so I accepted the offer. I was now an apprentice in the art of glazing – in fitting shower doors. Ironically, I was now learning the business in which my father had been involved during the Standerton days.

One day, while I was applying silicone to a shower door near Sandton City, my pager went off. (This was the pre-cellphone era – I had a small radio pager in case of emergencies.) It was a law firm. I found the nearest public telephone and called the attorney immediately.

With great excitement, I spoke to Reg Kossuth, who was acting for an insurance company called Commercial Union Life. Hillel Shapiro, the forensic pathologist I'd met at Wits, had suggested that he call me. The company had a problem and they wanted to know if I would be interested in investigating it. The documentation was delivered to me, and eagerly I started reading.

It was the case of a young woman who had been found dead in her bed, in Durban, with a packet of antidepressants and a bottle of wine by her side. She ran her own business and had recently taken out a substantial life insurance policy, with her husband designated as the beneficiary. Her death had occurred within the two-year suicide exclusion clause contained in most insurance policies, which prevents people from taking out policies with the sole intention of committing suicide and making money out of it for their beneficiaries. My brief was to determine whether her death had been a suicide or not.

I flew to Durban to investigate the case, and discovered that the woman had been a severe and chronic depressive. She was on significant doses of antidepressant drugs and had visited several doctors. She had had the scripts from these doctors dispensed at various pharmacies, using different names, and she'd even forged some of the prescriptions. These facts should have been disclosed to the insurers when she took out the policy. In instances where this does not happen, it is known in insurance jargon as a 'material non-disclosure'.

I did not conduct any analysis in this case – I obtained information from the mortuary. The results were puzzling. One particularly strange aspect related to her liver. The liver was weighed at the autopsy, but the recorded mass differed significantly from the mass of the liver that was received for analysis. I suspected that there had been a switch in the samples, and that the organs of another body had been sent instead. Whether her husband had had a hand in this was never established, but it was strongly suspected.

The claim was repudiated successfully because her state of depression had not been disclosed. No one challenged my finding. I now came to the daunting task of submitting an invoice: I didn't have a clue what to charge. My girlfriend at the time suggested that I charge R100 per hour, a figure that seemed exorbitant to me. I followed her suggestion and submitted my account with bated breath. To my surprise, I received a letter of thanks and a cheque for R10 000 in return! This was more than I had earned in an entire year as an academic, and I realised that a good living could be made in private consulting. My career as a budding glazier was cut short – all my energy would now be channelled into running a private forensic practice.

One of my first steps was to call Hillel Shapiro to thank him for referring the case to me. After some difficulty in getting through to him, I finally spoke to his secretary, Maureen Stroud. She told me that Shapiro had passed away the previous week and that she was busy sorting out the estate and tidying up his affairs. I was shocked and deeply saddened by the news.

It had become clear to me that I would need some administrative support in my practice, so I called Maureen about a week later to ask her what her future plans were. She wasn't quite sure, so I invited her around to my house to offer her a position as my secretary. (I had typed the first report with one finger on an IBM Golfball typewriter.) Over a cup of tea Maureen agreed to come and work for me, and we sealed the agreement with a bottle of marmalade and a jar of beetroot preserve, which I had made. Maureen was to work for me for the next twelve years, and she proved to be a godsend in many ways.

We set up office in a pair of semi-detached houses in Fox Street, opposite the Jeppestown post office in Johannesburg, and I began to establish a laboratory. Setting up a laboratory was no cheap exercise, and I decided to lease the equipment to start with. John Green and MLS Bank loaned me the money, and I spent it with gay abandon.

Shortly after Maureen had joined me, she sat me down one day and asked me what I thought I needed to earn in order to service my debt. The thought had not even crossed my mind – I hadn't a clue. My passion is for science, and once a case is completed, I have no interest in the financial side. This is perhaps a result of my childhood experiences of the terrible trauma caused to my family by my father's horse-racing addiction. I earn the money, and what happens to it after that is of no consequence to me.

Maureen took over and ran the business for me with little intervention from my side. She spoke to the bank manager, arranged an accountant to submit tax returns, and single-handedly kept the practice afloat despite my excesses. She set up processes that I still use today, and I owe her a huge debt of gratitude.

At one point, the practice was particularly slow and we needed to cover our overheads. I recall telling Maureen the story of the verger at St Peter's Church in London, who couldn't read or write. When a new vicar came into office, he told the verger that he should either learn to read and write or vacate the position. The verger felt that he was too old to start learning new things, so he left the employment of the church. As he was walking down the street, he felt like a cigarette, so he looked around for a tobacconist. There wasn't one anywhere. So he walked down the adjacent street, and then the next street – nowhere could he find a tobacconist.

He decided to start his own tobacconist. Within a few years, he had set up a chain of shops around London, and had amassed a great fortune. One day, he went to see his bank manager to discuss how to invest this money. When he was asked to sign some documents, he admitted that he couldn't read or write. The bank manager looked at him in horror and said, 'You have done so well in business. Imagine where you would have been today if you could read and write.' The tobacconist looked at him and smiled. 'Yes,' he said. 'I would still have been the verger at St Peter's.'

With this story in mind, I suggested to Maureen that she and I make sandwiches and find someone to sell them for us, as there were no food outlets around our offices. We got to work and made delicious sandwiches. We did not, however, have the same success as the St Peter's verger – our product hardly sold. We ate most of the sandwiches ourselves!

These were exciting times forensically, and the lack of cash flow at times was something that I did not take very seriously or worry about for any length of time.

I was contacted by a reporter from the *Sunday Times*, who came to interview me. A few days later, an article titled 'Forensic Scientist aims to show the other side' appeared in the newspaper, which brought me my second case, a drunken-driving case in Bronkhorstspruit.

There were major flaws at that time in the process of testing for drunken driving. When attempting to convict a man of driving while under the influence of alcohol, a blood sample is drawn and analysed to determine the alcohol content in the bloodstream. The law states that the sample must be sterile in order for it to be suitable for chemical analysis. In other words, there must be no micro-organisms in the sample. This implies a completely germ-free process when the blood is drawn.

Almost all alcohol that is produced for drinking purposes, however, is created by the fermentation of sugar by micro-organisms. The yeast that converts grape juice into wine is but one of a myriad small creatures that converts sugar and other chemicals into the wonderful, simple alcohol called ethyl alcohol.

The way in which doctors took samples in the mid-1980s was guaranteed to lead to contamination with micro-organisms. The government doctor would bare the driver's arm and, without cleaning the injection site, would draw a sample of blood. The sample would then be placed in a small bottle with a screw-top lid called a McCartney Bottle. This bottle contained certain chemicals that were supposed to prevent the formation of alcohol by any microbes that had inadvertently found their way into the bottle during the opening and filling process, thus making the analysis accurate. Unfortunately, about 40 per cent of the bottles tested by Dorothy Gill at the time contained living microbes, which could alter the alcohol concentration.

The moment it could be established that living microbes inhabited the bottle, the accused was perfectly entitled to ask if the state could prove that these microbes had not converted some of the blood sugar into alcohol. Of course, the state could not rule this out, and conviction under those circumstances was out of the question.

Drinking and driving was, and still is, one of the major problems in this country. I faced a moral dilemma in the Bronkhorstspruit case, and in some of the cases that followed, in that I was helping drunken drivers to get off scot-free. I wrote a letter to the then Attorney-General, raising the issue with him, as I was genuinely concerned by the fact that I might be assisting drunken drivers to walk away without facing the consequences of their crime. I also decided to raise the issue with the Deputy Attorney-General, Kevin Atwell. He was a man of great integrity, and one of the few state employees whom I had felt comfortable dealing with. I wrote to him, and he replied, saying that the matter was out of his hands and that I should contact the state health chemical laboratories.

I did this, and drove to Pretoria to see the head of the state health laboratories, Dr van Niekerk. He listened to what I had to say, politely thanked me, and indicated that they were quite satisfied with the way things were run, and that they would contact me if they felt the need. My meeting with Dr van Niekerk was the start of a process that, in retrospect, can only be described as a three-ring circus.

It would have been easy to solve the problem – all that the state needed to do was to take the blood in sterile conditions, something that any junior nurse could have told them. I explained this to

Atwell, but he was adamant that his hands were tied, and suggested that I try to win a case or two and then come back to discuss the matter with him.

It was around the same time that an attorney came to see me on the way home from court. He was accompanied by Advocate van Nieuwenhuizen, who was interested in my work. Shortly afterwards, I started receiving instructions from the attorneys who had briefed him. One of these was Nick von Wesel from the law firm Cliffe Dekker & Todd (now Cliffe Dekker Hofmeyr). Between Von Wesel, Van Nieuwenhuizen and me, we were briefed on around 100 cases of drunken driving, and we won all of them. Thanks to the total intransigence of the state over alcohol testing, I was comfortably kept in business for the first two years of practice.

Criticism was received from far and wide, and at one point I even had the organisation Mothers Against Drunken Driving (MADD) publicly criticising my role in helping drunken drivers to get off the hook. The reality, of course, was that I was not making the law, but simply taking advantage of it. The state's stupidity kept me alive for a good few years, and I started to earn a reputation for finding the loopholes. All we had to do was ask a few pertinent questions of the state prosecutors regarding the taking of blood samples. Their charts and graphs would mean nothing when the blood sample could not be guaranteed to be sterile.

The state hated me. General Lothar Neethling, who headed up the police forensic laboratory, in particular despised me. We were adversaries for many years, and he always used to say to me, 'Klatzow, I can't wait to get you in a witness box. I will crush you!' But, sadly for him, he never did.

Apart from the problems with blood testing, the police periodically made some other mistakes in their zeal to arrest drunken drivers. I was involved in one such case, in which Nick von Wesel had developed a malignant tumour of the parotid gland (one of the salivary glands near the ear). A mutual friend, Grant Kassner, had removed the tumour, but there was some facial-nerve bruising, as often happens in such cases. Nick ended up with a surgical Bell's palsy, which caused the left-hand side of his face to droop. It also made him slur his words and meant that he had a problem with his balance.

One day, while on his way home from work, Nick was stopped by the traffic police for a minor offence. The traffic officer took one look at him and immediately arrested him for driving under the influence. He was taken away, and at the forensic laboratory he was examined by the young district surgeon. Of course, there was no case for drunken driving.

Some time later, Solly van Nieuwenhuizen and I were in court on another drunken-driving case. Who should be the district surgeon who had been called to give evidence? None other than the same one who had examined Nick. She was being particularly stubborn, and would not concede that unsteadiness on the feet could be caused by a wide variety of conditions, of which inebriation was only one. State officials, as I had learnt, rarely make any concessions in court. The district surgeon took refuge in technical terms and kept referring to the positive Rhomberg sign, which is just another fancy name for being unsteady on the feet.

Van Nieuwenhuizen asked her to demonstrate the Romberg sign. She called for the court orderly, but the legal counsel insisted that she use the instructing attorney – Nick von Wesel. Of course, Nick swayed around like a branch in a storm, and the district surgeon had to concede that there may indeed be other reasons for unsteadiness on the feet!

According to law, blood samples taken within two hours from the commission of the crime will be presumed to be an accurate measure of the blood alcohol at the time of the crime. But what happens if there are two conflicting blood test results within the two-hour period?

A young man had attended his work office party and, after

consuming vast amounts of punch, was on his way home in his father's Mercedes-Benz. As luck would have it, he was stopped in a roadblock and asked to blow into a breathalyser. Of course, he was found to be over the legal limit, so he was promptly arrested and taken to the police station, where he was charged and then told to sit on a bench in the charge office. A blood sample was taken from him, and he sat waiting. When no one seemed to take any notice of him, and still in possession of his car keys, he eventually decided to sneak out and go home.

The man jumped into his car and drove off – straight into another roadblock! This time he decided not to stop, and an exciting chase ensued. He was rearrested and charged for a second time that evening, and a second blood sample was taken. Both blood samples were taken within the statutory two-hour interval after the first commission of the crime.

The two test results were poles apart, and the magistrate was not prepared to guess which was the correct reading. Theoretically, the two samples should have been identical, but because of the way the blood samples were taken, there were discrepancies and there was doubt. The young man was acquitted.

Over that time, I continued, unabated, defending people charged with drunken driving. The prosecuting authorities found it almost impossible to achieve a conviction using this flawed system. I discovered that the state would never admit that it was wrong. They would use tactics that included counter-arguments, personal criticism and throwing in irrelevant curve balls in an attempt to avoid the real issue at hand – namely that of taking samples correctly.

These times, for me, were not about game-playing. Drunken driving is very serious, and can lead to great tragedy. By not being able to prosecute effectively, one can argue that the state, in a sense, had blood on its hands.

It is interesting to know that alcohol can also form in the body through other means. On 28 February 1975, a great tragedy occurred when a London underground train crashed into a dead end in an unused section of the tube system at Moorgate. Forty-two passengers and the driver were killed. The accident site was a mangled mess, and it took several days before the body of the driver was extricated from the wreckage. At the post-mortem, his blood alcohol was found to be high. It was only after a substantial effort by forensic analyst Janet Corry that it was discovered that the alcohol in the driver's body had formed during the process of decomposition. This is the same process that occurs when bacteria or fungi get into a blood sample and convert the sugar in the blood into alcohol.

The explanation that alcohol has formed naturally in the blood is often offered by lawyers in cases where their clients have been killed in road accidents, but it is only a valid defence in cases where there are obvious signs of decomposition. In most other cases, the post-mortems are conducted within a time period that would not allow for alcohol to be formed naturally, as occurred with the train driver at Moorgate.

This is particularly significant for insurance companies. Many companies will refuse to pay death benefits if the driver of the car is over the legal blood alcohol limit. This often results in great hardship for those left behind, but there is no doubt that the devastating effects of alcohol on our roads should be combated by all available means: insurers should not be expected to pay for the damage caused by the hordes of reckless, inebriated drivers.

It took about six years for the state to see the light. Eventually, it adopted more scientifically accurate methods of collecting blood samples from drunken drivers that would guarantee a sterile sample. This was not without its teething problems, but the system that I recommended is now in place and the blood alcohol cases are tried fairly and in a more scientifically reliable manner. I have not given evidence in a drunken-driving case in many years.

These were exciting times and interesting years. At one point, I was branded as somewhat of a forensic outlaw. This label was to be reinforced repeatedly in the following years, especially with regard to my growing involvement in fire investigations.

CHAPTER 4

THE 'HIRED GUNS' OF THE INSURANCE INDUSTRY

'[There is a] myth that bureaucracies guided by scientific knowledge are efficient and benevolent.'

– IVAN ILLICH,

Austrian philosopher

Fire is a vivid manifestation of chemistry at work, and a very important part of forensic science. I had read a great deal about fires, but at this point in my career, in the early eighties, I had never actually investigated one. This was soon to change.

Each fire investigation presents a unique challenge: it is arguably one of the most demanding areas of forensic science, particularly with regard to finding and interpreting evidence. A fire can create misleading evidence, and it is easy, as the forensic scientist, to make a mistake.

Most solids do not burn; they must be heated before they will give off sufficient flammable gases, which will then ignite. Take, for instance, the familiar coal fire found in the living room of many homes. To light it, you need to place some paper under a quantity of thin wood kindling, and the coal has to be placed on top of all of this. The paper ignites easily, heating the wood to its ignition point, which in turn heats the coal to its ignition point. In the early stages of a fire, therefore, the principal form of heating is by convection – hot gas produced by the heating process must heat up nearby materials to their ignition temperature before they can catch alight. As hot gases rise – remember the hot air balloon – so the course of the fire will move upwards and outwards from the initial source.

Fire development always follows a pattern, which can be read and interpreted by the experienced observer. All too often, the arsonist performs his deeds as an act of desperation, or, in order to make sure of the total destruction of the property, he or she helps the fire along by using accelerants such as petrol or by setting multiple fires. These are the signs that we look for. When a fire has not developed normally, it is possible to document the actual development and to find out what the real cause of the fire was. It is also possible, using sophisticated equipment, to demonstrate the presence of accelerants.

There are very few things that burn away and leave no trace. In so many aspects, then, the investigation of a fire resembles an archaeological dig: it is by using the methods of the archaeologist that the investigator is able to reconstruct the scene and to inter- pret the causes and the origins of a fire properly.

My career in forensic fire investigation began in 1985, when a hotel in Middelburg burnt to the ground and I was approached by an insurance loss adjuster to investigate. My journey into the world of pyroforensics had started! I was to discover that the most common cause of fire is bank managers – the number of fires that occur after the bank has put financial pressure on a business is phenomenal.

I flung myself into this fire investigation with gusto, and the way in which I approached it became the general methodology for all of my subsequent investigations of fires. By sweeping the floors clean of debris, I was able to see clearly the fire patterns on the carpets. Long, narrow trails of burnt carpeting provided the first clue that an accelerant had been used in this particular fire. I interviewed the various players in the running of the hotel and those who had observed and fought the fire. When I compiled all the information, there was a clear indication that the fire had been deliberately started. This is what I reported to the insurers, and my first fire investigation was complete.

Within a short period of time, I was asked by a large insurance company to investigate another fire, this time a house that had burnt down in Ferndale, Johannesburg. I was able to excavate through all the debris and could show that there were trails along the floor where the fire had followed a flammable accelerant, which had been placed there prior to the fire. After analysing the remains, I could also show that the house had contained almost no normal house contents when the fire occurred.

In my report to the insurance company, I had referred to the accelerant as 'petrol'. By the time the matter came to trial two years later, my experience had taught me that the correct way to refer to the material that I had found was not 'petrol', but rather 'fossil fuel–based accelerant'. Petrol comes out of a pump, and, once ignited, it is altered by the evaporation and heat during the fire – after a fire it is technically no longer petrol.

I wanted to correct my report based on what I had learnt subsequently. The insurance company's legal advisor instructed me not to. I knew that using the word 'petrol' was blatantly wrong, and could result in stringent cross-examination. I was outraged that a legal advisor could dictate to me what my report should contain, particularly as this report was going to be used in a court of law. I refused point-blank to cooperate. The insurance company's claims manager vowed never to engage me again, and that was the end of my work with that company.

I was subpoenaed by the state to testify as a witness in this case. Two years later, at the civil trial, Deneys Reitz wanted me to testify on their client's behalf, which I ended up doing.

This was my first encounter with what I believe to be the unacceptable side of business, and the power that money holds. The larger insurance companies have vast sums of money at their disposal, and can decide at a whim whom to instruct. For a young struggling consultant, insurance investigations can be very tempting indeed. The danger comes in when the insurance company's agenda is different from the scientific agenda. I have always refused to bow to their requests and have exercised the utmost integrity in my work. I believe that once you start altering scientific reports to suit the client or submitting information that you know is incorrect, you become beholden to your client and your credibility suffers in the long run.

When giving evidence in a court of law, it is absolutely critical for the expert witness to be free from obligations; to be seen as completely independent. If the majority of a forensic investigator's work comes from a single source, such as the insurance industry, then he or she always risks being at the behest of the combined force of money and power. This is not a good recipe for honest behaviour. It is quite true that many claims submitted to insurers are false to the point of fraud, but dishonesty on the part of the insurers towards their clients – and there is no doubt that some of the insurers resort to dishonest business practices – is not a solution to the problem.

My work in the area of fires had a direct impact on my personal life, for which I am eternally grateful. After about eighteen months of fire investigation, I had completed a few cases with an American insurance company called CIGNA. The company invited me to speak at its conference in Johannesburg, and, unbeknown to me, my now wife, Shelona, and a colleague, Susan Edwards, were in the audience. Some two weeks later, there was a fire in Long Street in Cape Town, on a site that was being renovated by Resnekov & Nielsen. CIGNA was the liability insurance company, and Shelona and Susan Edwards asked me to investigate the fire.

It was a simple case to solve, and ultimately CIGNA paid the claim: the welder had dropped sparks onto the floor, causing the fire. After I'd inspected the site, we all went to lunch, and Shelona was part of the group. When I returned to Johannesburg, we remained in contact and, shortly afterwards, we were married. A fully qualified archaeologist, Shelona manages my practice, and it has been a fantastic partnership and marriage that has worked extremely well for twenty-three years. I have been doubly blessed in that she has been able to raise our children, James and Cathryn, as well as engage in her passion for archaeology. James is interested in physics and mathematics, and Cathryn has a passion for the arts, in particular Shakespeare, both following in the family traditions.

In 1989, a couple of months after the Long Street fire investigation, I was contacted by Vic Lewis, a loss adjuster who called me in to investigate in the *Maritime & General Insurance Co. v Sky Unit Engineering* case. Vic was a snappy dresser and was transported around in a chauffeur-driven Mercedes-Benz. He openly bragged that his suits cost R1 000 each, which was a fortune in those days. Mine cost around R75 each, and Vic was not shy to tell me, 'Yes, I can see that!'

Sky Unit Engineering was a company that manufactured spare parts for cars. There had been a downturn in the economy, and two lathes in their factory had spontaneously and inexplicably caught fire. The insurance company, facing a large claim for loss of profits, decided to pay out. The claim had hardly been paid when someone took a forklift truck and flattened the rest of the factory. The insurers were now in a bit of a state. They were deeply suspicious, but they could not prove any foul play, and decided to reinvestigate the lathe fire that had occurred some two years previously.

Fortunately, the burnt lathes were still in storage, and I was called in to investigate the matter.

These lathes were complicated assemblies of motors, hydraulics and electronics, and I soon found myself in an area about which I had little knowledge. With great persuasion, I managed to convince the insurers to allow me to appoint Professor Charles Landy, the then head of electrical engineering at the University of the Witwatersrand, to assist me in unravelling the complex electronics of the machine.

The lathe was made up of two sections, both of which had been burnt in the fire. One of the sections was a hydraulic part that was joined via a rubber grommet to the other section. The door on the one side had been closed, so the only way that the fire could have spread would have been through the grommet. I tested the potential spread of the fire myself by removing the grommet. It was easy to see: there was evidence of burning lower down and higher up, but there was a distinct unburnt section in between. The fire hadn't gone though the grommet. This meant that there had to have been two fires – which suggested that the lathe fire had been deliberate.

I needed to see one of these lathes in an unburnt state in order to compare it to the burnt lathe, confirm my finding and complete my investigation. There were no such machines in the country other than our burnt one, so the insurance company reluctantly agreed that I could travel to Cremona in the north of Italy, to the home town of these lathes. (Cremona, incidentally, is where the Stradivarius violin has its origins.) In Cremona, I was able to confirm what I had suspected. On investigating an unburnt lathe, I could establish how it worked and was then in a position to rule out certain allegations that were presented as causes of the fire.

The case eventually made its way to court. Sky Unit Engineering was represented by the legal firm Deneys Reitz, with John Neaves the appointed attorney. The attorneys had flown in an expert from London to deal with the case. His brief became obvious to me very quickly: he had clearly been instructed to deal with my evidence and to discredit it as best he could.

I was cross-examined by Jules Browde for the better part of a week. I will never forget his opening statement: 'Doctor, I am waiting with bated breath. My client is waiting with bated breath. The court is waiting with bated breath to hear how my client is alleged to have set his lathe alight.'

I replied rather flippantly, 'I think he poured petrol over the lathe, and put a match to it,' and then added, 'I may concede, though, that he may have used a cigarette lighter!'

After a hard three weeks in court, judgment was given against the insurance company. The matter was taken on appeal, and was won in the court of appeal before three judges. The judges were quite complimentary about my evidence. In their judgment, they said, 'While Klatzow may have been rather unorthodox in his approach and whilst he may have been a little over-enthusiastic, he was well qualified to speak and his views merited serious consideration.' I agree with the judges' opinion.

Maritime & General Insurance Co. v Sky Unit Engineering clearly illustrates the role of an expert witness, as well as the pitfalls that can occur when an expert is expected to act as a hired gun, as was the London expert in this matter. It has since become a leading case on the duties of the expert witness and his or her obligation to the court. Many dilemmas confront the expert witness. The client who briefs you expects that you will act in his best interests, but this is not where the expert witness's duty lies. His or her responsibility to the court is not to mislead the judge with science. Often, the scientific truth will imply that the client's case is bad, and that on the expert evidence it would be a mistake for the client to call you as a witness. Clients and their attorneys do not like this.

The claims manager of the insurance company SA Eagle, a man by the name of Jimmy McIntosh, was often quoted as saying, 'If you work against me, you will never work for me,' which epitomises the thinking so prevalent in the industry. Jimmy has long since retired and was in the Ombudsman's office for a while. I have grown to like and respect him as I have mellowed with age, but I have never understood his dictum. This belief of the insurance companies is counter-productive to honest expert evidence, and it exposes the expert to a charge of bias towards the insurance company.

Arson is a huge problem in the world of insurance. To catch the arsonist and to curb the occurrence of this type of fraud in the industry is an important task. However, the insurance industry has gone about this business in a rather foolhardy way. Quite often, the claims manager will proceed on a hunch, and will then resort to any means to avoid paying the claim.

One of the larger and more recent fire cases I have worked on is that of the Munitoria Building in Pretoria, which housed the municipality. The building was gutted in March 1997, causing between 300 and 400 million rands' worth of damage. The incident had strong political undertones – it took place around the time of transition in South Africa, and the press touted the idea that the Afrikaner Weerstandsbeweging (AWB) and right-wingers had started the fire.

I was called in by a consortium of insurance companies, including CIGNA, who had a financial interest. The police seemed pleased to have me involved, as they didn't want the responsibility of any problems or fingers pointed at them, so I led the investigation on behalf of the insurers.

All the evidence – the path of the fire, eyewitness accounts and damage to the exterior of the building – pointed to the fact that the fire had started as a result of an electrical malfunction in a downstairs office. Because of the political pressure, there was a need to make a public statement revealing my conclusions. We held a press conference on the steps of the burnt Munitoria Building, and I presented my findings. The police and other investigators concurred.

CIGNA was not happy. My findings had greatly limited their ability to find what I like to call 'wiggle room' – an opportunity for them to find a reason not to pay out. Yet paying out is a fairly simple concept: it's a case of fulfilling their obligations in terms of a contract that they have with the client.

CIGNA brought in an expert called Dr Newton, who was from Burgoynes, a company of consulting forensic scientists and engineers in the UK, to conduct the investigation. I accompanied him, drove him around and showed him the evidence, and he came to the same conclusion that I had. I wrote a report to CIGNA and said that Dr Newton had investigated and it was a case of I came, I saw, I concurred (a wordplay of mine on the old Julius Caesar statement '*veni, vidi, vici*' – I came, I saw, I conquered). My little joke was lost on the insurers. But, once more, the simple truth stood the test of scientific scrutiny, and the case was concluded accordingly.

Another pertinent case that illustrated insurers resorting to any means to avoid paying out a claim involved a farmhouse that burnt down. The incident left the owner outraged – not only by the loss of his property, but also by the attitude of the insurers. The owner, Piet Sandberg, a farmer from the Leeudoringstad area, had returned home one evening, in the middle of a huge thunderstorm, to find his house on fire. He had a collection of handmade rifles in a safe in the house, and had stood until daybreak with a hosepipe trying to douse the flames to protect his safe. He believed that lightning had caused the fire.

The insurance loss adjusters dragged their heels for six months. An exasperated Sandberg came to see me to ask me to assist. I thought it only right to inform the insurance company, SA Eagle, which was also a client of mine, that I was about to embark on a matter against them.

I called the claims manager, Wynand van Vuuren, and was taken aback by his response. 'David,' he said, 'I think you should know about your client. He is a bomb-maker who worked for the security police. Furthermore,' he added, 'I can prove that the house was not set alight by lightning.' Van Vuuren then told me that he had enough evidence to 'bring fraud charges' against my client.

I decided to examine the house anyway, and it was clear that the cause of the fire had been lightning. I also obtained the contents of the report made to the insurers by their own appointed expert, who had informed them that the cause was indeed lightning.

During some protracted correspondence with the man heading up the insurance company, it transpired that there had been no question of fraud relating to this unfortunate man. What the claims manager had told me was incorrect. The claim was paid and Piet Sandberg went on to rebuild his life.

I suppose that is where I should have left it, but I was outraged by what I had been told by Van Vuuren. The day after the claim had been settled, I phoned him and said, 'You, as a man and as a company, place a high value on integrity, so please explain to me why you misinformed me on the Sandberg matter. Please tell me why your clients should not lie to you when you are nothing more than a common liar.'

I don't think Van Vuuren was accustomed to such a direct approach, and he stalled me for two days, on the pretence of locating the files. Predictably, he never came back to me, so I continued the debate with Denis Burton, a more senior man at the company. Denis fenced with me for about three months, until I called him to ask what had been done about this matter. He replied that he had debated the issue with Van Vuuren, and that my version differed from Van Vuuren's. I was piqued by his suggestion that I was lying.

The answer was simple: I asked Denis to listen to the tape recording of the original conversation between Van Vuuren and me. That is where it ended.

One has to understand that the style of some companies in this country is that of totalitarian dictatorship, which seems to be tolerated within the broader political landscape. The so-called 'captains of industry' are sometimes little more than robber barons who will bear no criticism. This fails to allow for many subtle positions in between the two extremes.

After this, Denis immediately issued a banning order preventing anyone in the company from using my services. They could not control me, and they didn't like that. Ironically, about a year later, they needed me to give evidence in a case that I had investigated previously. I called them and said, 'You fellows have banned me. I rather like my banning, and I shall stay banned. Furthermore, you can go and give your own evidence in court.' They did not like this one bit (see Appendix C).

The pool from which an expert witness can draw paying clients is rather small and, to some degree, you are at the mercy of the larger firms, who like to call the shots. I have been extremely fortunate in that, in the eighties, when I was starting out as a pyroforensic expert, I had a number of strings in my bow. At the time, the country was in a state of total onslaught and the police and the army were behaving atrociously. There was simply no one else to call to assist the attorneys acting for the families of people who had been shot by the police or who had been mistreated in other ways. I was regularly briefed by the legal representatives of these people, and I gained experience beyond my years and beyond my station. To some degree, therefore, I was immune to the whims of the big insurers, although I did accept them as clients on numerous occasions.

Sooner or later, an expert witness who falls into the trap of accepting the patronage of the insurance companies to the exclusion of all others will be placed in a compromising position. It is not worth it, because eventually it is akin to drinking from a poisoned chalice. The secret is to stay true to yourself in your profession, always.

||||||||||||||||||||||||||||||||||||||||||||||||||||||||||||||||||

CHAPTER 5

THE EXPERT WHO NEVER WAS

*'"Entia non sunt multiplicanda
praeter necessitatum."*
*Entities should not be multiplied beyond necessity,
or, all things being equal, the simplest theory
is the one to be believed.'*

– OCCAM'S RAZOR, WILLIAM OF OCCAM,
English Franciscan friar and scholastic philosopher

Cases are won or lost based on the evidence provided by the experts. An expert is defined by his or her credentials, but this is not always infallible.

I recall the case of the expert who never was. A huge horse-and-trailer vehicle worth a considerable amount of money had been parked overnight on the premises of a garage in Kimberley. The following morning, it had vanished into thin air.

An insurance claim was lodged with Mutual & Federal Insurance Company, who claimed that they were not liable to pay the claim because there was no sign of forced entry. However, after protracted negotiations, they agreed that if the owner of the vehicle could show that the lock had been picked, this would count as a forcible entry.

The insurance company employed the services of Mr Sneeuberger, an expert locksmith, who testified that he had many, many years of experience: he designed locks; he lectured to the locksmith academy; what there was to know about locks that he didn't know really wasn't worth knowing at all.

The rather distressed plaintiff came to see me. He brought the lock with him and asked, 'Can this lock be picked?' The other expert had stated categorically that the lock could not be picked, but I was so ignorant about locks that I said, 'Well, as far as I'm concerned, any lock can be picked.'

I asked him to give me a weekend to see if I could pick the lock. I called various locksmith supply companies and discovered that there is a wonderful device called a pick gun, which enables one to pick locks rather more simply than by using more conventional methods.

Armed with this device and other lock-picking equipment, I settled down for the weekend. I clamped the lock in a vice and sprayed a little Q20 into the lock, and set to work with my pick gun. After about fifteen minutes, lo and behold, the lock sprang open. I tried it again, and I was faster: the more I practised, the better I got. While we were waiting for the day of the court case to arrive, I used it to practise and as a bit of a party trick. By the time we got to court, I was quite adept at picking the lock.

My expert summary was a very interesting construction. In the teeth of the expert summary from the locksmith, the true expert, I said, 'Look, I know very little about locks and I am, in fact, a medical biochemist, trained as a chemist, but I say this lock can be picked for the simple reason that I can pick it.' I got into the witness box in the Kimberley Court, armed with my lock-picking set, my lock, a little vice and some Q20, and proceeded to tell the judge the story of how I could pick the lock. At the end of my evidence in chief, I asked him, 'Would your lordship like to see it picked?'

'Yes,' he said.

So I screwed the vice to the bench in the witness box. I clamped the lock, and after a few seconds the lock was open, much to the astonishment of everybody – particularly Mutual & Federal.

It was time for me to be cross-examined, but it was also tea time, so my cross-examination was put on hold until after tea. The counsel for the other side asked me one question before the break, however, which meant that I couldn't talk to anybody during tea time because I was technically under cross-examination. I was left alone with the court orderly in the courtroom. I got bored after a while and I thought, well, I wonder if I can pick any other locks in the building? I leapt up and looked around, and saw that the door to the judge's chamber had a Yale lock on it. I said to the orderly, 'Should I see if I can pick that one?'

'Yes!' he replied.

So I climbed over the bench to where the judge sits, and within thirty seconds I was in the judge's chambers. Fortunately for me, he had gone to tea as well. I unpicked the lock and relocked the door.

After tea, everyone trooped back into court and counsel proceeded to complete cross-examining me: 'Doctor, that was a very impressive demonstration of your lock-picking abilities,' he said.

'Yes, thank you. It is kind of you to say so,' I replied.

'Doctor, have you practised on this lock?' he then asked me.

'Yes, indeed I have, my lord,' I responded. 'I've practised a great deal on this lock. In fact, it has become a bit of a party trick.'

'Thank you for your candour, Doctor,' he said to me, and then added, 'I'd like to put to you that the only reason you could open this lock with such facility is that you have practised a great deal on this lock, and that you would not be able to pick any other lock.'

I replied, 'Well, my lord, that's a nice theory, but unfortunately, during the tea break, I was able to pick the lock into your lordship's chambers, which took me about thirty seconds. I unpicked it to relock the chambers.'

The judge's eyebrows shot sky-high! There was no doubt about the way in which the case was going to go: since the lock could so clearly be picked, the insurers would have to pay out on the basis of forced entry. Cases can be won in the most surprising ways, and experts can be so wrong with their dogmatic statements – a fact illuminated by the story of the lock-picker and the expert who never was!

The idea that 'experts' are defined as such by their credentials leaves much to be desired if one considers the so-called 'lie-detector' or polygraph test. This was brought home to me in a case in which a young man's car was damaged when he swerved to avoid a taxi. His tyres had worn bare, so about two weeks later, he went to have them replaced. He was told that he had bent the struts of his car, and that this would cost a sizeable amount to fix.

He decided to submit an insurance claim, and the insurance company paid for the repairs. However, his insurance policy in-cluded a clause saying that the insurers could put him through a lie-detector test, using a polygraph. The insurers insisted on this, and the young man 'failed' the test: the insurance company wanted their money back from him. He came to see me.

What made this so ludicrous is that a lie-detector test is a farce, and is not accepted in South African law. I called the man who had administered the test, and pretended that I needed a test done on a client. I asked what his qualifications were, and was told that he had completed a stunning six-week course at the Maryland Institute of Criminal Justice and had a master's degree in theology from the Rhema Church!

A polygraph is all about psycho-physiology, a field that requires an understanding of psychology and physiology. This depth of understanding and knowledge cannot be obtained in a mere six weeks. Electrophysiology is a subtle component of the process, and

I doubt that any of the so-called polygraphers have a clue about any of this.

I then called the insurance company and asked them if they *really* wanted to run their case on these qualifications: a man who has completed a six-week course in physiology, psychology and other pertinent elements, which takes other people years to study. There answer was, 'Talk to our lawyers.' Well, I do not talk to lawyers, so I contacted journalists from *Business Day* and *Carte Blanche* and suggested that they contact the insurance company to get the story.

The next day my client called me and said that the insurance company had decided not to pursue the matter. They were great bully-boys, it seems, until there was a chance that their story would become public knowledge.

A polygraph measures a number of elements, including your blood pressure, heart rate, breathing speed and perspiration. In theory, if you lie, you heart rate will increase, you will perspire or you will demonstrate one of the other signs that the machine measures. But these are all based on a false premise, as people differ from each other. These physiological conditions can change for a variety of reasons – reasons that may not reflect dishonesty. Many factors can cause a positive spike on the polygraph, and the measurement of human honesty has not been verified by this method.

Polygraphs are not relied on in the judicial system, and are not legal tender. They are not even accepted by the South African Insurance Association (SAIA). I would advise anyone who is asked by an insurance company to take a polygraph test to refuse point-blank.

For the insurance company to use a polygraph test in the instance of this young man's case was completely underhanded, and would have bamboozled an innocent client if he had not sought help.

I have enjoyed challenging the large insurance companies, and I have enjoyed being truly independent. The thought of constantly being subjected to the whims of the various insurance companies' claims managers is utterly abhorrent to me.

An expert's evidence is only as strong as the scrutiny it can withstand. Invariably, there will be 'experts' who do not have the expertise they profess to have. However, scientific proof is always the deciding factor. There is no grey area: everything boils down to the hard facts.

||||||||||||||||||||||||||||||||||||||||||||||||||||||||||||||||

CHAPTER 6
QUEENSBERRY RULES

'Fair is foul, and foul is fair:
Hover through the fog and filthy air.'

– WILLIAM SHAKESPEARE,
Macbeth, Act 1, scene 1, lines 11–12

Having delved into an exciting career as an independent forensic scientist, people started approaching me to assist them in doing battle against the insurance companies. I became involved in a number of these cases, and started a company called Queensberry, to act specifically on behalf of insurance claimants. I chose this name because The Queensberry rules symbolise fair play, and were endorsed by the ninth Marquess of Queensberry for use in professional and amateur boxing matches. The rules are pertinent to both the world of boxing and the world of insurance claims.

One of my first encounters acting on behalf of a claimant was with one of the larger direct insurance companies. It is one of those insurance companies that encourages potential clients to insure directly – that is to say, without the advice and assistance of a broker.

When Mr Joffe, a humble shopkeeper from Alberton, submitted an insurance claim, he found the ball thrown right back in his court along with some serious threats.

Mr Joffe's children, who lived in the United States, were planning to visit with the grandchildren. The Joffes were delighted, and purchased a video camera to record their time together. The visit came and went, and their children and grandchildren returned to the United States, leaving the video camera, some tapes and many happy memories. Then fate stepped in, and the Joffes were burgled. They were cleaned out, and along with the microwave oven, TV set and other electronic goods, the video camera was stolen.

No problem, thought Mr Joffe, as he called his insurers. Within days, an internal investigator and loss adjuster came to see Mr Joffe and proceeded to interrogate him. Mr Joffe was asked all sorts of trivia relating to the equipment, leaving him feeling bewildered. Bewilderment turned to anger when he later received a letter signed by the assessor, stating that the insurers had rejected the claim because Joffe had 'failed to supply [the insurer] with true and complete information' and that he had 'failed to comply with our reasonable instructions and requests'. In addition, he had 'failed to supply proof of ownership and value of the items claimed for'. The letter further stated that the insurers had 'handed the matter over to the SAPS Fraud Unit for further investigation'.

Mr Joffe was horrified, dismayed and angry. Someone suggested to him that he come to see me, and we met shortly afterwards.

When he had told me the whole sorry tale, I phoned the loss adjuster, who immediately passed me on to the in-house legal advisor for the insurer. I asked if we could meet in person before the company embarked on its threat of criminal charges. The legal advisor agreed, and Mr Joffe arrived at my offices in Johannesburg at the designated time, and we waited.

After about forty-five minutes, I called the insurer's legal advisor, who informed me, abruptly, that the matter had been referred back to the loss adjuster. He was kind enough to transfer my call, and the loss adjuster told me in no uncertain terms that he was not prepared to discuss anything with either me or Mr Joffe, and that he was going to lay criminal charges immediately.

I smiled to myself as I said to him, Is it true that you have not laid criminal charges yet?'

'Yes,' he retorted, 'but I am going to do so now.'

I replied, 'But I have a letter from a few months ago where you said that you were going to do so then. It appears that you have not done so. I suggest the following to you: run down as fast as your little legs will take you and lay the charges. I will phone you for a police reference number. Following this, I can assure you that the following will occur. Firstly, I will charge you in your personal capacity with extortion. Secondly, I will assist Mr Joffe in bringing a civil claim against you in your personal capacity for defamation. Thirdly, I will involve your entire company in this activity. Go quickly,' I added, 'I need the money.'

Well, this caused an uproar at this insurance company, to put it mildly. Joffe phoned me to tell me that the insurer's legal advisor had called him, and that he had referred him to me. The legal advisor then phoned me and I questioned him as to how he, as an attorney, could contact a client directly when he knew that the client was being represented. He backed down immediately, and another meeting was arranged. This time, all parties attended. Bizarrely, they insisted that the meeting be held at a noisy restaurant in a nearby shopping centre. They obviously felt uncomfortable in my office. The childishness of the 'captains of industry' is truly astounding.

The end result was that Joffe received a cheque in the post, as well as a letter of apology from his insurer.

One may have thought that this insurance company would have learnt their lesson from all of this. Not so.

Michael Collison was asleep with his girlfriend one night when they were awakened by the sound of breaking glass. They cowered in their locked bedroom and, eventually, when the noises subsided, they ventured out. They were immediately met with a blast of hot air and smoke coming from the stairwell. They ran back into their bedroom and headed out to the balcony, but it was too high for them to jump. Back inside, they skirted the stairwell and managed to find a loft ladder, which they used to reach the safety of the ground. It was a highly traumatic experience.

Collison approached his insurers and submitted a claim. The insurers enlisted the services of the Council for Scientific and Industrial Research (CSIR) to investigate the fire, who submitted a report shortly afterwards. Collison received a call from the insurers, and was asked if he would come in to see them. Sitting in their plush offices in Pretoria, Collison was shocked by what he was told.

'Look, we know what went on in this fire,' the claims adjuster said. 'You must realise how seriously the courts view arson. You are not going to be the only one who suffers here: I prosecuted a man with young children and he was sent to jail. You do not want to go the full fifteen rounds with us. I will do a deal with you, withdraw your claim and I will not prosecute you.'

Collison was outraged and came to see me. I approached the insurer on his behalf and met with the legal advisor and the claims manager. I warned them about the flimsiness of their case, but my cautioning fell on deaf ears. I was sent away, and departed with their statement ringing in my ears: 'We are quite confident about our case and we will be happy to see you in court.' My reply to them had been, 'So be it, but when you hit problems in the court case, don't cry. You are big boys.'

The insurers seemed to try their level best to make this case as difficult as possible. The first hurdle we had to overcome was their denial that Collison was insured with them – they claimed that they had not been receiving premiums! This was purely a tactical move, and in any other situation it would clearly be called dishonest. They were quite capable of checking their records to see that

Collison had been paying premiums. However, to the dismay of the insurance company, Collison was made of sterner stuff than they had anticipated, and he emerged from the gruelling cross-examination on the first day having proved that he was, in fact, a client of theirs.

That afternoon, at close of play, the insurers again took us by surprise. They had sent out their expert to gather more evidence, and he arrived back at court and presented us with a new bundle of photographs that we would have to consider before the case resumed the next morning. This was not proper in terms of the rules of evidence, which expressly forbids this type of ambush tactic.

Collison was running his case on a shoestring budget. Although he was well within his rights to insist on a postponement at the insurer's cost, both he and they knew that we did not have the funds to pay for an entire rerun of the proceedings at some later date. We elected to continue.

I looked at the photographs in court when they were given to us that afternoon, and then, in a voice loud enough to be heard by the insurance company's representatives and their lawyers, I said to Collison's legal counsel, 'John, please thank them. They have unwittingly provided me with more evidence that refutes their case and they have saved me a trip back to the scene.' There was wide-eyed silence from the opposing team.

The next morning, the advocate acting for the insurers came sidling up to our lawyers and asked for a second experts meeting. I readily agreed, insisting that no lawyers be present.

Their expert had made a complete hash of his investigation. He asked me if we could work this out, and in the spirit of proper expert cooperation – noticeably lacking from the insurers up to that point – their expert and I drew up a new expert minute that put their case in an entirely different light. Their expert backed down completely from the view that was contained in the court papers. We went into court and recorded that the insurers had conceded the merits of the case.

After emerging from the courtroom, the insurer's legal advisor was standing outside, and there was some tension between us. In later years, we mellowed and we can be quite civil to each other. In fact, on the rare occcasion he even recommends my services to various people, as long as they are not clients of his insurance company!

This case is just another shameful example of the behaviour of industry leaders. One would have expected them to show some remorse. Not so. This insurance company proceeded to offer Collison R750 000 in full and final settlement, despite the fact that they had valued the property at R2.2 million. They were banking on the fact that Collison would be unable to fight a protracted and unfair court battle to get what was rightfully his. No amount of correspondence and discussion by Collison's attorney would move them.

Finally, in desperation, Collison turned to me again, and I called the overconfident claims manager once more. The conversation went roughly along the following lines: 'I have,' I said, 'a tape recording of a conversation between a member of your staff and Mr Collison. I am not a lawyer, so I called my friend, the Deputy Attorney-General, and he tells me that this attempt to get Collison to withdraw amounts to extortion. I am giving you an opportunity to persuade me why I should not discuss this live on radio.'

There was a prolonged silence, followed by the plaintive response, 'Well, it would be very bad for the company.'

A meeting was set up between us for early the following week, and a much more equitable settlement was reached.

To date, I have dealt with about 1 800 cases, and the experience has done little to diminish my cynicism regarding the so-called 'captains of industry'.

The insurance industry is organised on a number of levels. There is the central managerial section, under which falls the underwriting department, whose function is to evaluate the risk to be insured and to assess a fair value for the premium. The underwriters are supposed to take into account all the risk factors and problems at the onset of the insurance contract.

Then there is the claims department, which deals with and processes all the claims that are lodged with the company. Claims and underwriting should function as a harmonious whole. When a claim is lodged, the company appoints a loss adjuster to investigate the claim. These loss adjusters claim to be independent and to act fairly to adjudicate the claim, but this does not happen in practice. The loss-adjusting fraternity – like many forensic investigators – is critically dependent on the goodwill of the insurance companies, which leads to the loss adjusters grovelling at the feet of the insurers to retain their goodwill. This often results in the insured being short-changed. I have been embarrassed to see the abject servility exhibited by some of these loss adjusters when dealing with their principals, the insurance companies. There are some loss adjusters, of course, who do not exhibit such servile behaviour, but they are not in the majority.

I realised this fairly early on in my dealings with the insurance giants. When I started my consulting career, there were approximately forty different short-term insurance companies doing business in South Africa. This number has dwindled over the years; there are now only about five large players. The effect on customer choice, support and, above all, equity, has been devastating. Although difficult to prove, I believe that there is collusion between the large role players and, at the end of the day, the client is the one who suffers.

I have tried to bring this to the attention of the large insurance companies. I have given numerous talks at their congresses and also at several high-placed meetings, such as the Thursday Club, a monthly gathering of senior managers from the industry at which they discuss relevant issues. All of this has been to no avail. Money and power, as I have mentioned, are an evil combination.

In the early hours of the morning of 21 October 1994, a fire gutted a small family business in Brakpan – Brakpan Superette – leaving severe fire and smoke damage in its wake. The owners, two Greek brothers, had worked late the previous evening and, some time before leaving the shop at about 10 p.m., they had deep-fried some potato chips.

I was called to the fire the very next day by Commercial Union Insurance. Peter Evans, the former claims manager, would use no one but me. Peter was a straightforward person and wonderfully fair, who always said to me, 'Give me a reason to pay the claim.' He liked the way I worked. I would present him with a full exposé on what I had found, a report with all the details – both the good and the bad. By this stage, Peter had retired and been replaced with Hugh Gardiner.

I found a typical single-source fire that had started in the region of the chip fryer and had spread to the adjacent aisle. The rest of the damage to the shop was purely smoke damage.

In any fire investigation, if the cause is claimed to be innocent, that must be taken seriously until other compelling evidence emerges. There was no evidence to the contrary in my view: my report reflected that the fire had been caused by the chip fryer, which had been left switched on.

About two weeks later, I received a phone call from Commercial Union's new claims manager, Hugh Gardiner, to say that he had obtained two other expert reports that disagreed with mine. He sent these reports to me, and I spent an entire Saturday perusing them and writing a report on them. I disagreed with the two other experts, and motivated my reasons in the report. All the role players were called to a meeting at Commercial Union, where the matter was discussed. Certain observations of mine were challenged by a loss adjuster called Basil Pahl. The upshot of the meeting was that we all reconvened at the burnt-out premises, where we established that my observations were correct.

After another two weeks, I received a phone call from the claims manager to say that it was a case of 'two against one' and that they were going with the numbers. I replied that I was naturally disappointed, but asked if they would release me from the case, seeing as they thought I was wrong. I gave them an undertaking that I would not approach the insured, but we agreed that if I were to be approached, I would take the case. My words to Gardiner were, 'Let us all get into the ring and box and see who will win.'

My wife was outraged by the behaviour of the insurers, and urged me to proactively fight the case. I resisted the temptation and waited. I was eventually approached by the insured, and two years later, the matter came to trial. The crux of the matter was now whether there had been a single fire or two fires. Two fires would have meant that it was a deliberate burning. In court, my expert opponent from the CSIR claimed that the fire could not have spread across the aisle.

Anyone who has been in a supermarket would know that the aisles are often festooned with brightly coloured bunting that hangs across the ceiling. My view was that the bunting over the chip fryer had caught alight and burnt across until it had burnt through and fallen into the second aisle, causing the fire to spread (see photo). I had several photographs of the burnt bunting in the appropriate places across the aisle and, to make doubly certain, I purchased two rolls of the bunting from Koo products in Midrand.

I took my son, James, who was four at the time, to the Brixton Fire Brigade, where we tested my theory. He had dressed up in fireman boots and a helmet, and was very excited about the visit!

At the fire brigade's premises, I festooned the firehouse with the bunting, set a fire under it and sat back to photograph it as it caught alight. The streamers behaved exactly as I had predicted. Armed with this evidence, I returned to my laboratory to write the report for the court proceedings.

The counsel for the supermarket owner was Bernard Ancer. He and I were having a drink in chambers the night before the court case when in walked Johann Strauss, who was acting for the insurance company. Their expert had scorned my explanation of how the fire could have spread across the aisle. He had reasoned that the bunting was made of plastic and would have melted at temperatures well below those needed to ignite them. It was a good theory, but completely wrong.

Strauss joined us, and I felt it perhaps appropriate to spare him some humiliation the next day. I happened to have some bunting flags with me, and in a spirit of mischievousness, I suggested to Strauss that he tear one of them in half. He did so, and to his dismay he discovered that they were not made of plastic, but of paper. That was the end of the case. He could not go into court with an 'expert witness' who had failed to notice such a basic thing, and he advised his client to settle the matter immediately. It was settled that evening, and Commercial Union ultimately paid about twice as much money for costs as they would have paid had they settled the case in the first place.

I always believe in going the extra mile – putting in that little bit more effort, digging that extra area or taking additional samples. This story illustrates perfectly the dangers of theory over practical experiment, and also demonstrates the nature of insurance company thinking. I had believed that the insurers in this matter would have learnt their lesson, yet they chose to ignore my advice and made utter fools of themselves. They never briefed me again. I was hurt at the time, but as time passed, I realised that it was good riddance.

I learnt afterwards that Peter Evans, when he heard that Hugh Gardiner had gone with the other experts against me, took him on before the court case and bet him ten rand that he would lose against me!

In all fairness, evidence left by a fire can be misinterpreted if one does not have enough experience in this field. Low burns, for example, do not always indicate foul play. In other instances, traces of certain substances found at the scene that seem to be the source of a fire may have been introduced only afterwards: firemen may have traipsed through a fire scene carrying flammable substances on their boots; or the water they used to douse the flames could have carried flammable substances. One has to be very cautious about approaching the evidence at a fire scene, as it is easy to make mistakes or become confused.

This kind of confusion was well illustrated in the case of the Buccaneer Shoes factory fire. The factory is based in Maitland, Cape Town, and, as the name suggests, it manufactures shoes. On 5 May 2003, the factory burnt down, and it was alleged that the managing director had paid two of his employees to set the place alight. Three sets of experts ended up investigating the scene – one from the police, one from the insurance company, Mutual & Federal, and me. I was acting on behalf of the managing director.

Each expert had his or her own interpretation of the fire scene. Theresa Bester from the police said that there had been five separate fires. The insurance expert said that there had been four fires in completely different places, which did not correspond with the police findings. A so-called 'arsonist' had made a statement containing much of what the insurance investigators wanted. This statement had been made under duress, but, even so, the place where he had admitted to setting the fire did not correspond to where the police and CSIR expert alleged it had been found. In the end, the prosecutor did not rely on the state forensic expert. This is rare, as generally the state would go to great lengths to protect their own expert.

The truth was that the Buccaneer factory blaze had been a single-source fire. Advocate William King, who was representing the managing director of Buccaneer, brought me in to investigate. It could be shown quite clearly that there had been only one fire. There was clear evidence of the so-called 'arsonist'.

It eventually came out that one of the workers on the factory floor had started the fire. He, in fact, was never prosecuted, as he turned state witness. He admitted to deliberately starting the fire, and another arsonist who was not a state witness said that they had started the fire to cover their tracks: they had been stealing components of shoes – soles and uppers – and would take them home, glue them together and sell them to craft markets and other outlets. In no instance did they involve the head of the factory. The managing director was acquitted. Mutual & Federal, in trying to avoid paying the claim, had alleged that Buccaneer was on the brink of financial ruin. At the end of the day, the full claim was not paid out, yet the business is still in operation today.

A fire in which the rage of controversy is almost as hot as the flames is that of the Paarl Print factory. Just before 8 a.m. on 17 April 2009, a devastating fire broke out at Paarl Print in the Western Cape. Employees felt and heard a shock wave and then saw a wall of flame spread across the entire roof of the 300-metre building in a matter of seconds.

The building housed offices, printing equipment, a bindery and a storage area, and of the 300 employees, around 150 were on the premises at the time of the fire. Many were trapped inside: thirteen people died as a result of smoke inhalation, and many more were injured. Firefighters battled the blaze for hours, and by 1 p.m. it was under control. The entire building had been gutted.

I was called in by one of the directors of the company to investigate the cause of the fire. When I arrived at the scene the following day, Paarl Media chief operating officer Emarie Botha and chief executive officer Stephen van der Walt gave me a very hostile reception. I was not allowed onto the scene, the excuse being that only the police were allowed access at that point.

I was also surprised to find Anthony Young investigating on behalf of the insurers – he should not have been on the site: he has previously been discredited in a court case and is not registered with the South African Council for Natural Scientific Professions, which is illegal if you are operating in this capacity. Any person operating in the field of forensic science needs to be registered, just like a practising doctor is registered with the Medical and Dental Council. I was very unhappy with the fact that he was there.

I was also extremely irritated by the fact that the police objected to my presence there. The forensic policewoman, Theresa Bester, had come across me before in court, during the case of the Buccaneer fire. In that case, her evidence had been largely discredited by William King and me in cross-examination. She did not approve of my presence now, and one could only wonder why.

A major fight erupted on the scene, and I withdrew. The directors of the company wanted to discuss the matter with me further, but I declined, and I removed myself from the investigation.

The Paarl Print fire is a very strange story, of which the basis has not yet been established, I believe. There has also been an ominous silence in the press about it. The reports at the time stated that a microwave oven had blown up, causing the fire. I do not believe this. Some of the evidence was allegedly disturbed, which apparently caused subsequent problems.

More recently, the inquiry into this fire appears to indicate serious dereliction on the part of the owners. Allegations of malfunctioning fire equipment, blocked escape routes and little attention paid to fire regulations may well see the light of day when this matter gets to court, and we shall see if there is any truth in it.

The extent to which Paarl Print is liable *can* be established, but only if the evidence from the fire is properly examined by an impartial forensic investigator. What is crucial is that the Queensberry rules apply: only if there is fair play will the truth come out.

CHAPTER 7

KINROSS: A BLACK DAY IN SOUTH AFRICA'S HISTORY

*'Research is to see what everybody else has seen,
and to think what nobody else has thought.'*

– ALBERT SZENT-GYÖRGYI,
Hungarian biochemist and winner of the Nobel Prize in Medicine

On 1 October 1986, 177 miners died and scores more were injured in one of the worst mining disasters in South African history. A welder's spark had ignited the foam linings in a mining shaft in Kinross, in the former Eastern Transvaal. The political ramifications of the accident were felt far and wide: black miners had died because the white mine management appeared to have cut corners, compromising the safety of their workers.

Kinross is a sleepy town situated on the far eastern side of the gold reef. It owes its existence to the gold mines, which dominate the landscape. Gold mines employ thousands of black South Africans, and were notoriously dangerous places in which to work in the 1980s. The men were usually unskilled and had to work at depths of up to 3.658 metres and in temperatures reaching 30 °C.

This particular mine at Kinross was owned by Gencor, one of

the big Afrikaans mining houses that had established a foothold in the traditionally English industry, which was dominated by Anglo American at the time. Mines are extremely vulnerable to the gold price: when prices are high, it's all systems go; when prices are low, every last cent counts. Kinross deep-level mine was no exception.

New mining areas were being developed at the time, and huge haulages were being cut into the unforgiving rock. Once a passageway has been cut into the rock, the workers have to be protected against large chunks of rock breaking off from the roof (known as the hanging wall). Large steel rods, similar to Rawlbolts, are driven into the exposed surfaces and a steel mesh is secured over this to prevent rock falls.

The steel meshwork has to be covered with some protective coating, as the chemical atmosphere down the mine is somewhat corrosive due to the explosions that produce corrosive gases. Traditionally, the meshwork is coated with gunnite, a thick slurry of cement sprayed on by huge compressed air guns. While very effective, the disadvantage of using gunnite is that it is relatively slow to apply. In the mining industry, time is money, and money is king.

When a salesman approached the Kinross mine management and offered a faster solution to the problem, their attention was riveted. The salesman suggested that the mine use a type of foam – polyurethane foam – down the mine shaft, which could be sprayed on and which would harden in a matter of minutes. The management saw the opportunity to finish the tunnel in about half the time it would have taken using gunnite, and they were sold on the idea. Within a very short period of time, the walls of the tunnels were coated with the foam. All went reasonably well for a year or two.

This new method, however, was not without risk. An incident occurred at a coal mine in England, with disastrous consequences, and the dangers of polyurethane foam became well known to most mining engineers. The alarm was raised, and the salesman was called back to the mine to explain why he had recommended polyurethane foam. His explanation was as simple as it was dishonest: 'This is not polyurethane,' he said. 'It is polyisocyanurate.' Strictly speaking, he was right. He produced a journal article showing that polyisocyanurate was more resistant to ignition than polyurethane, and the work continued.

What he failed to tell the mine management was that this foam, if subjected to a powerful ignition source, would also ignite, and that once ignited, there would be precious little difference between this and the much-feared polyurethane. The substances look similar and have a similar chemical composition – both of them contain nitrogen atoms in their make-up. When they burn, they produce copious quantities of cyanide gas, which means that the smoke and combustion products produced by this substance are extremely dangerous to all living things.

Then disaster struck at Kinross. On the morning of 1 October, a platelayer took his welding equipment, consisting of an oxy-acetylene kit, down to do some repairs on the railway line in the tunnel lined with polyisocyanurate. During the process, he accidentally knocked over the acetylene bottle and damaged the valve, which started emitting acetylene, and it caught alight. It became like a huge flamethrower, the flame playing directly on the wall of the tunnel.

Within seconds, the side wall of the tunnel ignited, and the fire spread rapidly down the rest of the railway line, fanned on by a strong, forced air draft produced by the ventilation fans. The result was an underground inferno that produced lethal fumes. The platelayer managed to escape quickly and ran for help, but it was in vain.

It was a disaster on a grand scale, and the political implications were enormous. Cyril Ramaphosa, the then secretary general of the National Union of Mineworkers, was quoted as saying, 'We are obviously back to the dark ages of mining,' and accused the mine owners of not placing enough store in the safety of their employees.

I was called in to investigate this disaster about three days after it happened. It came as no surprise to me when, a few days after the Gencor team had contacted me, I was phoned by the legal firm Cheadle Thompson & Haysom, which specialised in, among other things, politically sensitive cases. They wanted to involve me in the case for the National Union of Mineworkers. By then, however, I had accepted the brief for Gencor. My declining the law firm was to have interesting consequences later on in my career.

I travelled to Kinross to inspect the scene. Cyril Ramaphosa and I visited the devastated mine, along with a whole delegation. We travelled down the mineshaft in a wagon that worked on pedal power. A burly black miner pedalled furiously as we sat in the cart, propelling us along the railway tracks within the mine. Arriving at the level where the fire had occurred was a frightening and eerie experience. We traipsed along the blackened mine tunnel along a distorted disrupted railway line for about a kilometre and a half. The temperature and the humidity were almost unbearable, and the smell of death was everywhere.

After examining the mineshaft, I proceeded to the mine managers' office, where I started the tedious process of taking a full history of the shaft and the events leading up to the disaster. As is so often the case, the secret to proper investigation is to get the fullest possible history. Within a few hours, it became clear to me that the mine had coated the shaft with polyurethane foam because it had been misrepresented to them by the salesman.

Direct evidence in the form of an invoice and correspondence showed that the mine management had queried the use of the foam. The subsequent correspondence made it quite clear that the salesman had allayed their fears by producing literature that detailed the fire behaviour of the polyisocyanurate in small-scale fire tests.

This invoice and the subsequent correspondence proved to be the central feature of the defence when the matter was later tried in the criminal court in Witbank, near Kinross. The other information that proved vital in the case against the mine was the data I gathered in Germany, where I went to pay a visit to the Bayer factory, on the outskirts of Cologne, which is the font of all knowledge on the family of polyurethanes. I established that, although polyisocyanurate was a different substance, it was nevertheless possible to ignite it – it just needed a larger ignition source.

In South African law, in order to be guilty of a crime, one needs to have the so-called 'guilty mind' or 'intention to commit a crime' (*mens rea*). If, through no fault of your own, an accident such as the one at Kinross happens, provided you have not been negligent, you may escape the criminal consequences of the accident. After a long trial, the fact that the Kinross mine management had queried the use of the foam, coupled with the fact that they had been misled by the unscrupulousness or ignorance of the salesman, was sufficient to eventually result in an acquittal for most of the accused.

I involved Dr Len Anstey in the matter, as we had to determine the cause of death of the 177 mineworkers. Len is a pathologist in Cape Town, and he travelled with me to Kinross when I went to examine the scene. The only place nearby that could provide us with the most basic facilities needed to conduct the autopsies was Standerton. There, we found the bodies piled one on top of another in a makeshift mortuary fridge that, in happier times, had seen service as a cold room for beer and cold drinks.

It was quite clear that the men had suffered from asphyxiation in some way, but it was very difficult to pinpoint the exact cause of death. We had even found a group of men a kilometre away from the fire, clustered around an air hose, stone dead. These men probably died as a result of the cyanide produced by the burning foam, together with other highly toxic gases emitted during the fire.

The case finally went to trial. The accused included an array of seven employees from the mine, from the platelayer who had caused the fire to the directors – they all sat in the dock. Our counsel in the case was Chris Plewman, who went on to achieve great things on the Supreme Court bench and later as a judge of appeal.

The entire case was fraught with political tension. Kinross mine was heavily criticised for not announcing the disaster until hours after it happened, and for identifying the dead black miners by ethnic group only. Despite all of this, I believe that the accused were given a fair trial and were, in my opinion, correctly acquitted. The Congress of South African Trade Unions (COSATU) subsequently established a National Health and Safety Day in recognition of the tragedy.

Despite this terrible tragedy and the fact that it showed clearly that polyisocyanurate should not be used underground, about two years later, Anglo American had a fire in one of their mines, when the same substance caught alight. The Kinross disaster had obviously not been enough of a warning to them. Fortunately, there were not too many casualties in the Anglo American fire. The occurrence of this second, preventable tragedy indicates that the bosses of big business seem to be driven purely by profits, irrespective of the risks they take and the potential danger in which they place their employees.

A strange irony arose for me from this story. Some years later, I was called again by an attorney called Helen Seady from the firm Cheadle Thompson & Haysom. A young man called Padi had escaped from police custody. (I have never quite understood why he went to all the trouble of escaping, because he would in any event have been released a few weeks later.) The police tracked Padi down and, just to show him that it was wrong to escape, emptied their firearms into him and his girlfriend, Faith.

One of the attorneys wanted me to investigate the shooting for the family. During my conversation with this attorney, she informed me that the firm had been displeased with me for accepting the brief from Gencor in the Kinross matter and, as a result, had decided not to brief me from then on. I replied that I was grateful they had

My father, Cyril Klatzow, in his army uniform just after World War II

My mother, Winifred Mabel, was a woman known for her forthright nature, a temperament that probably derived from her Cornish ancestry

My brother, Peter (right), and me, aged four, enjoying a sandy ice cream on a South Coast beach in the early fifties

Happy times: Peter, my mother and me at Scottburgh in the early sixties

Shelona and me on our wedding day on 10 April 1988

A family photo taken on my birthday in 2009 at Hermanus, where we had all been attending a court case for an unfortunate drunken driver. From left to right: James, Cathryn, me and Shelona

The Brakpan Superette, where a fire I investigated in 1994 had started slightly to the right of the chip fryer (in the background of the picture), which had been left switched on the previous evening

Dr Mark Froneman, my opposition in the matter at the Brakpan Superette, examining the scene where a supposed second fire had occurred. This fire damage was caused by the falling All Gold bunting, however, some of which can be seen on the burnt bags of charcoal and on the floor immediately in front of Mark

My assistant, Richard Baloyi, helping me to examine the behaviour of bunting in a staged fire. This Koo bunting was identical in every way to the supermarket's burnt All Gold bunting. The burning Koo bunting caught alight after being placed close to the fire

A view of the Brakpan Superette's interior, showing that no effort had been made to deliberately spread the fire and destroy any of the other goods. The only damage was to the far side of the shop

Left: The police's gas mask from the 1983 Saul Mkhize matter. According to the police, they had shot Mkhize in self-defence after he had attacked them with a knobkierie. Microscopic examination of the mask showed clear damage to the canister and lenses but not to the nose piece or rubber, indicating that the damage could not have been made by a knobkierie

Right: Seen under the microscope, grains of sand are visibly embedded in the gas mask from the Mkhize case, which reveals that the mask had been on the ground, and not on the policeman's face, when it was damaged

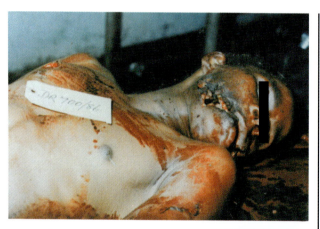

A victim of the Gugulethu Seven incident, a shoot-out that occurred between the security forces and a group of 'terrorists' in Gugulethu on 3 March 1986. This man was shot at close range

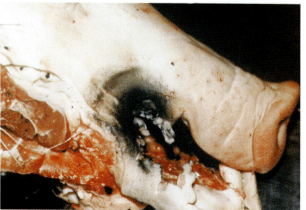

The effect on a pig's jaw of a close-range shotgun shot, fired from a distance of about twenty centimetres. The wound to the pig's jaw matched the injury to the deceased, putting to rest the notion by the police that the shot had been fired from twenty metres away. Pigs are used in forensic ballistics tests as their skin is almost identical to human skin

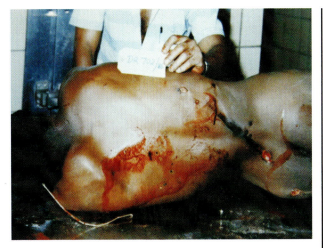

Another victim in the Gugulethu Seven tragedy. Note the burn marks across the small of his back, which were claimed by the police to be the marks of a bullet traversing the skin. The bullet's entrance hole can be seen immediately above the left buttock and the exit hole immediately below that to the right

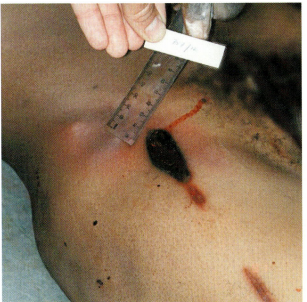

This photograph shows what a bullet traversing the skin actually looks like: it produces an abrasion, caused by the bullet skimming over parts of skin and touching it in other places. This should be compared with the above photograph, in which the marks in no way resemble an abrasion

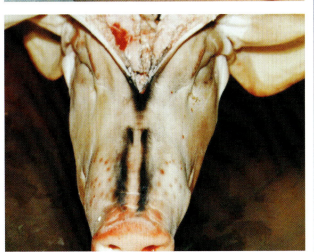

Our faithful pig having had an R1 rifle placed on its snout and the trigger pulled. The blackened colour of the mark resembles the burn mark in the above (top) photograph of the victim's back, indicating that he was shot at point-blank range

An exact replica of the cheap-and-nasty Walkman labelled 'Evidence – Hit Squads' that killed young attorney Bheki Mlangeni in 1990. An explosive had been placed inside the headphones, which detonated the moment he switched it on

An aerial photograph of the Komati River area (bottom left-hand corner), where two anti-apartheid activists were murdered by Vlakplaas men. Lothar Neethling's poison drops had failed to work on the men, so they were shot instead. The crooked, vegetation-free Mozambique border is visible on the mountainside

The cartoon drawn for me by Dov Fedler after the 1991 *Vrye Weekblad* case, which was linked to the Komati River disappearances. The sinister-looking fellow standing behind the poison bottle is Lothar Neethling, who headed up the apartheid-era forensic labs. Max du Preez is in front and Jacques Pauw is at the back. 'Exhibit A' is the animal on which Neethling had tested his potions

The slain activist Ashley Kriel, 15 July 1987. Note the handcuffs and bear in mind that there were circular abrasions around both wrists, a detail that the court would not take into consideration

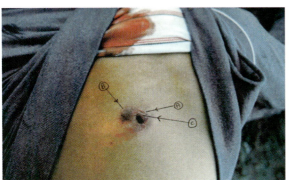

The bullet hole in Ashley Kriel's chest. The bullet entered his heart and killed him, but I believe it was really one of two bullets. 'A' shows the mark made by the skin being blown back against the muzzle of the pistol, while 'C' is the elliptical burn mark indicating that it was an angled contact wound

The exhibit showing the small hole in Ashley Kriel's jacket. The police alleged that an accidental contact shot had killed Kriel, yet the shot that produced this hole was clearly fired from a distance of greater than two metres … the story did not add up

The hole made by the shot I fired into a similar jacket to that of Ashley Kriel during my investigation, showing a much larger hole than that found on the victim. This is what a contact shot through clothing actually looks like

The .22-calibre weapon used to murder Ashley Kriel

The state pathologists demonstrating the marks made by the pistol in the Ashley Kriel case. Note, however, the lack of clothing when Kriel had been wearing clothing when shot. Inadvertently, the pathologist proves that one of the shots that made the marks on Kriel's back had to have been made with the clothing out of the way – impossible in the terms set out by the police of the incident. The state pathologists' test was inappropriate

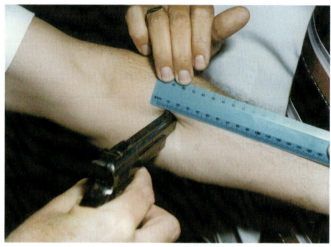

The shotgun pellet lodged in the skull of little Kwanele Moses Bucwa in the early eighties, showing its circular shape. It was this case that led to my mistake in the Trojan Horse matter of 1985

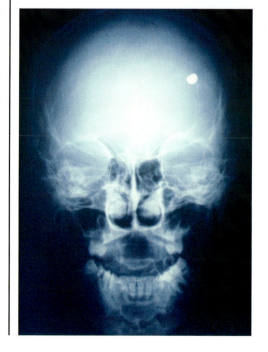

put aside their annoyance and that they were prepared to hire me for this case. Some time into the discussion, she asked me if I could recommend a good pathologist to perform a post-mortem for the families. I had no hesitation in recommending Jonathan Gluckman, a private pathologist who had been involved in the inquiry into the death of Steve Biko in the late seventies.

Her answer to me was at once both revealing and exceptionally irksome. 'Can't you recommend someone else?' she said. 'Gluckman is regarded as something of a left-wing sympathiser.' I was utterly astounded and told her that she seemed to be suffering from schizophrenia.

'What do you mean?' she said, bridling immediately.

'It is quite simple,' I replied. 'Here you have told me that you took exception to my working for Gencor in the Kinross matter when they had briefed me first, and now you tell me that you don't want to appoint Gluckman because he never acts against you and is seen to be a left-wing sympathiser as a result.'

Despite these comments, however, I ended up working on the case. Lawyers can be funny creatures.

|||||||||||||||||||||||||||||||||||||||||||||||||||||||||||||||||||

CHAPTER 8

IT'S SAD WHEN
THE STATE GOES BAD

*'Nothing in all the world is more dangerous than
sincere ignorance and conscientious stupidity.'*

– MARTIN LUTHER KING JR,
leader of the African-American civil rights movement
and Nobel Peace Prize winner

The 1980s in South Africa were violent and unstable years. We were
in the stifling grip of apartheid, a system based on discrimination,
denial and segregation that was applied to every aspect of South
African life. It permeated the social, political and economic fibre
of our country, grossly violating human rights in numerous ways
and on many different levels.

I was to get extraordinary insight into these injustices from an
unusual and very different perspective. Because I was the only
independent forensic consultant in the country at the time, I became
involved in many cases where human rights violations had taken
place, often finding myself in situations far beyond my experience.

In 1985 I received a phone call from Geoff Budlender, who
headed up the Johannesburg office of the Legal Resources Centre,

the first public-interest law organisation in South Africa, co-founded by Arthur Chaskalson (later Chaskalson C.J.) in 1979.

A man by the name of Saul Mkhize had been shot and killed by the police. Under the Group Areas Act, certain areas were declared 'white areas', and families of colour occupying these areas were forcibly relocated to 'black areas'. The Mkhize family and Mkhize's community were in the process of being forcibly removed from their East Rand dwelling, which they had occupied since time immemorial. Mkhize had objected to being removed, and was shot as a result.

The police claimed that Constable Nienaber had shot Mkhize in self-defence, after Mkhize had attacked the policeman. A severely dented and damaged gas mask had been handed in as evidence of the alleged frenzied attack by Mkhize on the policeman. Nienaber was exonerated – policemen were not often found guilty of shooting blacks in those turbulent days of police rule.

Mkhize's family were unhappy with the outcome, and had lodged a claim against the Minister of Police for damages that they had suffered as a result of his death. It was at this point that I was called in.

I asked Budlender to secure the gas mask for me. Examining it closely, I was struck by the symmetry of the damage to the canister: each dent on the canister was separated from another dent by about 180°. Looking at the canister under a microscope, it was quite easy to see that the damage consisted of three pairs of dents, one set of dents containing wood fibres embedded in the metal, and the opposite set of dents containing sand particles embedded in the metal. This could never have happened in the manner alleged by the police. Also, the canister was damaged, but the rubber surrounding it was intact. The damage did not appear to have been caused during an attack.

I realised that what had, in fact, happened to the canister was that it had been placed on the ground and there had been beaten with a wooden club of some kind.

My findings were quickly drafted into a court report. The police forensic and legal teams then backed off, and Mrs Mkhize was paid some compensation. The advocate handling the matter was Arthur Chaskalson, who was later to go on to become Chief Justice of the Constitutional Court. Budlender informed me afterwards that the police legal team had backed off so quickly because there was a decent judge on the bench and due to the high calibre of my report. It was not a case they could dispute.

This was the first politically overt case where the police were taken to task, and it was my introduction to the sort of political police violence that was flooding the country at the time. Many other cases were not as easy to win.

A while later, I was approached by the Legal Resources Centre in Cape Town to investigate a series of fires that had taken place in Crossroads, in Cape Town, in 1985. There were two opposing factions in Crossroads at the time – the 'witdoeke', who were agents provocateur, secretly employed by the apartheid government to cause mayhem in the townships, and the 'terrorists', political groups who were trying to bring about change in the country. Through my investigations, I was able to prove without a doubt that the fires had been started deliberately by the unofficial police agents. The 'witdoeke' had fired flares into the humble dwellings, setting them alight. No one was punished at the time.

Around this time, the *Cape Times* published a story about a matter that was to become known as the 'Gugulethu Seven' case. Gugulethu is a township on the Cape Flats, and in the days of apartheid rule, it was viewed by the authorities as being a kind of breeding ground for subversive elements.

On the morning of 3 March 1986, a shoot-out occurred between the security forces and a group of 'terrorists' at the corner of NY1 and NY111 (Native Yard 1 and Native Yard 111) in Gugulethu. Seven young black men – 'terrorists' – were killed. According to police testimony, the police had been informed that an attack by these terrorists was to take place at this particular crossroad, so they had set up a counter-ambush.

The case enjoyed high media publicity at the time, particularly on television, and we, the public, were entertained by the police commissioner explaining to us just how lucky we were to be protected against the evil performed by the 'terrorists', and that we should value the gallantry of the police.

There was another side to the story, though, and *Cape Times* reporters Chris Bateman and Tony Weaver told it, producing an article about the incident that seriously contradicted the official reporting. Bateman had done some prior investigation at the Dairy Belle hostel, which looked over the scene of the shoot-out, during which he had taken some disturbing statements from eyewitnesses. Bateman was completely fluent in Xhosa, the language spoken by most of the black inhabitants of the Cape. The police version of events simply didn't add up.

Based on their investigation, Weaver gave an interview to the BBC African service, stating that the men had been shot despite the fact that they had surrendered. He reported that they had been lying on the ground when they were shot in cold blood.

This interview resulted in chaos in Parliament. There were calls for Weaver's blood, and the debates raged furiously, taking up much space in Hansard. Outrage was expressed by the Minister of Police, Louis le Grange, and by Adriaan Vlok, who took over the position after Le Grange had been promoted to Speaker of the House of Parliament.

Amidst the cries for his head on a platter, Weaver was charged with the contravention of section 27(b) of the Police Act, for, among other things, unlawfully publishing untrue information relating to this particular shoot-out. Brigadier Leon Mellett, who was the personal secretary to Vlok, attended the trial, which was held before Magistrate J.M. Lemmer.

I was contacted by Jonathan Gluckman, the private pathologist who had been involved in the Steve Biko inquest. By 1984, Gluckman had started to dabble in forensic science and was doing post-mortems.

Weaver had employed the legal firm of Findlay & Tait, with Gordon Rushton and Jeremy Gauntlett acting as the legal team. Gluckman had been briefed on the forensic work, but he felt that the ballistics, which involves studying the dynamics of the relevant projectiles, was too far outside his field of expertise, and so passed the work on to me.

I flew to Cape Town and consulted with the legal team at Gauntlett's house in Llandudno. Bits of string were produced and trajectories were measured, with various members of the legal team acting as the deceased. Angles were estimated. At the end of the consultation, I flew back to Johannesburg with various photographs and post-mortem reports to begin my real work.

Two of the deceased were of particular interest to me. One had very different types of wounds – a protracted blackened strip across the small of his back and a grievous wound through the fleshy part of his buttocks. The second was a man who had fled into some nearby bush and had been tracked down and shot by a policeman called Warrant Officer Barry Barnard, a particularly brutal and nasty product of the apartheid police force. This man had been shot in the face and had had part of his jaw blown away by the shot.

I set up experiments using fresh pig heads and tried to reproduce the results seen in the post-mortems. Pigs are the tried-and-tested animals for use in forensic ballistic tests. The skin is almost identical to human skin and, consequently, the test results are much more comparable to the effects seen on human skin than they would be if any other animal's skin was used.

The police version was very simple: they had been given prior intelligence about the ambush and had set up a counter-ambush. A number of statements had been compiled under oath for the inquest into the death of these unfortunate men.

The statements were themselves quite interesting. They had been compiled by a single individual: the grammar, diction and syntax showed that this person had gone to considerable effort to make the versions neatly dovetail with each other. Normally there would be slight differences in the accounts given by people, particularly when caught up in violent and distressing events, as these surely were. Yet the policemen's statements were all beautifully turned out, with not a hair out of place. The problem with them was just that – they were too perfect. In addition, I had done a great deal of research into the Weaver matter, and the police versions simply did not fit the frightful injuries to the deceased.

These statements did have one important benefit for the defence team: they resulted in each policeman being saddled with the version that he had given under oath. This was to have unfortunate consequences for the police.

Having conducted in-depth research into the injuries of the deceased, I recognised that there were several inconsistencies between my findings and the versions laid out in the police statements.

The man running through the intersection from right to left, and who was shot by one particular officer, had no bullet wounds on his left, but only from his right, and those were not made by a weapon matching the one carried by the police officer.

The man who was pursued by Barnard and shot twice in the head while allegedly turning to shoot at Barnard from some twenty metres away, was in reality killed from a distance of under a metre. A photograph of the deceased reveals the devastating injury produced by the discharge of a shotgun at close range. When I tested this on a pig's jaw, the similarity of the wound produced on the jaw was quite apparent, with all the features of a close wound (see photo). Not only was the blackening reproduced in my test scenario (caused by the unburnt propellant from the shot), but the shot had been fired from such close range that the pellets did not have time to spread. These details matched the injury of the deceased.

All the angles of the shots were in conflict with the police versions. A photograph of the deceased who had a long, blackened burn mark across the small of his back showed this wound clearly. He could only have been shot at point-blank range. At the subsequent inquest, however, the state pathologists stated that this was an abrasion caused by a bullet fired from a distance, which had tracked across the man's skin. Yet a bullet abrasion looks completely different. There can be no doubt that the state pathologists were prepared to twist the evidence and perjure themselves to suit their political masters and the police.

During the Weaver trial, not only did it come out that the police had lost vital pieces of evidence, as was reported in the *Argus* of 3 August 1987, but none of the state forensic experts gave evidence. This was peculiar: normally the state is obliged to lay out all its evidence, and in this case the ballistics and other forensic evidence were of crucial importance to support the police's version of the story. Yet there were no state forensic experts to be seen; they were not even present to aid the prosecutor in cross-examining me or Johan van der Spuy, who assisted in giving evidence about gunshot wounds in general. The state experts put in an appearance several years later only, at the second inquest – and not to give evidence, but primarily to assist the prosecutor in cross-examining me.

This was something that always bothered me about this case, and about others, too. The function of a court expert is to assist the court in coming to the correct conclusion. As I mentioned in Chapter 4, the expert is not there as some sort of hired gun to assist 'his' side, as it were. Experts do not have a 'side' – they are equipped with only the truth, as far as it can be ascertained.

During the trial I prepared large diagrams of the crime scene. Each policeman who had participated in the shooting was asked to place himself on the plan and to indicate which of the deceased had been killed by him. In doing so, they claimed to have shot the men at a distance. Yet it could be shown that many of the wounds were contact gunshot wounds, which are created when the muzzle of a weapon is really close to the skin when the shot is fired. This was proved in all seven instances, and showed that the inaccuracy of the police version of the incident – an ambush and shoot-out – was untenable. The carefully doctored affidavits prepared by the police were thrown into total disarray.

There could only be one result: Weaver was acquitted and left the court a free and very relieved man. For me, it counted as another black mark against my name as far as the state was concerned. The head of the police laboratory detested me: General Lothar Neethling was an arrogant, harshly militaristic type of person, and he marked me down for special attention after the Weaver trial.

I interacted with Neethling often over the years, and his dislike of me seemed to grow with time. He was a German war orphan who was brought out to South Africa after the Second World War and rapidly rose through the ranks of the police force. He was no fool, and started a modern police forensic laboratory in 1971, the first of its kind in South Africa.

At heart, though, Neethling was a political animal. He loved to parade around in his medals, enjoying the pomp and ceremony. I recall the first time I ever spoke to him – it was in 1984, before I became involved in any serious political cases. I had attended a lecture of his and made a point of approaching him afterwards. 'Colonel Neethling,' I said, 'I want to start a forensic laboratory, and I am sure we will have dealings with each other.'

His reply to me was: 'I would say you are stone deaf, because I am a general, not a colonel.' I was a little taken aback, but that was the man as I soon came to know him. I could not understand the basis of his intense dislike for me in the beginning, and the real reasons only dawned on me some time later, when the full extent of his hatred for me became apparent and the police atrocities mounted up.

A couple of years after the trial, I was informed by the police that a new inquest into the death of these seven men had been ordered, and I received a subpoena to attend the hearing. These unwelcome instructions to attend court for criminal trials and inquests were a bane of my life in those days. Invariably, the inefficiency of the court wasted a great deal of time and the state paid expert witnesses R18 per day. The state pathologists delighted in my discomfort.

I appeared at the new inquest, which was held in the Wynberg Magistrates' Court. The presiding magistrate was Magistrate Hoffmann, and a battalion of medical minds grilled me. Jurie Nel, a professor of forensic medicine at Tygerberg Hospital, acted as assessor, and I was questioned by Pietman Mostert, a senior public prosecutor at Wynberg Magistrates' Court, retired professor of forensic medicine at the University of Cape Town (UCT), L.S. Smith, Theo Schwär, a current professor of forensic medicine at Stellenbosch, and Deon Knobel, successor to Smith at UCT. They never took me on single-handedly in those days; they came in brigades.

The result of this inquest was quite predictable. Hoffmann made a few mild disapproving noises about the police falsifying affidavits. The government pathologists attacked each and every part of my evidence, and the end result of all this was predictable: there was 'no one to blame'.

These were frustrating days for me, and it was to be many years before I was vindicated in this and many other matters. The vindication came only during the Truth and Reconciliation (TRC) amnesty hearings, when the full, squalid truth came out. We had all believed at the time that the entire episode at Gugulethu had been a police set-up, that weapons had been planted on the deceased, and that the entire affair had been seized upon by the propaganda machinery of the SABC.

It's so sad when the state goes bad. It was admitted at the TRC hearings that the entire event had, indeed, been set up. The group of unwitting young black men had been infiltrated by government agents, and the plot hatched by a greater force operating in the country at the time – the men of Vlakplaas, home to the 'death squads' of the eighties and early nineties.

||||||||||||||||||||||||||||||||||||||||||||||||||||||||||||||

CHAPTER 9

A PLACE CALLED VLAKPLAAS

'Injustice anywhere is a threat to justice everywhere.'
– MARTIN LUTHER KING JR,
leader of the African-American civil rights movement
and Nobel Peace Prize winner

The truth was a complete misnomer in the turbulent 1980s. The state propaganda machine trumpeted out 'official' versions of events, portraying the 'successes' of the government in fighting the total onslaught in an attempt to brainwash the public at large. Unbeknown to most average South Africans, a common denominator in many of the political stories at the time was a place called Vlakplaas.

Vlakplaas was a farm near Pretoria, and the headquarters of the South African Police counterinsurgency unit C10. It rehabilitated 'turned terrorists', known as 'askaris' – the Kenyan name for 'warrior' – but actually operated as a paramilitary hit squad. Anti-government agents were arrested, taken to Vlakplaas, and asked whether they would switch allegiance and start working for the government. If they refused, they were shot at point-blank range in front of the others – a sure-fire way to persuade anyone to agree!

Similar units were established in Camperdown in KwaZulu-

Natal and in the Eastern Cape, but Vlakplaas was the flagship of this operation. It was truly a place from hell: on entering its gates, all decent and honourable conventions were abandoned as murder became a way of life and torture an entertaining diversion. No law applied here other than the eleventh commandment: Do not get caught. The men from Vlakplaas lied, raped, murdered and thieved their way around the country, behaving in the vilest way possible.

They were led by a number of individuals, including Dirk Coetzee and later Eugene de Kock, who was dubbed 'prime evil' by the press. The tale of these men is told in many books, such as *In the Heart of the Whore: The Story of Apartheid's Death Squads* by Jacques Pauw. I do not wish to repeat what has already been told, save to say that Vlakplaas existed to aid and abet the grotesque policies of the successive National Party governments. These were men who operated outside the law and who were devoid of any decency whatsoever.

The men of Vlakplaas needed money to further fund their operation, and they required something spectacular to show the political masters just how useful they were. That is when the bizarre scheme leading to the murder of the Gugulethu Seven was plotted.

As discussed in Chapter 8, a number of young men were duped into thinking that they were to attack a police van. They had no idea that this was a trap, and that they were to be the victims of a police murder squad sent to create good publicity so that the political leaders would be grateful and open the national Treasury to provide more money for even greater obscenities. That is exactly what happened. The seven men were all murdered, weapons were planted and the national propaganda machine revved into action.

The plot would have worked had it not been for the courage and integrity of Bateman and Weaver, who investigated it and told it as it was. The Minister of Police at the time, Adriaan Vlok, knew about the whole squalid affair, as did the generals in the police force. We average citizens were docile, indoctrinated fools, accepting the pronouncements of the various government departments. It was obvious to anyone prepared to look a little deeper that something was not quite right. However, like the Germans in Hitler's Nazi state, we chose not to see.

I was involved in many cases during these years. Many of the askaris were truly vicious. One of them was Joe Mamasela, whose handler was Dirk Coetzee, one of the first commanders at Vlakplaas. Mamasela was responsible for the brutal murder of Griffiths Mxenge, a human rights lawyer and anti-apartheid activist, and his wife, in Durban. With violent savagery, this agent of the apartheid government mutilated Griffiths' face and sliced off his ears.

Another askari, Butana Almond Nofemela, became a celebrity in his own right for unravelling much of the story behind the hit squads. Nofemela was arrested and sentenced to death after murdering, of his own accord, a farmer and his wife in Brits.

He was paid a visit in his death cell by his former associates from Vlakplaas, who promised him that they would see to it that he was not executed, as he was 'one of theirs'. Ten days before Nofemela was to be executed, they informed him that they had tried their best, but could not prevent the execution. His commanding officer visited him on death row and told him, 'Sorry, you are going to have to take the pain.'

Nofemela used his head. Backed by a legal team, he blew the whistle on Vlakplaas, Dirk Coetzee and the others, and in all the mayhem, torture and terror that had transpired, he was granted a stay of execution.

This sparked a huge exposé of Vlakplaas, with the law taking its course. Dirk Coetzee, who had left the police force in a hurry, had started a new career as a private investigator. Coetzee was an irritation to the police, and they were eager to pin something on him. The police labelled him a maverick, but Dirk contacted Max du Preez from *Vrye Weekblad*, a newspaper started by Du Preez and Jacques Pauw that had the courage to challenge and question the state's 'official' versions of events. It was a logical place for Dirk Coetzee to tell his story, and it was the biggest story this fledgling newspaper had dealt with.

The newspaper arranged for Coetzee to fly to Mauritius, where he unfolded the whole tale of murder, torture, political assassinations and lies to Jacques Pauw. After the story broke, Coetzee eventually found asylum in the Netherlands, and on 17 November 1989, the story about Vlakplaas broke on the front page of *Vrye Weekblad*. The local mainstream media in South Africa preferred, by and large, to ignore the story or to deny its truthfulness, but it received widespread coverage outside South Africa's borders.

The floodgates were open. Dirk Coetzee's revelations prompted other policemen and government officials to start talking. As an upshot of all of these revelations, Colonel Eugene de Kock, who headed up Vlakplaas at the time, was given two life sentences and an additional 212 years in prison, on charges ranging from murder to kidnapping to assault and corruption. Like most South Africans, I watched this horrific story unfold, but so much of what was revealed made sense to me from the political cases in which I had been and would be involved.

Coetzee found himself moving around a lot, as there were regular attempts on his life. In 1990, he was in a safe house in Lusaka when a parcel was delivered to the local post office addressed to him. He took one look and suspected that it was a bomb sent by the security police, so he returned it to the apparent sender, who happened to be Bheki Mlangeni, a young attorney working for Cheadle Thompson & Haysom. Innocently, Mlangeni opened the box when he received it. It contained a cheap Walkman with a tape labelled 'Evidence – Hit Squads'. He put the headphones on, plugged them in and pushed the start button. This detonated a massive explosion, which blew his head off.

Mlangeni's family approached the legal firm of Cheadle Thompson & Haysom, and I was called in to investigate the case. The more I looked at it, the more certain I was that this was a police hit. The parcel had been sent to Coetzee by someone who knew where he was. The explosives were suspicious. Bomb builders were usually explosives experts from the mines who used gelignite that they smuggled off their work premises. The explosive material used in this case was PETN – pentaerythritol trinitrate – a substance not readily available outside military circles. It was also not a standard South African detonator, and appeared to be of Eastern Bloc or Russian origin. The Eastern Bloc had no interest in killing Dirk Coetzee. Quite the opposite, in fact.

However, the police had access to all kinds of weaponry seized from Eastern Bloc operatives. The prime suspect at the time was Waal du Toit, who headed up the bomb unit of the SAP. He ran a specialist bomb laboratory and was a guru in his field. I had a heavy suspicion that General Lothar Neethling – South Africa's own 'Dr Mengele' – had a finger in the pie too.

The police could not investigate the matter, as they were the prime suspects in the case. I was asked to oversee the investigation, and worked closely with the South African Bureau of Standards (SABS) on the matter. One of the first things I did was voice my dissatisfaction with the involvement of Klippies Kritzinger, a policeman. I asked who he was answering to, and established that, of course, it was General Neethling – a prime suspect. Kritzinger took a back seat because of my objection, and this made me no friends during the investigation. He also denied the existence of key elements in the investigation, such as the bomb laboratory of Waal du Toit, which I asked about.

The evidence included a handwriting sample and a fingerprint. I obtained a court order so that we could acquire handwriting samples and fingerprints from the men of Vlakplaas. Court order in hand, I arrived at Wagthuis, the police headquarters in Pretoria, and was met by Krappies Engelbrecht. One of the darker forces of apartheid, Engelbrecht headed up the Brixton Murder and Robbery Unit, and was a murky character. People around him were responsible for murders and torturing, yet he always managed to evade prosecution. The mere mention of his name to Judge Richard Goldstone, who headed up the important commission investigating political violence in South Africa in the early 1990s, used to send Goldstone into apoplexy!

Engelbrecht greeted me with his standard 'Hello, Duif.' He always called me 'Duif' for some unknown reason. I wanted to see the Vlakplaas men three at a time – I didn't want all the papers handed out simultaneously, as it could result in switching and confusion of the process. But the men were all seated at one long table, and Engelbrecht told me that this was the way in which it would be done. I said no, and we argued bitterly. I left Wagthuis saying that I would see them all again in two weeks' time.

I obtained yet another court order, and this time managed to get all the fingerprints and handwriting samples on my terms. This was a clear message to the men of Vlakplaas and the South African Police that the tide was turning, and that we would start investigating them. No one was above the law any more.

There was no particular finding at the trial, and the feeling of the courts at that time was echoed well in the title of a book that George Bizos wrote subsequently, *No One to Blame: In Pursuit of Justice in South Africa*. The courts were extremely reluctant to reach decisions that were anti the police or authorities. Anybody can manipulate a crime scene if they hold all the evidence, and there were many devious examples of this happening during the 1980s. Evidence was also often damaged or destroyed or lost, severely hampering any meaningful investigation. The Gugulethu Seven case illustrated this perfectly. The environment was truly toxic in those days.

Vrye Weekblad went on to reveal the secrets of the Civil Co-operation Bureau (CCB) in May 1990, and described how CCB commander Pieter Botes had tried to kill anti-apartheid activist Albie Sachs in Maputo in 1988, as well as destabilise the run-up to the Namibian elections in November 1989. In 1991, a bomb destroyed the *Vrye Weekblad* offices. A CCB operative by the name of Leonard Veenendal later confessed to having planted the deadly explosive.

The demise of the newspaper came that same year, when it was sued by Lothar Neethling in a defamation case linked to an investigation in which two activists had gone missing on the banks of the Komati River. Neethling was linked to this incident, and the court case took place over a protracted period of time. The police had not wanted another Steve Biko on their hands, and Neethling's 'silent, undetectable potion' had been their answer.*

What is sad about this is that Neethling was a well-qualified man who put forensic science on the map in South Africa. In normal criminal cases, he was excellent. Unfortunately, when politics entered the fray and state interests were on the line, he showed a different side of his character.

Vrye Weekblad published allegations that Neethling had synthesised poison in his laboratory, 'remedies' that were referred to as '*Lothar se doepa*' – Lothar's potions. These were formulated in order to kill African National Congress (ANC) activists without a trace. He showed himself to be a dishonest man who had little regard for science and the truth. I even question his application to the TRC for amnesty.

In this case, Neethling's concoction should have resulted in the two activists dying from heart attacks. The only problem was that

---

* Despite the excellent cross-examinations of the security police and the doctors who were involved in the 1977 death of Steve Biko, which revealed that Biko had been in custody when he died, that he had been chained naked in a puddle of his own excrement and driven in this form to Pretoria, and that he had suffered a severe head injury brought on by vicious assaults by the police, the magistrate found himself unable to lay the blame for Biko's death at anybody's doorstep.

the potion did not seem to work: after numerous doses the men were drowsy, but not dead. So they were shot, their bodies burnt and thrown into the river.

I visited the alleged murder scene as well. It was remarkable how accurate Coetzee's memory was regarding this event. He described every minute detail, such as a fork in the road and the topography, and when I investigated it, I was able to find the exact spot where the murders had taken place. I photographed the area from the air (see photo), and what Coetzee had described was virtually 100 per cent accurate. We never found any remains in the area.

After a long trial, Judge Johann Kriegler ruled in favour of *Vrye Weekblad*. The appeals court overturned Kriegler's decision on a legal technicality, and ordered the paper to pay R90 000 plus costs. The ensuing battle cost both sides two million rand over five years, and forced the paper to close. Neethling was free. I have never understood why Michael Corbett C.J. reversed the court's initial findings.

Judges were bending over backwards to fulfil the needs of the government. Because of my involvement in a number of political cases, on request, I became known as an 'ANC man'. However, I never took sides and was not a member of any political party. I simply conducted my investigations to the best of my ability. In some cases, the police were right: if the evidence stood up to scrutiny, I would not waste time and money refuting it.

I would never manipulate evidence or create a defence for a person, though. In recent years, I was approached by a man accused of the illegal manufacturing of drugs. He showed me all of his equipment and chemicals, and I asked him how he had obtained them and what he used them for. In response, he asked me, 'What could I have been doing with these chemicals and equipment?' He was looking for a defence – a valid excuse as to why he had all the chemicals and equipment in his possession. I would not sit and dream up something in order to invent a defence for him. I told him that it didn't work that way – he should tell me what he was using it for, and I would let him know if his explanation was feasible or not. In the end, the man was found guilty and his house was one of the first to be seized by the asset forfeiture unit.

The various murders, torture and disappearance of individuals in the 1980s took place behind the cover of massive government propaganda. Most South Africans were blissfully unaware of the truth that lay behind these horrors. This blindness was truly reprehensible in those groups who should, by virtue of their training and position, have known better. The state forensic practitioners saw evidence of the atrocities arriving in their mortuaries every day. The evidence of torture and assault was there to see, yet they chose not to see it.

As a newcomer to the forensic scene in the eighties, I could recognise the gaps in the story; I could see that the police versions could never explain the forensic evidence. The state forensic experts were in a better position than I was, but they never raised the alarm. They failed in their duty as professionals and as human beings. They allowed gross abuses of human rights to continue and, as a result, in my view, they join those in the trash can of history, people like Joseph Mengele and the other Nazi doctors and professionals who chose evil over good.

There was one notable exception to all this. Wendy Orr was a young district surgeon in the Eastern Cape who had found herself in the position of having to pay back student loans. The Department of Health had seconded her to the area where Doctors Tucker and Lang were working. They had been involved in the Steve Biko inquest, and admitted later to having behaved in a manner that was contrary to their Hippocratic Oath – they had protected the security police and, by their actions, had allowed abuses of prisoners to take place.

Not so Wendy Orr. She lodged complaint after complaint against the rampant security police abuses, which she saw on a regular basis as part of her duties. The existing forensic infrastructure should have sprung to her assistance. They did nothing of the sort – there was not a single word of support for her courageous actions. Not even Tucker and Lang, who should have learnt from their past mistakes, gave her a single iota of backing. That was unfortunately the state of the official circles at the time.

Other examples of state abuse covered up by the authorities included the mysterious disappearance and death of Siphiwo Mtimkulu, who had been poisoned with thallium while in prison in 1981 by the security forces. Frances Ames, who was a neurologist in Cape Town, became involved in the matter. She was outspoken and made public her findings. Of course, nothing was done. Ames, together with Trevor Jenkins, Philip Tobias and three other doctors, later raised the matter of Tucker and Lang's involvement in the Biko inquest and forced the Medical and Dental Council, the statutory registration body that had exonerated the doctors, to take some belated action against the pair.

These were not isolated actions: the unholy alliance between the state pathologists and the police was played out, yet again, in the killing of Ashley Kriel.

||||||||||||||||||||||||||||||||||||||||||||||||||||||||||||||||||

CHAPTER 10
THE MURDER OF ASHLEY KRIEL

'Science is the organized, systematic enterprise that gathers knowledge about the world and condenses the knowledge into testable laws and principles.'

– EDWARD O. WILSON,

American biologist, researcher and theorist,

Consilience: The Unity of Knowledge

On 15 July 1987, Ashley Kriel, a curly haired, intense and fun-loving youth, had his life cut short, just a few months before his twenty-first birthday. His death shocked his own community as well as the broader public, and he is recognised today as one of the tragic victims of the struggle against apartheid.

While growing up in Bonteheuwel on the Cape Flats, Kriel was painfully aware of the impact of gangsterism in the community. Together with two friends – Gavin Adams and Paul Jansen – he set up an alternative to gangs for the youth, a movement called the GAP brotherhood. The acronym derived from the initials of their first names, but the aim of the group was to provide a 'gap' for youngsters through which they could escape gangsterism. Interestingly, Kriel was taught by Cheryl Carolus, who rose to prominence and high government office after 1994.

Being an active community member, the implementation of the tricameral system of government in 1984, which excluded the vast majority of South Africans, led to Ashley Kriel establishing a network of revolutionary militants who debated and explored alternatives to what the apartheid government was proposing. He became one of the leaders of the anti-apartheid United Democratic Movement (UDF), and left South Africa in 1985 to join the ANC and its military wing, Umkhonto we Sizwe (MK).

Kriel was seen by the community as an agent of change, but the authorities viewed him as a serious threat to the stability of the country: a powerful orator, he was able to stir up crowds and cause significant unrest. Something had to be done about him.

The 'problem' of Ashley Kriel was permanently solved by a particular Western Cape policeman, Warrant Officer Jeffrey Benzien. Acting on a tip-off, Benzien went to the house in Athlone where Kriel was staying. According to the police report of the incident, Kriel produced a firearm and, in the ensuing struggle, Kriel was shot in the back.

The official story, which was reiterated in Benzien's submission for amnesty in 1995, at the TRC hearings, goes as follows:

> On [15] July 1987, Benzien and Sergeant Ables went to
> 8 Albermarie Road, Hazendale, Athlone. They had been
> instructed to do surveillance of the house and its immediate
> vicinity as the police had received information that Ashley
> Kriel, a trained ANC terrorist, might be hiding out there.
> He and Ables went to the house disguised as municipal
> employees pretending to check the sewerage ... Sergeant
> Ables knocked at the [back] door. Moments later a man
> opened the door. Benzien immediately recognised him as
> Ashley Kriel. Kriel held a jersey and towel in front of his

trousers in his right hand and his left hand was pressed against the covered right hand. Benzien told him that they had come to inspect the drainage on the property. Kriel said nothing and tried to get back into the house. Benzien suspected that Kriel might be armed with a pistol or hand grenade, so he moved quickly, put his arms around Kriel's arms and chest trying to pin his arms to his body. Benzien identified himself as a policeman and told Kriel that he was arresting him. In the process the towel and jersey fell off revealing an automatic pistol in Kriel's hand. Benzien disarmed Kriel and struck him a heavy blow on his forehead causing him to fall to the floor. Sergeant Ables then tried to handcuff Kriel, but Kriel sat up and grabbed Benzien's right hand in an attempt to retrieve his pistol. While Ables was trying to handcuff him, Kriel suddenly stood up, but Benzien held him from behind with the pistol still in his hand.

Then a shot went off and Kriel fell to the ground. He had been wounded and blood came out of his mouth and nose. Ables handcuffed Kriel while Benzien went to his vehicle and radioed for help. When Benzien returned, he found that Kriel was dead.

– *Truth and Reconciliation Commission Final Report*, AC/99/0027

According to Benzien, he and Ables then searched the house for weapons, only to find a hand grenade under the pillow on Kriel's bed. Benzien insisted that it had not been their intention to kill Kriel, but merely to arrest him, and that the shooting had been accidental.

Kriel's family was not happy with the official explanation, and I was requested by them to investigate the matter. I flew to Cape Town and started my work.

The wound on Ashley Kriel's back was clearly a contact wound. It would have to be in order to support the police version. Because the pistol had been in contact with the skin on firing, it had left black burn marks on the skin in an elliptical shape.

There was only one difficulty: Kriel had been wearing a tracksuit top at the time he was shot. I called for it, and discovered that a neat calibre-sized hole was located in roughly the right position. Kriel had been shot with a .22-calibre automatic pistol. I managed to secure the pistol from the police and took it back to Johannesburg with me, where I researched the types of ammunition available and then started my experiments.

Using the same ammunition and the same type of clothing involved in the Kriel killing, I again enrolled the help of a pig because of its skin's similarity to human skin. Covering the pigskin with identical clothing to Kriel's, I fired a contact shot.

The results were spectacular. Any shot fired with the muzzle of the weapon either in contact with or at very close range to the skin, with the clothing interspersed, produced a whopping great hole in the material. The reason for this was quite simple – the clothing was made from cotton polyester, through which a huge hole burnt as the heat spread from the muzzle of the weapon. Yet, when I inspected Ashley Kriel's clothing, the hole was not more than half a centimetre across – the size of the bullet. I repeated the experiment a number of times, but could not get a calibre-sized hole in the garment when I fired at close range. It was impossible to recreate the alleged contact shot that had killed Kriel without simultaneously blowing a great big hole in the tracksuit top.

Interestingly, the state pathologist didn't comment on the bilateral abrasions that Kriel had on each wrist. These clearly indicated that he had been handcuffed while alive. It was obvious that this story did not add up.

The only explanation I could think of was that he had been handcuffed and Benzien had fired a shot from a distance, which had hit Kriel in the heart and killed him. Benzien then realised that he had a problem: how could he admit to having shot a handcuffed, unarmed man? Based on my findings, I speculated that they had lifted Kriel's top, put the gun against his skin through the same hole, and fired a second shot. That was my version, anyway, but it was extremely difficult in those days to appear in court and allege that the police had murdered someone.

I was present and testified at the inquest, which was held in the Wynberg Magistrates' Court in May 1989, with the same magistrate on the bench who had ruled that there was 'no one to blame' in the Gugulethu Seven case. The prosecutor was again Mr Mostert, and the whole forensic establishment was out in force, including Deon Knobel from UCT, and my old adversary Theo Schwär, who was there to aid the magistrate in assessing the technical evidence. Assisting was Jurie Nel, forensic pathologist at Tygerberg Hospital, as well as Lionel Shelsley Smith, the former head of pathology at UCT.

The police were aware of my version and were desperate to counter it at any cost. The state called on a police 'forensic ballistics expert' to argue against my evidence.

Amazingly (or not), the police expert freely admitted under cross-examination that he kept only that data which suited him. In this case, therefore, he had fired some 180 to 200 shots, and selected those that corroborated his theory.

In the court record of the case, this police expert states that 'he wanted to get a hard contact shot on the "right background" without getting a large torn hole in the clothing'. A little later on, he says that he 'began to realize that whatever was behind the clothing played a huge role in the effect of the shot on the clothing'.

He kept altering the background, commenting that it made a huge difference to the size of the contact shot. When he used a sandbag and fired a contact shot, he found he could get a calibre-sized hole in the clothing. The reason for this is clear: a sandbag has a porous surface, which would allow the weapon to be held firmly in place. This did not apply to what had happened to Ashley Kriel.

Later, the magistrate questioned the state expert, who confessed that with all the shots where he used a pig-belly background, he produced only large blown-out holes quite unlike the one on the tracksuit of Ashley Kriel. The magistrate asked, '[S]o it is only with the sandbag that you got the same effect as with a contact shot as that seen on the deceased's clothing?'

'Yes,' responded the expert.

There can be only one explanation of the forensic evidence placed before the court, and it tied up with the theory that I had formulated: Ashley Kriel was gunned down in cold blood by Benzien. Realising that he would need an explanation, Benzien had lifted Kriel's clothing and fired a second shot through the existing bullet hole, this time in contact, to give support to the story that there had been a struggle.

One would have thought that the 'evidence' given by the police expert would have vindicated me and caused an embarrassing refutation of the state version of the story. Not so. Not one of the four state pathologists raised a single criticism of the nonsense spoken by the state witnesses. It beggars belief, but such was the mindset of the time.

Deon Knobel conducted an experiment in court: he pressed the weapon against his arm, and it left muzzle marks. All Knobel's experiment did was show that the muzzle would leave impressions on the skin. This was perhaps innovative, but it was completely immaterial, as there had been clothing between the muzzle and Ashley Kriel's body.

One of the tenets of science is that like always has to be compared with like. In a controlled experiment, the scientist eliminates variables, keeping constant the element he or she wants to investigate. This was clearly a loose-contact shot – there was a gap between the muzzle and the skin. (The further away from the skin the weapon is on firing, the more debris is visible on the skin.) So why did the state pathologist test for a close-contact shot?

Why did he change the background, when pigskin, as I have mentioned, was and still is widely accepted as the closest to human skin for ballistic experiments? He also tested only on a skin that had no clothing over it. It was ridiculous experimentation and completely irrelevant. Four senior men sat there and said nothing about how unintelligent the experiments were.

Cross-examination was interesting: they had to ensure that they were right, so they ignored scientific evidence to prove their point. They wanted to prove that the shot that had killed Kriel was a contact shot, and not a loose shot, and they could do that only with a sandbag. It didn't prove their point, in my view; it just illustrated their stupidity, or their blind determination to prove the police story. None of the so-called expert advisors said anything about using a sandbag. Interestingly, too, no comment was made on the number of bullets found in Kriel's body. There should have been two bullets if my hypothesis is correct.

These pathologists sat in the bench and said nothing. I felt as helpless at the Ashley Kriel inquest as I had at that inquest of the Gugulethu Seven.

Equally sad was the findings of the inquest magistrate, who seemed to be more intent on protecting the police than finding the truth.

The outcome of the Ashley Kriel inquest was that no one was to blame – as I've said, a common outcome in many of the political cases in the 1980s.

An interesting footnote to this saga was played out in front of the TRC. Benzien features on the cover of Volume 2 of the TRC's final report, where he is photographed holding a bag over the head of a person in a demonstration of how he had obtained 'free and voluntary confessions' from the people he arrested. This was known as the 'wet bag' approach: a suspect was made to lie on the ground with his hands handcuffed behind his back. Benzien would then sit on the small of his back, with his feet between the suspect's arms. A bag soaked in water was pulled over the suspect's head and twisted tightly around his neck, cutting off the air supply. The suspect was then questioned. From time to time, the bag was released to avoid the victim losing consciousness. It was removed only when he showed signs of wanting to talk. Benzien claimed to get a confession within thirty minutes or so every time he used this approach! Each and every time a confession was obtained, Benzien would have gone to court with it, and he would have sworn under oath that the confessions had not been obtained by illegal means.

Truth had no meaning for the boys in blue during those dark days. I was once asked by a judge, 'Well, doctor, why would this policeman lie?'

I longed to reply, 'My lord, just to keep in practice.'

Of course, to give such an answer was unthinkable before some of the judges of those days, just as it will become again in the not too distant future if we are not careful.

At the TRC amnesty hearing in 1995, it was found that Benzien did not convey a clear picture of the events or the sequence in which they occurred. There were inconsistencies and even contradictions on some aspects, one of them being that it was not clear whether Kriel was shot while he was attempting to get up or when he was standing. Nor was it apparent whether Benzien had climbed onto Kriel's back when the shot went off (see Appendix D).

What is beyond doubt is the fact that Kriel was initially shot through his clothing, as Benzien alleged and testified. This must lead then to the fact that there was a second shot, which was fired without clothing between the muzzle of the pistol and the skin. Kriel was murdered, and Benzien lied about the events.

The ANC's legal team was ineffectual in their cross-questioning at the TRC hearing: they didn't come close to exposing Benzien. His version of the events that had played out that day in July 1987 was quite different from the report given at the inquest. I was upset at the time, as I felt that Benzien had not told the truth, not only at the inquest, but also at the TRC hearing. It was concluded that it was possible that Benzien had not intended to kill Kriel, but that he was negligent in the way he had held the youth with the pistol in his hand while Ables was trying to handcuff Kriel.

Jeffrey Benzien was granted amnesty for the killing of Ashley Kriel. It is an enormous travesty that Kriel was denied justice by the TRC.

CHAPTER 11

THE TROJAN HORSE MASSACRE: NOT MY FINEST HOUR

*'Reason is, and ought only to be
the slave of the passions.'*

– DAVID HUME,
Scottish philosopher and historian

On 15 October 1985, a group of policemen burst out the back of a truck in Athlone and started firing on the crowd, wounding and killing several people in the process. The so-called 'Trojan Horse Massacre' is well documented in the history of the struggle against apartheid. It was, however, one of the few occasions that I made a glaring error – an error I learnt from and have never repeated.

On that fateful day, a group of anti-apartheid protesters were gathered at the corner of St Simon's and Thornton Roads when a railway delivery truck drove down Thornton Road. Hidden in the wooden crates at the back of the vehicle were members of the police force and the South African Defence Force (SADF). The truck passed the crowd, where some serious stone-throwing was taking place.

The security forces suddenly emerged from their hiding place, and, without warning, began firing into the crowd with automatic weapons. Most people scattered, but three young people, Michael Miranda (aged eleven), Shaun Magmoed (aged sixteen) and Jonathan Claasen (aged twenty-one), were gunned down and killed. A further thirteen adults and two children were injured.

The whole ambush was caught on camera and was broadcast both locally and internationally, causing an outcry among anti-apartheid supporters worldwide.

An inquest into the incident took place in March 1988, at which the magistrate ruled that the actions of the police had been un-reasonable. The police were found to be responsible for the deaths. The case was then referred to the Attorney-General of the Cape, who refused to prosecute.

South African legal history was made when the families of the deceased decided to launch a private prosecution. Provision is made for this in the Criminal Procedure Act, and I was called in to investigate on the families' behalf.

The police had used shotguns, which are capable of firing ammunition of varying sizes. Birdshot cartridges contain large numbers of very small lead pellets, which do not travel very far and will cause very little damage to a human when fired at a range of thirty metres or more, unless the victim is struck in the eye or in a superficial large blood vessel. The same shotguns are capable of firing much larger ammunition, the so-called AAA and SSG ammunition, also known as *skerppunt ammunisie* – sharp-point ammunition. These cartridges contain fewer but larger lead pellets and are much more lethal over greater ranges than birdshot.

One of the crucial issues in the Trojan Horse trial concerned whether the police had used this larger variety of ammunition or the smaller, less damaging kind. The police records showed that the police had been issued with the birdshot type of ammunition. Unfortunately, the police records were not always accurate – it was not unusual for police officers to pocket some of the larger, more deadly ammunition to use at their discretion.

I was able to examine one of the survivors of the random shooting, a young child. He had a pellet lodged in the upper part of his leg, in the femoral groove near to the femoral artery, the large blood vessel supplying the whole leg. It was easy to see the object pulsate as the artery pulsed. The piece of lead embedded in his thigh was considered too dangerous to remove under local anaesthetic. The child was very lucky that the shot had not penetrated this vessel, as he would almost certainly have bled to death on the scene.

This situation reminded me of my experience with the Kannemeyer Commission some years before. The Eastern Cape was a political hot-spot at the time, with some serious political unrest taking place. On one occasion, the police had opened fire on a crowd that was being troublesome, wounding a small boy called Kwanele Moses Bucwa in the head. This resulted in the boy being paralysed. The police claimed that they had fired into the air and on the ground and that, if anything, this was a piece of shrapnel from a ricocheting bullet. I was called to give an opinion on the metal lodged in the child's skull. I was able to take X-rays from the side, from the front and from the top to the bottom of this bit of metal, getting a three-dimensional view. On each X-ray, the object appeared to be circular.

An X-ray is a shadow cast by the object of interest, and only one shape will cast a circular shadow seen from three different aspects at right angles to each other: a sphere. A piece of shrapnel from a ricocheting bullet is most unlikely to form a sphere – I have seen many such pieces of twisted and tangled metal. The most likely item to have produced the metal in Kwanele's head was a shotgun pellet, which had to have been fired at him directly. This was in conflict with the police evidence. I went to see a professor of radiology, and we were able to show that the object in the child's head had lodged there as a result of a direct shotgun hit on the head. It was large ammunition – probably *skerppunt ammunisie*, which has the ability to wound and kill.

I was rather pleased with myself that I had proven this. In the cross-examination, counsel could show that they had fired directly at the child.

Now, after the Trojan Horse Massacre, I faced the situation of the metallic fragment in the young child's leg from the police's firing at him. Of critical significance was the size of the pellet: my X-rays of the leg showed that the fragment was considerably larger than the birdshot claimed to have been issued to the police.

I was faced with an interesting problem. I could get side-to-side X-rays of the leg, as well as front-to-back views, but, because of the awkward position of the fragment, I could not obtain a third view. I worked out the film focus of the X-ray machine – an X-ray magnifies as the beam moves from the X-ray tube and can make an item appear larger than it is. Looking at the X-ray view, and calculating the extent of magnification, the object seemed round. Based on my reasoning, and without the benefit of a third view, I assumed that the parent shape had to have been a sphere. That assumption was incorrect, as it turned out.

The whole matter came to trial and was heard in the Cape Town Supreme Court. In my evidence, I gave all my reasons for concluding that the larger and more lethal shot had been used. A radiologist from the Stellenbosch University medical school gave evidence to counter my testimony. I was cross-examined by Flip Hattingh, who had made a name for himself in acting for the police. He also later acted for Eugene de Kock in a marathon trial in Pretoria.

The cross-examination was quite acrimonious, and when the matter stood down, I was warned to expect to appear some weeks later. When I arrived back in Cape Town, I wanted to get to the bottom of the matter, and decided to request that the piece of metal be removed from the leg. I found a willing surgeon and an anaesthetist and, having obtained consent from the boy's parents, we took him to theatre at the Gatesville Medical Centre. The piece of lead was removed. The moment it was in my hand, my heart sank: it was flat, clearly a ricochet, and its weight corresponded to the smaller shot that the police claimed to have used.

I went back to court with my tail between my legs and, before being cross-examined further, I asked the judge for permission to address him. I told him the whole story, but it didn't make matters any better – I had clearly screwed up. The thirteen men accused were all acquitted in December 1989. It was not my finest hour.

Some of the less intelligent legal people saw my mistake as a reason to question my competence, and stories went around that 'Klatzow made a mistake' and 'Klatzow is fallible.' I believe that it was more of a testimony to my honesty than my incompetence, but some people will grasp at any excuse to cast doubt over a person's abilities.

The expert for the police, who was, at the time, a professor of radiology at Stellenbosch University's medical school, urged me to publish the results in a learned journal. Before I could get around to it, one of his associates obtained the data and published it. Interestingly, the same professor told me afterwards that I had had him convinced in court. It is not about giving the most cunning evidence, however; it is about giving evidence that is true.

In the eighties, the legal system did not seek justice for certain people who had been injured or killed. Instead, it protected the perpetrators, and was a sad indictment on the prosecutors and judges, many of whom were real old National Party war-horses whose sole purpose was to protect the state at any cost. Sadly, we again seem to be moving in that direction today: judicial benches are being packed with party cronies, reflecting cadre redeployment.

A memorial was unveiled on 24 September 2005 to the victims of the Trojan Horse Massacre. It is located at the site of the ambush, adjacent to what is now the Athlone Technical College, previously

Hewat College. The memorial incorporates a section of wall on which messages honouring the victims, as well as messages protesting against state violence, are spray-painted. It also includes a steel structure portraying armed police in a truck.

The Trojan Horse Massacre was one of many tragic events to take place in the 1980s in South Africa. On a personal level, it was a case that led me to extreme caution when making assumptions and statements. I made a huge supposition in error, and it is a mistake that I hope never to repeat again.

CHAPTER 12

ORDERS TO ELIMINATE, NOT ILLUMINATE

'The ultimate measure of a man is not where he stands in moments of comfort and convenience, but where he stands at times of challenge and controversy.'

– MARTIN LUTHER KING JR,
leader of the African-American civil rights movement
and Nobel Peace Prize winner

Getting rid of a problem rather than solving it was often the chosen path in the dark days of apartheid. Numerous 'strange' deaths occurred, and the official versions of stories were blatantly touted as the truth, while the struggle organisations had their own accounts of events. It was only many years later that the *actual* truth would come to light. As an independent forensic scientist, I found investigating many of these murders to be extremely frustrating.

The deaths of the Cradock Four were cases in point. The bodies of Matthew Goniwe, Fort Calata, Sparrow Mkhonto and Sicelo Mhlauli were found in the Eastern Cape on 29 June 1985, sparking a huge outcry from the Anti-Apartheid Movement and liberation fighters. The four had been active members of the UDF, so their deaths were not likely to have been an accident.

Matthew Goniwe, who was thirty-eight years old, hailed from Lingelihle, a black township outside Cradock. He trained as a teacher at the University of Fort Hare, and his teaching career spanned areas such as the Transkei, Graaff-Reinet and Lingelihle.

He was passionate about his community, but ran into trouble with the authorities when he was arrested in 1977 under the Suppression of Communism Act. He spent four years in jail in Umtata, during which time he obtained a BA degree from UNISA, majoring in education and political science.

Goniwe played a central role in the formation of CRADORA, the Cradock Residents' Association – an unofficial township organ-isation – as well as CRADOYA, the Cradock Youth Association. At the time of his death, he was also the rural organiser for the Eastern Cape region of the UDF, and he was an associate member of the Black Sash.

In March 1984, Goniwe and a number of others were arrested under Section 28 of the Internal Security Act, and were held in Pollsmoor Prison. They were released without being charged in October 1984. From that point onwards, Goniwe was under con-stant police surveillance.

On the morning of Thursday 27 June 1985, Goniwe, Calata, Mkhonto and Mhlauli left Port Elizabeth to head home to Cradock after attending a UDF meeting. The next morning, Goniwe's wife phoned Port Elizabeth to find out what had happened to the men, as they had not returned home. Goniwe's gutted car was found on the outskirts of Port Elizabeth that afternoon. In the evening, Sparrow Mkhonto's body was discovered near the road to Persever-ance, a few kilometres from the burnt-out car.

Sicelo Mhlauli's body was found on Saturday 29 June in the sand dunes near Bluewater Bay, on the outskirts of Port Elizabeth, and the following Tuesday, after an extensive search by members of the police and the Defence Force, the bodies of Goniwe and Calata were discovered in the dunes, lying near each other on their backs, with burnt arms outstretched. The bodies were so charred that it was difficult to see whether they had been mutilated.

I was approached by Molly Blackburn, from the Black Sash, to investigate this case. The 'official' explanation of the deaths was that the four men had been killed by their own informers, which everyone intuitively knew was nonsense.

The evidence that I found told an entirely different story. When I examined the car, I could see that it had been driven away from where Goniwe was shot. It was clear when looking at the car that he had been shot by someone taller than him, as the seat had been set right back on its tracks. We also knew that Goniwe would not have stopped for anyone except the police. None of this added up.

The involvement of the police in the investigation was predictable – their body language and attitude showed that they had no interest in investigating these murders. They seemed to know what had happened. The dockets were empty, and we had limited access to the evidence; the police used every tactic in the book to prevent us from getting to the truth. There seemed to be no such thing as an independent police forensic person. The sham of an investigation was a waste of everybody's time, and it was one of those cases where the truth emerged only many years later.

Some fourteen years afterwards, in 1999, George Bizos revealed at the TRC hearings the minutes of a state security council meeting in March 1984, in which a reference was made to Goniwe by the former apartheid government minister Barend du Plessis. The minutes indicated that certain 'agitator' former teachers be 'removed'. Du Plessis later stated that he was referring to the redeployment of Goniwe due to the political climate in Cradock. But the truth did come out, eventually.

Cases like this cast a terrible shadow over the state at the time. It was the same with the David Webster murder (which I discuss in

Chapter 14). People started to assume that the state was responsible for all kinds of atrocities, even when it was not.

Another tragic and frustrating case in which I was involved was the Piet Retief massacre on 8 June 1988, an event that was typical of the unspeakable things that occurred during the years of 'total onslaught'.

One of the methods used to fight the unholy war of apartheid was to capture certain of the 'enemy' and offer them a stark choice – summary execution or the opportunity to turn collaborator and work for the security police. This happened predominantly at Vlakplaas, but also elsewhere, as discussed in Chapter 9. It was not much of a choice, and most took the latter option and betrayed their former comrades to become askaris.

In the Piet Retief case, information arrived in the hands of the security police that certain ANC cadres – members of MK – were planning to cross the border from Swaziland into South Africa on a given date. A 'secure' vehicle driven by an undercover askari was arranged for the MK members by the security forces, and they were duly picked up. They were driven to an ambush site on a lonely part of the road outside Piet Retief, a sleepy hamlet close to the Swaziland border. The askari then, using the pretence of relieving himself, left the car, and the security police stepped out from the shadows and riddled the vehicle – and all those in it – with bullets.

No attempt had been made to arrest the occupants of the vehicle prior to the ambush. The result of the shooting was a set of bullet-riddled corpses, and the normal falsified affidavits were prepared for the inquest. The photographs included in this book illustrate the savagery with which these killings were performed. Some time after the inquest, one of the constables who had been on duty at the Piet Retief police station that night unburdened himself to Max du Preez of *Vrye Weekblad*, and an article revealing what had happened was published on 26 January 1990.

I was called in after the article appeared by the attorneys acting for the families of the deceased, and I went up to the scene. We asked to see the car in which the killings had taken place. During the examination of the car at the Piet Retief police station, I found a bullet that had not been removed by the police during the original examination. I asked the policeman overseeing us whether I could remove the bullet, and he attempted to obtain higher authority. The legal team for the families contacted the magistrate in charge of the inquest, but there was silence from all concerned.

I took the bull by the horns and cut the bullet out of the seat. The angle at which it had entered the seat would have serious consequences for the police version of the story. I also wanted to perform ballistic comparisons on the bullet. No sooner had I arrived back at my laboratory in Johannesburg with the bullet than I was visited by Krappies Engelbrecht, by then a general in the police force. He instructed me to hand over the bullet and threatened me with prosecution for tampering with a crime scene. I was forced to give it to him.

Of course, nothing more was ever heard of the bullet.

The problem in this case was access to evidence. When one party has sole access to the evidence, it can be manipulated in any way. Government agencies should not have this privilege. In the United States and the United Kingdom, private forensic agencies are allowed access to all evidence, and the investigations can take place openly, standing up to the scrutiny of the public at large.

Nothing was conducted in the open during the apartheid years. The magistrate at the hearing of the Piet Retief massacre issued veiled and not-so-veiled threats about charging me with obstructing the course of justice. It has never ceased to astound me just how dishonest and politically servile the state officials were. They forgot their oath of office to uphold the law of the land, and in many instances they were so politically motivated that it was beyond reasonable belief.

Our counsel in the Piet Retief matter was Zac Jacoob, who was blind, but who constantly amazed me with his incredible courtroom acuity, eyes or no eyes. He made use of a little Braille typewriter, and he had a phenomenal memory. His work on this doomed case was excellent, despite the somewhat inevitable outcome, given the time and circumstances.

It was clear from the angles of the gunshots that this was nothing more than cold-blooded murder of people that the police considered politically undesirable. There was room to arrest them; the laws were robust enough to deal with any crimes committed by such state officials. But the police had learnt well from Steve Biko and others, and they wanted to eliminate rather than illuminate. A report in *Vrye Weekblad* at the time said that the policemen stood around drinking sherry while the bodies were being booked into the mortuary, attesting to their utter callousness.

At the TRC hearings some years later, I stated to Bishop Desmond Tutu and Alex Boraine that these atrocities could never have happened without connivance at all levels of the public service, including police, prosecutors, magistrates and some of the judges. Many of the judges and magistrates behaved impeccably during those times, and several sought to frustrate the worst of the apartheid legislation by their interpretation of the law. There were, however, those who saw it as their duty to twist and bend the law, the evidence and anything else to achieve results that were in line with the wishes or needs of their political masters.

These were insecure times for me. The state loathed me with a passion and never appointed me to act in any matter. They regarded me as someone who tried to pervert the course of justice. People like Lothar Neethling must have known of the involvement of the police in underhand activities, and he knew I would doggedly pursue true justice. I became ever more vocal in my beliefs and started tape-recording the policemen I spoke to. I would walk up to them with a microphone and record them openly as I asked them questions, something with which they were extremely uncomfortable.

The state was not above eliminating adversaries. One particular incident severely rattled me. Shelona, our son James and I were on our farm for the weekend. While I was busy putting up a fence quite a distance from the farmhouse, a car pulled up and a man climbed out. As he swaggered towards me, I could see the bulge of a pistol on his belt. He was Afrikaans, and wanted to know where the owner of the farm was. When I asked for his name, he refused to give it to me. I informed him that the owner was not there. The man said that he had heard that the farm was for sale, to which I replied that it wasn't, asking him where he had learnt that. The lady at the bottle store in town had told him, he responded.

As soon as the man left, I went to the only bottle store in town and asked the woman there whether she had discussed the sale of my farm with anyone. She denied having spoken to anyone about such a thing. I went straight back to the farm and relayed the incident to Shelona. We felt extremely uncomfortable and unsafe, especially because James was just a baby at the time. That evening, leaving the house lights switched on, we packed James into the car and drove to a friend's house with our car lights off. We never went back to the farm, and we sold it years later. Those were very scary times for me, both personally and for us as a family.

Despite the fact that I was labelled an 'ANC man', I always tried to carry out my investigations with the utmost impartiality. In one case, two young activists were killed at Duduza in the East Rand. It was alleged that the police had murdered them by shooting them, and the community was livid. At the post-mortem, it was clear that there were hand-grenade fragments in their brains, but also interesting was that their hands had been blown off. The truth was that the security forces had infiltrated these ANC groups and tampered with the hand grenades, substituting the four-second detonator with an instant detonator, so that when the pin was pulled out of the grenade, it went off immediately.

I was never there to favour one side or another – I was there simply to ascertain the truth. In this case, the two activists had not been murdered; they had died as a result of the hand grenade going off in their hands. I suppose it was a murder of sorts, but they should not have been tossing hand grenades around in the first place.

As time progressed, we seemed to be getting closer to the truth, but I was often on the wrong side of the fence. This caused me no end of worry. It would have been easy for the state to take me out at any point, and I do not understand why they didn't – perhaps I simply didn't cause enough damage. My personal safety, however, was a genuine concern of mine.

In 1988, I went to London on an Anglo American scholarship to study fingerprinting. I recall speaking to various individuals, particularly media people, about my concern for my safety. Their advice was to 'hide under the light', and that became my method of protecting myself – I worked on my public profile, making sure that people knew what I was doing and what I looked like, and I interacted with the media on a regular basis. This ensured that people knew about me, and would ask questions if anything happened to me.

I also made sure that I never went off on solo investigations without informing someone of my whereabouts. I remember one instance where I was asked by Geoff Budlender to go to a place where a witness said they had found a mass burial site. I knew that if I found it, I would not come back alive. I called Advocate van Nieuwenhuizen and told him that if I was not back by 3 p.m. that afternoon, he should send a search party. I called Helen Suzman and told her as well. Fortunately, in that case, the witness cancelled and we never went.

The 1980s were dangerous times, politically and personally. Fortunately, normality started returning to South Africa in the early nineties, and I began to feel safer in my ongoing quest for the truth.

||||||||||||||||||||||||||||||||||||||||||||||||||||||||||||

CHAPTER 13

THE DEVIL
IS IN THE DETAIL

*'Anything could be made to
look good or bad, important or unimportant,
useful or useless, by being redescribed.'*

– RICHARD RORTY,
American philosopher

Are they real or are they fake? That was the million-dollar
question asked in 1987 in a huge legal wrangle over a collection
of early Japanese stamps. My training and experience in the world
of forensic science came into full force as I endeavoured to find
scientific evidence that would answer this thorny question.

The story of the Japanese stamps started long before I became
involved in the matter. A man by the name of Cyril Abrahams
worked for Sterns, a chain of jewellery stores. He decided to start
his own business, and obtained a significant overdraft facility with
the then Barclays Bank in Pritchard Street, Johannesburg, to do so.
After a while, the overdraft started reaching alarming proportions,
and the bank manager contacted Abrahams to ask him to provide
some security for the loan.

Abrahams went to see the bank manager, taking with him an A4 stamp collector's book, filled with stamps. He explained to the bank manager that this was a valuable collection of early Japanese stamps, which would more than cover his overdraft facility. The bank manager accepted the book of stamps as security and locked it in the bank vault.

Abrahams's overdraft continued to grow, to the point that it was well over a million rand, a significant amount of money, especially in the 1980s. The bank wrote Abrahams a polite letter asking him to settle the overdraft or reduce it to a more acceptable level. He replied that he was unable to do so, and correspondence travelled between the two parties as the bank became increasingly edgy about the risk they were carrying.

Finally, the bank decided to sell the stamps. After insuring the book of stamps, they sent them to Christie's in London with a request for the stamps to be sold for one and a half million rand, from which Christie's would take their commission before paying the bank the balance. Christie's wrote a very polite letter back to the bank, saying that they thought the bank was being over-optimistic, as the stamps were all forgeries. The London art dealers estimated the value of the stamp collection to be about two hundred rand.

The stamps were sent back to South Africa, and the bank informed Abrahams that they were forgeries. Furious, Abrahams went down to the bank to examine the stamps. After taking a look, he declared that they were a clear forgery, and that they were not the stamps he had handed to the bank months before. According to him, there had been foul play. Abrahams started legal proceedings against the bank for one and a half million rand.

Representatives from the bank arrived on my doorstep in a state of considerable agitation. I examined the facts surrounding the case. When Abrahams had given the stamps to the bank as security for his growing overdraft, they had been valued by a stamp dealer, Tibor Major. As part of the valuation process, photocopies had been made of all the stamps, page by page, which had been signed by both Major and Abrahams, agreeing that each page was a copy of the original stamps in the book.

Abrahams went to a huge amount of trouble to prove that these copies did not match the stamps in the book that the bank was now presenting as a forgery, implying that the bank had substituted the original stamps with worthless ones. His argument centred on the fact that, when you photocopy, there is an enlargement, which should be equal across the length and breadth of each stamp. He measured certain marks on the stamps and the copies, arguing that the ratios should be the same. Because there were differences in measurement, he claimed, these were not the stamps that he had given to the bank.

What Abrahams didn't know was that photocopy machines don't use a lens to copy entirely – they use a moving lens or a moving light to capture the image on a rotating drum, which determines the lengthwise magnification. The sideways magnification is determined by a lens and a slit. If these two are not exactly in sync, minute changes will occur. These may not appear significant, but will result in differences in measurement and a change in ratios. I had gone off to Rank Xerox and had spent some time at their plant near the airport so that I could fully understand how these machines worked.

Another important factor that had to be considered was the paper used to produce the photocopies. Paper is a living thing; it is made out of wood fibres that can swell and change in length and shape. Any printer will attest to the impact of humidity and other factors on the quality of printing. Accurate registration – the correlation of overlapping colours on a single image – is often difficult to obtain. This can sometimes be seen at the edges of a newspaper, where the colours are 'blurred' or imperfectly printed. When examining the photocopies of the stamps, I had to establish whether a change in the paper had resulted in the differences between the copies and the stamps.

During my investigation into paper and its potential pitfalls, I came across stamp paper, which is a very specific type of paper. At the time, the only company in South Africa that supplied stamp paper was Wiggins Teape, and I went to see them to learn about this specialised paper.

The key to this case happened quite by chance. I discussed the matter with various philatelists, one of whom told me about *Album Weeds*, a book written in 1905 by Reverend Robert Earee, a parson in England who was an avid stamp collector. His very authoritative book was still very relevant in 1987, and I scoured the world for it. Because these were pre-internet days, the task was not easy, but I eventually managed to locate a copy in England, and it was posted to me. I learnt some incredibly interesting facts from this book. I had noticed that each stamp had the same two symbols on it, and, intrigued by this, I found the explanation for it right there in *Album Weeds*.

The originals of the stamps were exceedingly valuable, and were prone to being forged. The Japanese did not take lightly to this practice: forgers had their heads chopped off if they were caught – there were no repeat offenders! So the Japanese forgers became cunning: they included a mark on the stamps to indicate that these were facsimile copies. These were the symbols that I had noticed on each stamp. On the originals of these stamps, there would have been no symbol, yet on the photocopies signed by Abrahams and Major of the book of stamps that Abrahams had handed in to the bank, these symbols were clearly visible. The stamps had been fake from the word go.

I then had to prove that the photocopies were, in fact, copies of the book of stamps handed to the bank by Abrahams. I used the process of comparison that you would use when comparing ballistics or fingerprints – I photographed each photocopy and each stamp, and compared the minute details on the stamp with the same minute features on the photocopy. For example, where the stamp had been cancelled and there was a mark, this could be seen on the original and on the copy. The same holds true with small details of damage, which you ascertain by examining the gaps and the size and position of the damage. Stamps are not perfect, and I studied the printing on each stamp. In some places it was stronger, in others weaker and faded.

Exactly the same features could be seen on the stamps and on the photocopies. I also showed that there was no significance in the nature of the paper in this matter – the paper could not have produced that particular finding. Even though there were differences between the stamps, there were also many similarities, which will always be the case. If you take two photographs of a person, for example, there will be differences depending on the photographic process, the camera, the lens, and so on. These differences will be random. Certain features, however, will be the same – such as a mole on the person's face, for instance – and these are more difficult to explain away when comparing the two photographs.

With an array of photographs as evidence, we proceeded to court. Since Barclays Bank was the plaintiff, we started. It was a hard-fought case, but very entertaining, and it was handled in a pleasant manner by Judge Johann Kriegler, a sharp man who quickly grasped the concepts and understood the evidence. I was cross-examined by Jonathan Heher, who is a judge of the Supreme Court of Appeal today – a real gentleman.

We won the case. Abrahams ultimately had to prove that someone had forged stamps of comparatively little value for a benefit that was not worth the effort – or, as Kriegler put it, that someone had gone to such extensive ends for a small crock of gold at the end of the rainbow that was not worth it. These were clearly forgeries – some stamps were worth a pittance. Why would anyone go to all this trouble? The originals were worth every cent that Abrahams had claimed they were, but Tibor Major had not realised that Abrahams's stamps were forgeries when he valued them.

This was a fascinating case and illustrated yet again the multi-faceted approach necessary when investigating a problem. On the face of it, it seemed a simple comparison, but digging deeper, there were other issues that came into play: I had to understand the impact of paper and how it could have changed the dimensions of the photocopies, how the printing process could have impacted on the stamps and the copies, how the basis of comparison works – that similarities are easy to explain, but differences are very difficult to explain away. On top of all of that, I had the immense good fortune to have discovered a book of which there are probably only a few copies left in the world, in which I found out about the Japanese symbol for a facsimile.

I was so intrigued by the case that I offered to buy the book of stamps from Barclays for the amount that Christie's would have given them. I still have it in my possession today.

The work of a forensic scientist can be extraordinarily varied, yet it always centres on solving a particular problem, no matter what shape or form it takes. The answer always lies in the detail. Despite the fact that there are some heavy odds at times and the obvious facts sometimes seem to be the only plausible solution, it's a fascinating business in which to be involved.

||||||||||||||||||||||||||||||||||||||||||||||||||||||||||||||||

CHAPTER 14

NEVER SEND THE FOX TO INVESTIGATE CRIMES IN THE HEN HOUSE

'Quis custodiet ipsos custodes?'
Who will guard the guards themselves?

– JUVENAL,

Roman poet

One of the major frustrations of the late 1980s and early 1990s was that the state police policed themselves. Allowing the fox to guard the hen house never works.

In August 1988, a massive bomb rocked Khotso House, the former headquarters of the South African Council of Churches (SACC). Placed near the lift shaft, the bomb reduced the entire building to rubble. Fortunately, no one was killed. An ANC supporter, Shirley Gunn, was falsely accused of the bombing, and spent more than two months in prison with her infant son after her arrest. During the presentation of evidence at the TRC, horrific facts were presented about her imprisonment, one of which was that the police had removed her sixteen-month-old son from her for eight days and then used tapes of him crying to torture her.

It emerged years later, at the TRC, that Adriaan Vlok – Minister of Police at the time of the bombing – had, on the instruction of P.W. Botha, arranged for the demolition of the building, as it was seen as a 'house of evil' used to store hand grenades, limpet mines and other weapons. I was not aware of these allegations at the time, and during my investigation I saw absolutely no evidence of any weaponry kept at Khotso House.

I was asked by the SACC to investigate the bombing. From the outset, I could see that it was yet another cover-up case. The attitude, body language and actions of the police investigators betrayed the fact that they were merely going through the motions of an investigation. They knew the truth, but were determined to hide it at all costs. In addition, evidence was concealed. The case, ultimately, was a disgraceful reflection on those people who were supposed to be serving and protecting the citizens of the country at that time.

In the case of the Khotso bombing, as in many other cases then, the police issued incorrect and misleading press statements, falsely arrested people, and tried to create an entirely artificial picture while they were planning and executing bombings, murders and torture. Years later, I prepared a report for the TRC on the failure of forensic science services during this era.

Similar institutional failures occurred after the assassination of David Webster, who was gunned down in cold blood on 1 May 1989. His assassination followed the same pattern as so many of the state-sponsored murders in which I had been involved, where political opponents were viewed as outlaws by the state and were simply taken out.

Webster was born in 1945 in Northern Rhodesia (now Zambia), and he later immigrated to South Africa with his family. After deciding to follow a career in anthropology, he joined Wits as a lecturer in 1970. Because his doctorate focused on the traditional anthropological topic of kinship, he was exposed to the effects of migrant labour, particularly in the southern Mozambique region.

This steered him in the direction of related issues: he began to explore with zest the social history of tuberculosis and the social causes of malnutrition. Living with the people as a researcher, his academic critique of government policies led to anti-apartheid activism.

In 1976, Webster was invited to lecture for two years at the University of Manchester, after which he returned to Wits. It was the detention of some of his students in 1981 – specifically Barbara Hogan – that was to catapult him into the role that eventually resulted in his assassination.

Webster worked for the Detainees' Parents' Support Committee, a support group for relatives of detainees and banished people. In addition to assisting with tracing banished and detained family members, he organised regular social gatherings, known as 'David Webster tea parties'. At these meetings, families of detainees could share information and pool ideas on how to find those who were in prison or had disappeared at the hands of the state.

Webster, who was involved in the End Conscription Campaign, the Five Freedoms Forum, and the Detainees' Education and Welfare Organisation, interacted with many anti-apartheid activists, and was a dynamic activist himself. In the late eighties, he wrote a research report with his partner, Maggie Friedman, about repression under the state of emergency, exposing the increasing state repression and how liberation movements were finding new and creative methods of resistance. I never quite understood why he was seen as a threat so large that he had to be removed from society. He was one of my wife Shelona's lecturers at the time of his death, and we knew him as a quiet, gentle, scholarly man of unquestionable integrity.

On 1 May 1989, just nine months before Nelson Mandela's release from prison, Webster and Maggie Friedman returned to their home in Troyeville, Johannesburg, after buying plants from a nursery. A car pulled up, and Webster's name was called out. As he turned to see who it was, a gunshot was fired and he fell to the ground, clutching his chest. He called out to Maggie that he had been shot, and that she should get an ambulance. A few minutes later, he was dead.

I was contacted within an hour of the shooting to investigate on behalf of the Webster family. I immediately went to the crime scene, accompanied by Shelona, who had known Webster well, and found it swarming with police. The investigating officer was Colonel Floris Mostert.

I spent a long time looking for the bullet as I tried to piece the crime together. The bullet was likely to have passed right through Webster, and would have ended up somewhere on the premises. Wollie Wolmarans, the police forensic ballistics expert, assisted me. He was another one of the scientifically inept people in the police force, but he was a good foot soldier and did what he was told to do. Mostert also assisted us in the search, and we overturned flower-pots and such, combing the entire area. Eventually the police brought in a sniffer dog to help us look.

I didn't have sight of the body or clothes, and after many frustrating hours of searching, I insisted on seeing Webster's clothing. The moment I saw his blood-stained T-shirt, I realised that the shot that killed him had to have been a shotgun wound, so the pellets would still be in him. Pellets would have gone straight into the body and not emerged out the other side. It was blatantly clear that the police, including Mostert and Wolmarans, must have known about the weapon and had kept us running around on a wild-goose chase while they covered their bases.

It was always obvious that there were crimes the police wanted to solve and crimes they didn't want to solve. Again, the telltale signs were there – they were milling around, failing to make proper notes, and were disorganised. Basically, they were treading water until everyone went away, when they would cover everything up.

Webster's assassination was a politically organised crime, and the police knew who the killers were from the outset. This murder was the subject of seven investigations, including the Harms Commission of Inquiry and an internal military inquiry, but no one was prosecuted at the time – an utter waste of time and money. I removed myself from the case once I had identified the body and established that the murder had been police-initiated. Nobody was found guilty of the crime.

The Harms Commission started making inroads into these political murders and started the process of unveiling the hit squads. The commission found that the CCB was run by a number of people inside the police force, and that Staal Burger, Wouter Basson and many others knew the true facts. Their involvement infiltrated all ranks of the police force, including the Brixton Murder and Robbery Squad.

The problems with the Harms Commission were multifaceted. Judge Harms could not absorb the mindset of the people with whom he was dealing. When Dirk Coetzee gave evidence in London in 1990 relating to the existence and activities of hit squads, Judge Harms could not contain himself and cried out, 'This is all bullshit!' When Judge Harms wrote his report, he found no evidence of hit squads. Part of the reason may have been that the terms of reference of his commission were very narrow, but perhaps he simply could not bring himself to believe that his fellow Afrikaners in the police force could perform such atrocities. The result was that the hit squads appeared to have got away with murder.

However, the truth behind David Webster's killing came out years later, when Ferdi Barnard, a CCB member, bragged to a TRC amnesty applicant that he had murdered Webster. He was eventually arrested and prosecuted for the crime, and a more just jailing of an individual cannot be conceived.

Barnard had been paid to murder David Webster, and had rented a room at the Oribi Hotel down the street from Webster's house to keep surveillance. On that fateful May day, Barnard drove down Eleanor Street, leant out of the car window and fired the shot.

He is indeed the lowest piece of scum that I have ever had the misfortune of encountering, a cold-blooded murderer who showed no remorse or emotion for what he had done, and who was not worthy of cleaning the shoes of the man he had murdered.

The police never investigated the Oribi Hotel surveillance, nor did they follow up on any clues or try to determine who had paid for the murder. Their plain disinterest mirrored the attitude they had exhibited after the Cradock Four murder, when they knew, too, that the culprits were among their own.

The Elim church fire was another textbook case of foxes in the hen house. Eight children died on the night of 12 March 1992, when the church building became an inferno, leaving many of the children trapped in the dormitories on the third floor.

The old Elim church in Sunnyside, Pretoria, was semi-derelict. Jeremy Kruger, a community-spirited man, had decided to convert it into a shelter for street children, with the aim of providing the children with food and some kind of support structure. Kruger obtained donations of blankets, beds and rudimentary cooking equipment, and ran the shelter as a community project.

Some of the children had had run-ins with the local police, and a particular altercation with a policeman from the Sunnyside police station had taken place. One day, this police officer caught one of the children allegedly stealing from a car, and he chased him, wanting to arrest the boy. The child ran straight to the Elim church building, where a number of his friends ganged up on the policeman. The end result was that the policeman jumped out of a window and broke his ankle. This was to have tragic ramifications a short while later.

On the night of 12 March, the children living in the old Elim church woke up to flames and choking smoke. There was no way to get out of the third-floor dormitory, where many of them slept, as the doors were locked. Some of them jumped out of the window, sustaining injuries, while one boy hung out of the window and directed others to slide down his body to safety. Amidst the flames, panic and chaos, eight children died in the blaze and many others were seriously injured.

The police enlisted Gawie Basson from the CSIR to investigate the fire, as they lacked a proper fire investigation team. Lawyers for Human Rights, an independent human rights organisation, called me in. From the beginning, it appeared obvious that this was no accident. The various signs were present, one of them being the speed with which the fire had developed. As mentioned in Chapter 4, deliberate fires develop much quicker than accidental ones, as they are normally set to burn in a number of places at the same time. They also burn at a lower level, starting slowly and burning upwards, following the path of heat. This fire seemed different: it appeared to have crept around on the ground. There was also the inexplicable fact that the fire had spread to a pile of wood in the church. All of this pointed to the obvious fact that the fire had been started deliberately.

The next logical question related to who would have wanted to set the building alight. The policeman from the Sunnyside police station was the prime suspect, as he had been seen in the area at the time of the fire. When he was confronted, he claimed to have been nowhere near the place, saying that he had been at home the entire evening.

I went to see his landlady, who informed me that on the night of the fire he had been out the whole evening, but that he had told her to sign an affidavit stating that he had been there that night. When she'd asked him why she should lie, he had said to her that it was police procedure. Clearly he didn't have an alibi.

I took a statement from the landlady and confronted the police with it. The way in which they dealt with the matter was extremely underhanded: they sent another policeman to speak to the landlady, confusing her with different time-and-place facts and causing her to doubt her own initial affidavit. They thereby neutralised her statement to me. Taking all the evidence into consideration, I concluded that the truth was that the policeman, either alone or with accomplices, had set fire to the building in an attempt to wreak revenge on the troublesome children.

The matter went to an inquest before a magistrate in Pretoria, and became a mere repetition of many other inquests of its time. The prosecutor, who was supposed to be a neutral leader of evidence for the state, was aggressively biased. The magistrate was viciously pro the police. In the end, the police were never brought to task and the outcome of the inquest was a non-event: predictably, no one was to blame. Like the Ashley Kriel inquest, like the Cradock Four case, like the David Webster assassination – like so many others – it was a travesty of justice in my opinion; a sham aimed at exonerating the police.

Of course, one cannot ignore the fact that there were political overtones in this case, which involved a white policeman and black children. Proper justice would have meant the prosecution of the white policeman, yet in those days it was not considered a *real* crime to kill a few black children – a tragic reflection of the times. The police knew about the various incidents that had occurred over the years – Khotso House, the murders, the hit squads – yet there prevailed an apathetic attitude that permeated investigations concerning black people.

The way in which the Elim church fire was handled led to an increased cynicism on my part. These seemingly pious individuals – regular churchgoers, supposed upstanding citizens of society – were entirely dishonest when it came to matters of a political nature.

In an ironic twist, the state threatened to prosecute Jeremy Kruger, the man who ran the Elim orphanage, for culpable homicide, because some of the doors had been locked and the children had not been able to get out. This would have been an extremely unfair prosecution; they were simply trying to turn the tables to find a scapegoat.

Around the same time, in 1992, I was involved in another politicised case where we actually emerged victorious. I was approached about a matter concerning a black child who had been caught stealing by a farmer. To punish him, the farmer had handcuffed the boy and welded him to a steel table. The farmer had then carried on welding close by, and the boy had caught alight. He was badly burnt. The farmer claimed it had been an accident, and that he hadn't known that the boy would catch alight.

The police were being their usual disinterested selves in the investigation, walking around smiling and paying lip service to the whole process. Mark Froneman, who was leading the police's forensic investigation, was not making any satisfactory headway, so I was called in by the law firm Deneys Reitz.

The child had been doused with petrol. During the welding, the sparks that had flown towards him had caused his clothing – a woollen top – to ignite. I decided to conduct an experiment, filming it with a video camera. I was able to show evidence in court that one could weld near a woollen top and sparks would not set it alight. (This, incidentally, is why firemen used to wear thick woollen coats.) If an accelerant such as petrol was added, however, the top would quickly ignite from the sparks.

The farmer's actions had been intentional, in my opinion. It was an important victory for us when the farmer was found guilty in court: it demonstrated that slowly the wheels of justice were starting to turn.

Sloppy police work almost prevented justice from being served in a truly frightening incident in which a plot had been hatched to expend black lives for financial gain. The Witbank Kombi Murder took place in Witbank, east of Pretoria, in 1992, when a group of black people in a burning Kombi plunged over the edge of a cliff. Five or six of the passengers were burnt beyond recognition.

The police investigation was totally incompetent: the police even went so far as getting one of the accused to interview a survivor. I was asked by the Legal Resources Centre to investigate the matter, and the story was chilling. Some unscrupulous insurance salesmen had offered employment to a group of black people, and had insured their lives as part of the deal. Shortly afterwards, these men were found in a burnt-out Kombi at the bottom of a cliff.

During my investigation, I was horrified at the sheer brutality of what I found. The Kombi had been prepared for the murder: there were no handles on the inside of the doors, so no one could escape; petrol had been poured over the vehicle; and it had been set alight before being pushed over the cliff.

As the investigation progressed, the whole sordid plot was exposed. I am not aware that any prosecutions occurred in this terrible case – once again, no one was held accountable. The days of shoddy police investigations and cover-ups were beginning to come to an end, but they were not entirely over yet.

||||||||||||||||||||||||||||||||||||||||||||||||||||||||||||||||

CHAPTER 15

DEATH, DRUGS AND DIRTY TRICKS

'If only there were evil people somewhere insidiously committing evil deeds and it were necessary only to separate them from the rest of us and destroy them. But the line dividing good and evil cuts through the heart of every human being. And who is willing to destroy a piece of his own heart?'

– ALEKSANDR SOLZHENITSYN,
Russian novelist, historian and winner
of the Nobel Prize in Literature

The cracks were beginning to appear in the apartheid government's armour, and I, along with many others, welcomed the truth with open arms. The Harms Commission of Inquiry into hit squads, the CCB and the mockery of justice was a sham, however. Louis Harms was and still is a good judge, but I fear he was a prisoner of his own ideology. A good, solid Afrikaner, he could not believe, as mentioned in the previous chapter, that his own people could possibly have committed the atrocities that were being alleged.

Despite Harms's findings, people were starting to run scared. Sparked by those coming out of the woodwork – starting with Butana Almond Nofemela, who blew the whistle on Vlakplaas (see Chapter 9) – various inquiries sprang up, and the whole can of worms, including the inner workings of the CCB, slowly began to creak open. Nofemela's admission started the slow leak that became a widening crack, until the floodgates burst open, with more and more former operatives coming out with the truth.

In spite of this, the tradition of foul play was still alive and well in the world of forensic science, and I was not immune to these dirty tricks. I viewed Lothar Neethling, the head of the police's forensic laboratory, as an intensely evil person – I believe that he perverted science in the name of a political agenda, and that is unforgivable. He and many others did not see it that way, but I believe in honest and truthful scientific applications.

Drug cases brought me into close contact with Neethling, and he used these opportunities to make my life as uncomfortable as he could. In 1988, I worked on a big Mandrax case, defending a group of drug dealers who had set up a Mandrax factory in Kempton Park, Johannesburg. The business had been operating smoothly until one of the dealers boasted about it in a pub one evening. The police were tipped off, and the entire business was seized – right down to the vehicles that were used to transport the drugs.

During its period of operation, this factory had produced a massive amount of Mandrax – estimated at around R186 million in value at the time. It was a huge case for the police. The drug industry was a cash-rich business, and when the police entered the home of one of the drug bosses – the Castle, in Roodepoort – they found themselves literally neck deep in cash!

I was approached by the drug dealers to act in their defence, and I accepted. The police claimed that the substance they had seized was Mandrax, and I had to determine if this was the case. To do this, I needed a sample from the state of the seized drugs so that I could test to see if it was, indeed, Mandrax. They refused, saying that we had to obtain a court order. Louis Virtue, the magistrate, granted us the court order, and I proceeded to take samples, followed around by Lieutenant Twigge, Neethling's *handlanger*, who then took samples of my samples.

The very next day, I received a visit from the police and a representative from the Medicines Control Council (MCC). My registration with the MCC permitted me to be in possession of certain illicit drugs in order to test them scientifically. The policeman and MCC representative had a warrant for my arrest, claiming that I was manufacturing illicit drugs.

The drugs that they were referring to actually arose from a previous case I had worked on. An Indian woman had been stopped at the airport and her luggage searched. Two two-kilogram packets of brown powder were found – presumably heroin. I had approached Neethling to obtain samples of the substance, so that I could test the brown powder against known heroin.

Testing for a drug is a complex procedure, and there are various ways of doing it, using a combination of methods. The first step is to conduct a paper chromatography test: a small spot of the solution of the drug is placed onto a chromatography plate, which is a very thin layer of silica stuck to a thin glass plate. A line is drawn across the plate about a quarter of an inch from the bottom, and the drugs are 'spotted' at regular intervals.

The plate is then placed into a solution of volatile substances, such as benzene or pentane, and the 'spotted' substances move up along the plate, much as a piece of paper would absorb water. This is called a 'capillary effect'. Different substances move at different speeds, so as they move up the plate, you can get a presumptive idea of what the substance is – whether it is tea leaves, sugar or something that comes from the family of opiates.

The second step, in those days, was to shine an infrared light through the substance and measure the wavelength and intensity of the absorption of the light using an infrared spectrometer. The pattern of light absorption would give an indication of the substance, as each chemical compound has its own pattern of absorption.

Today, a gas chromatograph mass spectrometer is used, which consists of a tiny oil-coated tube. A gasflow of nitrogen or helium is sent through the tube, into which a minute amount of the substance being tested is injected. It is carried by the flow of gas through the tube, and as it comes through the other end, it flows over a detector. The time it takes to pass through the tube will indicate what substance it is. Here one is measuring the retention time, of which each drug has its own.

Another method is to use a mass spectrometer as a detector. This test is much more definitive. Effluent from the end of the tube is fed into the mass spectrometer, where it is bombarded with electrons. This fragments the molecules and they shatter. If the same strength of electron bombardment is used, the molecules will always shatter in the same way, depending on the chemistry. These fragments can be picked up as separate entities by passing them through a magnetic field, which produces a fragmentogram – effectively a fingerprint of the substance under investigation.

Before embarking on any drug testing, it is important to run a sample of the known substance to ensure that your equipment is working and to make a comparison with the unknown sample. You also want to make certain that you get the same results – in other words, compare the fragments of your substance to the fragments of the known substance – in the case of the powder found in the Indian woman's luggage, heroin. So it was important for me to have a sample of heroin before I could embark on any testing.

I was having difficulty obtaining the legal sample of heroin that I needed. Eventually I managed to track some down through the United Nations drug control centre. It was not easy to find an airline to transport it for me: eventually Lufthansa agreed, but they could not get it to me in time.

I was under pressure from Neethling, who wanted the heroin case wrapped up so that he could attend the opening of Parliament. As I desperately needed the heroin to conduct my tests, I decided to manufacture it myself – I am a chemist, after all. It was not difficult, and within a few hours I had 100 milligrams of the purest heroin. When I compared the brown powder found in the Indian woman's luggage to the known heroin, it was clear that it *was*, in fact, heroin that she was transporting, and not herbal tea, as she claimed.

So the unexpected visit from the policemen and MCC representative just after I'd obtained samples of the substances seized during the Mandrax factory case arose because I was in possession of heroin that I had manufactured myself. In that quantity, however, I was entitled to possess it. Neethling was just trying to make life difficult for me. The matter was sorted out easily with a few phone calls to the magistrate and the then Deputy Attorney-General, Kevin Attwell. I was never prosecuted, and the matter died a natural death. The incident showed to what lengths the man would go. He tried a similar trick later on, but that was also quickly quashed by Kevin Attwell.

The case of the Mandrax dealers in Kempton Park illustrated the extent to which the state forensic department bent the rules in the testing procedures. A matter ended up in the Kempton Park Magistrates' Court, and when I looked at the results of the state's analyses, I realised that they were too good to be true.

We had used Neethling previously to establish the ground rules for the Mandrax case: in an earlier trial in Cape Town, I specifically had questions posed to Neethling that we could use as a point of reference in this trial. I had asked things like, 'Is it possible to get the same results each time?', to which the answer was, of course, 'No.' If one didn't ask the questions so pertinently, and in such a focused manner, the police experts would lie.

In the Mandrax matter, all seven test results were identical, which is simply not possible. To test the substance, a solid solution of it is made by grinding a small amount with pure potassium bromide. The powder is then compressed into a tablet, which is placed in the infrared spectrometer. When you analyse a substance using potassium bromide, you never quite get the same result: each result will be slightly different due to noise on the baseline – you find ripples on the line that are never quite the same, such as a fingerprint. The only explanation for the identical results in this case was that the state analyst had taken a single reference sample and repeated the test seven times, using the same reference sample, instead of taking seven different samples. I caught them flat-footed!

The analyst in the Mandrax case was lazy, so he had cheated. His laziness resulted, in part, in the drug dealers being acquitted. I have never been pro drug dealers, but I do believe in fairness. Even a drug dealer is entitled to a fair defence, and there is no excuse for having the evidence against you tweaked. It was no wonder Neethling detested me.

The accused in the Mandrax factory case were eventually convicted on something completely different: one of the chemicals that they had purchased had no other use than to manufacture Mandrax, which ensured their conviction. One of the accused set up another Mandrax factory to pay for his defence, and he was prosecuted for that as well!

Neethling eventually left the police laboratory and was replaced by Hein Strauss, a more honest man with whom I developed a healthy working relationship. Neethling died recently of prostate cancer, but he will always be reviled for the role he played in perverting justice during the apartheid era.

Laziness on behalf of the state forensic department has resulted in reasonable doubt over a man's innocence more than once. A few years ago, in the early 2000s, a man in Swaziland was accused of murdering his cousin. His defence was that there had been a third person in the house at the time: he said that he had attacked the third person, injuring him, and that his cousin had died in the battle. The third person managed to escape, even though he was injured.

The murder scene bore evidence of a bloody fight. There appeared to be multiple bleedings, with about fifty different blood splashes all over the place. An expert was sent down from Pretoria to carry out the analysis because Swaziland had no forensic department of its own. A young man who had trained in 1994 conducted the DNA analyses on the blood splashes, but to save money he analysed only four of them. All four contained the blood of the deceased. He testified to this in court.

The fact that he had taken such a limited number of samples meant that the version told by the defendant could not be ruled out. Testifying in the trial, I had no choice but to say, 'Well, my lord, the defence has always been that there was another person who was injured and who bled. If your lordship were to ask me whether his blood could have been in the fifty samples that weren't analysed, my answer to your lordship is that I cannot rule that out.'

There are no short cuts in forensic science. It's about doing the job properly so that there can be no doubt as to the meaning of the results. The judge in the lower court in Swaziland convicted the young man and sentenced him to death. The case was taken on appeal, and a full bench noted the concerns I'd expressed about the lack of completeness of the analysis done by the state forensic expert. They reversed the sentence, and the man was acquitted of the crime.

The authorities had so many dirty tricks up their sleeves in the late eighties – sometimes it defied logic. One such instance concerned the foul smell emanating from the Regina Mundi church in Soweto.

Regina Mundi was at the centre of political resistance to the National Party in the townships. A large gathering at the church had been planned, but on the Friday before the meeting, a foul smell permeated the entire place. The priests came to see me for help.

Fearing poison, they brought some items with them that displayed this foul smell, so that I could examine them.

I discovered that these items contained a substance called butyric acid, among other things. A short-chain fatty acid produced by bacteria as part of their metabolic process, butyric acid is one of the compounds that releases the smell of unwashed feet and unwashed people, and also, incidentally, gives some of the taste to cheese. It is not fatal and it is in no way poisonous, unless you drink vast quantities of it. I was able to reassure the priests quite happily that they could clean out the church and use a bit of deodorant, but that no lasting harm would come from the butyric acid.

Many years later, before 1994, a laboratory belonging to Armscor burnt down in Pretoria. I was asked to investigate the laboratory. Being cautious, and because the process of investigating a fire involves crawling around and sniffing things, I wanted to make certain that there was nothing toxic in the laboratory. I turned to the head of the laboratory and said, 'I need to sniff around your laboratory. Please bring me a shovel.' I duly dug around and finally discovered a foul smell. It smelt to me like butyric acid, so I asked the laboratory head if it was, in fact, what I thought it was.

'Yes,' he replied. 'It is. In fact, this is the place where the butyric acid used in the Regina Mundi church incident was produced. We used to manufacture those foul-smelling things for the forces.'

It was going way beyond acceptable limits for the National Party to spray such substances all over a church, no matter what the political persuasions were. I wasn't prepared to analyse the fire any further for the laboratory people because, as far as I was concerned, there was a conflict of interest – I had acted for the Regina Mundi church. Because the church had placed itself on the other, opposing side of the political spectrum, they had been subjected to these dirty tricks. I felt it my duty to reveal to everybody the fact that the Armscor laboratory had done this. Politics is such a dirty game; I did not want to be involved with any organisation that had stooped to using such dishonest techniques in a place of worship.

Political overtones and filthy tricks had a strong impact on Henry Burt, the first white person to be convicted of the 'necklace' murder of a black man. Necklacing entailed placing a petrol-filled tyre around the neck of a victim and setting it alight, and was fairly common in the apartheid years. Burt's trial and conviction caused quite a stir in its day.

Henry Burt was a young fitter and turner who lived with his girlfriend, Moekie, in Laezonia, near Lanseria Airport. In 1986, the body of a black policeman was found necklaced in the veld about 15 kilometres from Henry's home, near a place that would later turn out to be Vlakplaas. During the police investigation, it was established that Burt and another man had given the policeman a lift shortly before his death.

The police questioned Burt and the other man, who then, suddenly, went to the bank one day, withdrew all his money, left his house, his car and all his possessions, and fled to England. Burt was eventually taken into custody for questioning, where he was tortured almost to the brink of death. He suffered electric shocks, mock suffocations and other cruel methods of torture. After verifying his alibi, the police released him later that evening.

The next morning, Burt went to the Pretoria Murder and Robbery Unit to make a statement. He took a tape recorder with him in the event that any pressure was placed on him, or he suffered further torture. After making the statement and going for medical treatment, an attorney advised him to apply for an interdict against the police that would prevent them from any further acts of brutality. The interdict was granted at 8 p.m. that evening, after which Burt started criminal proceedings against the police.

Burt's civil case against the police seemed to trigger grossly intimidating behaviour by them – they would arrive at his house with no search warrant, force their way in, scratch through his possessions and leave chaos in their wake. About three weeks after the policeman's body had been found, the police decided to take Burt's car in again. They told him that the forensic department would 'definitely find something this time'.

And 'find' something they did. On the second investigation of the car, the police discovered fresh specks of blood on the edge of the back seat – almost as if someone had cut their finger, releasing tiny drops of blood. The car had bucket seats in the front and a bench seat at the back that could be removed to be cleaned.

The previous investigating officer, who had assaulted Burt, was no longer on the case. His successor came to see Henry at work, and asked him whether he would be prepared to withdraw the charges against the police. He also wanted to know how much money Burt had in the bank. He threatened Burt with arrest and a murder charge if he did not give him a statement explaining how the back seat of the car had come to be covered in the deceased's blood. Unable to comply with the investigating officer's request, Burt was arrested for the murder of the policeman.

The issue of blood testing played an enormous role in this trial. I was brought in by the defence to advise them on the analysis of the blood and the interpretation of the results, as well as on the non-specificity of luminol for detecting blood.

The police expert testified that, after finding the blood spots, he had examined the entire back seat of the car using the luminol technique. Luminol identifies haemoglobin by fluorescing in the dark. It is very sensitive, detecting haemoglobin traces down to the rate of one part in six million parts (i.e., one part of blood diluted six million times). Using this technique, the police expert could show that the entire back seat had been covered at some stage by haemoglobin, or, as the police expert put it, 'primate blood'. The sample was too minute to obtain a blood group, but they deduced that the chances were good that the blood was that of a human.

The court was faced with the picture of a seat having been fully exposed to blood and so thoroughly washed that the blood could be detected only faintly by luminol. I was not convinced that there had ever been blood on the seat – I could not understand the presence of the blood drops or the test result. At the time of the second examination of the vehicle, the blood drops would have been there in full view – anyone could have seen them. Yet the police had scoured the car several times on their first examination and did not see any blood: they had found it only after the interdict. I believe that the drops of blood could only have got on the back seat by being planted there afterwards, which I told the court.

The police may have used some blood left from the post-mortem of the necklaced man. Yet their submission that the seat had been covered with blood and cleaned – which meant that it must have been removed, soaked, scrubbed and rinsed at least two or three times – would have ensured that the spots of blood would have been washed out. The theory was that the victim had been carried from where he was killed to where he was necklaced, fitting in with the state's theory of blood on the back seat.

After three weeks in the Pretoria Supreme Court, Henry Burt was found guilty of murder, and sentenced to death. He spent two years on death row. He always protested his innocence, and eventually his sentence was commuted to twenty years on petition to the state president.

At the TRC, Henry Burt was declared a victim of gross human rights violations, and was paid R30 000 in compensation, a pittance if one considers the course of events that robbed a young man of his life and his future. He had clearly not been guilty, yet he had been convicted on circumstantial and false forensic evidence. Burt and I are still in contact every now and then. He has managed to get on with his life.

Justice Human was on the bench at Burt's trial. If you mention his name today in legal circles, people say, 'to err is Human'. He is dead now, but he was a typical National Party man, in court to do the government's bidding. The trial was so full of holes: the cause of death was never determined; there was no DNA to show that the blood sample belonged to the deceased. There was never any proper explanation as to how this murder happened. Yet Justice Human would never have found Henry Burt innocent. A policeman had been murdered, and someone had to pay: the police, whether black or white, were paramount in those days.

This case continued to bother me, in particular the luminol test, which delivered such damning proof of haemoglobin. Moekie, Henry's girlfriend at the time, knew nothing about the murder, yet it was in her car that the blood spots and evidence of 'primate blood' was found. She was a paraplegic who took part in paraplegic games. Henry had made fibreglass coverings for the stainless-steel rims of her wheelchair so that she had better traction for her hands when playing sport. The fibreglass was moulded over the rims, and Henry had sanded them down so that they were smooth and comfortable. I discovered many years later that polyester resin from fibreglass gives a positive luminol result. This could have been a logical explanation to the whole case.

Luminol testing has proved to be accurate and incredibly useful in reaching the truth. In the eighties, I was asked by Cape Town advocate Paul Hoffman to assist with the matter of a Malay messenger, who had been shot and killed by the police. They had mistaken him for a criminal and had ordered him to stop moving. In those days, if the police told a coloured man to stop, he ran. They were entitled to shoot to make an arrest, but, in this case, they shot him in his head.

An action was brought against the police, and I worked with luminol and the blood stains on the man's shirt. The police claimed that the criminal they were chasing and had shot was wearing a striped shirt. Yet the man who was killed had been wearing a blue shirt at the time. Even though the shirt had been washed, I was able to show, using luminol, that the shirt worn by the innocent dead man had been covered by his blood.

The defendant's advocate in the case was Jeanette Traverso, who subsequently went on to become a judge of the Supreme Court and is now Deputy Judge President of the Supreme Court in Cape Town. My testimony was accepted, and the police were forced to pay compensation to the widow.

These were difficult days. As an independent forensic scientist, I always had to be one step ahead of the so-called police experts. This was not always easy, as the techniques and methods they used changed all the time, presenting challenges and frustrations. From a forensic point of view, though, these years were interesting – I was always kept on my toes.

||||||||||||||||||||||||||||||||||||||||||||||||||||||||||||||||||||||

CHAPTER 16

POST-MORTEMS: THE GOOD, THE BAD AND THE TOTALLY INEPT

Disabling Professions

– IVAN ILLICH,
Austrian philosopher, book title

Investigating a crime – getting as close to the true sequence of events as possible – is like solving a puzzle. One of the critical steps in this process is the post-mortem. Sadly, in South Africa, the quality of work in this arena is far from ideal. I have been outspoken on this issue over the years, which has not earned me any popularity: it seems we are expected to keep quiet when we see things going wrong. I refuse to do that, and, as such, am often labelled public enemy number one.

In the 1980s, the post-mortem conducted on young activist Ashley Kriel was appalling. It failed to address the issue of whether or not the gunshot that had killed Kriel had been a contact shot. As I mentioned in Chapter 10, I am certain that there was a second bullet, the presence of which would have had significant ramifications at the inquest. Yet the scientist who carried out the post-mortem simply never looked for it or did not report on it.

Some post-mortem reports that I have seen have been blatant lies. One such case involved a policeman accused of shooting a suspect who had been running away. I was hired to defend the policeman. At the time, it was considered acceptable behaviour for a policeman to shoot and kill a fleeing suspect, and the pathologist's report reflected this: there were records showing that the pathologist had opened the body before he examined the bullet wounds in the back. This did not cohere with the report at all, because if he had conducted the post-mortem as he said he had, the organs would have fallen out when he turned the body over to study the bullet wounds! The pathologist had simply not conducted a post-mortem: his report was a patent lie. He was eventually cross-examined and admitted to his dishonesty.

At every crime scene, you, as the forensic investigator, have to start off with a high index of suspicion. If you accept too easily that a death appears to be natural, you fall into the trap that the British police did with Harold Shipman, who murdered old ladies after persuading them to change their wills in his favour. The police in this case had initially failed to find sufficient evidence to bring charges, assuming that the old ladies had died of natural causes. Instead, they had been poisoned by Shipman, their doctor, who had administered lethal doses of diamorphine and then forged their medical records to indicate that they had been in poor health.

A 'crime' can be downgraded to a natural cause of death; it is impossible, however, to go back to suspecting a crime if your starting point is that the death occurred as a result of natural causes.

Many people are clothed when they die. A post-mortem should be started with the clothed body in order to understand how the death took place. The clothing needs to be examined in relation to any wounds on the body itself to reveal the context in which the injury occurred. For example, if the hands of a person who has been shot were above their head when they were killed, their shirt would have moved up. The position of the bullet hole in the shirt would not, therefore, correspond with the position of the actual gunshot wound on the body. So the position of the clothing in relation to the wound is extremely important, as it will provide the forensic pathologist with valuable information about the way in which the shooting took place. In addition, the manner in which blood spills onto the clothing is different depending on whether the victim was sitting, kneeling or lying down.

Another crucial aspect of the post-mortem is that of microscopic investigation. Whenever two objects touch each other, there is a transfer of minute materials – something is always left behind, whether it is skin, hair or clothing fibres. This often requires microscopic research. The position and type of the fibres in relation to the clothing and the wound are also important – there may be a lack of burns on the body, for instance, because there was clothing in place. The wound ultimately has to be interpreted in terms of whether there was clothing on at the time of the shooting.

Ideally, the body should be examined in situ. The hands of the deceased need to be examined, as do the wound, the clothing, and the scene of the killing and its surrounds. In the recent case of Chris Drummond, a high-profile property developer who was pushed off a balcony in Claremont in April 2010, I observed blood on the pillars nearby, so I thought there might have been a fight. When the state mortuary staff arrived to remove the body, they did not have any plastic bags to bag the victim's hands. I would not allow them to move the body until the hands had been bagged, which I did myself, on the scene. This should have been done by trained, professional mortuary staff, not by me. The hands may have had bruising, material under the fingernails, blood or DNA on them, all of which would be vital evidence.

The current post-mortem procedure in South African mortuaries begins with a person called a prosector, who opens the body, takes out the organs and lays them out on the slab. The major downside of this is that the body needs to be seen intact first.

This was highlighted in a recent case I worked on, in which a man died as a result of a suture that had occluded his internal mammary artery, which was the main blood supply to the heart. Although a mammary is not normally a supply to the heart, in bypass surgery it is often used in this way, as was the case here. The man was eighty-two years old and was undergoing the surgery to replace his heart valve. The final metal suture – to pull the sternum together – was to be located close to the mammary artery. Normally, the surgeon would place a metal plate between the internal mammary artery and the sternum, but in this instance the surgeon did not use a plate, as the patient had scarring from a previous triple-bypass operation. The surgeon took a chance and put the suture right through the mammary artery, killing the patient on the operating table. The post-mortem did not reflect this fact, as the whole sternal plate was removed at the post-mortem and no one looked at it. The surgeon knew what he had done, though.

Examining a body in its entirety to determine how the person died is a major part of forensic pathology: it should be done by a pathologist, not a policeman with little or no training, as is often the case. Frequently, crimes are taken at face value, with very little actual detailed investigation taking place. This simply does not serve justice, as I have witnessed time after time.

When examining the scene of death in cases of suicide by hanging, the noose should not be removed from the body, as this evidence has to be compared to the marks on the structure from which the noose was hung, as well as the marks on the skin. It may be possible that the person was hanged after they died, for example. If you disturb the noose and the evidence, the exact cause of death will be difficult to determine.

Part of the problem with post-mortems is that families who wish to be present at these sessions find it very difficult to do so. Family representation should be encouraged, in my view. People like Jurie Nel, the chief forensic pathologist at Stellenbosch University, would always insist on the family obtaining magisterial approval, despite the fact that he could decide who attended the post-mortem on his own authority. The pathologists have also always tried to keep me out on the basis that I am not medically qualified. Even when I represent families, it is almost impossible for me to observe the post-mortem; in the past I have been allowed to examine the body only when the pathologist was finished with it.

The most important thing for a forensic pathologist to remember is that he is a man of science. If this critical piece of investigation is done badly, it leaves wiggle room, in my opinion – and the state pathologists like to have wiggle room.

The blatant laziness in performing proper post-mortems was illustrated vividly by the death of Isaac Miggels, a young boy who supposedly drowned in 2004. A story appeared in the press about this boy, whose body had been found in the Faure Dam in the Western Cape. Miggels, who was eight years old at the time, had been out with friends when he died, and the pathologist found that he had died as a result of drowning.

Miggels's father, to his credit, was unhappy with the post-mortem report, which resulted in a second post-mortem, in which it was found that Miggels had a fractured skull, as well as a fractured hyoid bone. I was approached by the press for comment, and I had less than complimentary things to say about the pathologist who had conducted the post-mortem. I found it very difficult to believe that the pathologist had missed the fractured hyoid bone during the initial post-mortem, as the first step in a medical examination is to open the body, and the neck, in particular.

The hyoid bone is part of the larynx, in the neck. Where there is strangulation or any manual pressure, this bone normally breaks. A fractured hyoid is almost always an indication of pressure brought to the neck. Thanks to the work done by the late Professor Okkie

Gordon, it is now possible to carry out a bloodless dissection of the neck to examine the hyoid bone. Previously, there would have been blood all over the place, making it extremely difficult to see if the bone was fractured. Clearly, the pathologist had not opened Miggels's neck when she had conducted the first post-mortem.

The second thing the pathologist should have done was to look at the boy's skull to examine the brain and the base of the skull. It is very easy to see if there has been a fracture of the skull: the skull is sawed open and a scalpel is used to cut the attachments that fix the brain to the base of the skull. The brain is then lifted out by hand. The pathologist is left with an empty skull lined with transparent membranes. The brain is inspected, and the membranes are then peeled back – they come away from the skull bone quite easily – leaving the white inside of the bone of the skull. If any fractures have occurred, they would have caused bleeding against the white inside of the skull, which shows up tiny blood lines.

My first experience with post-mortems was when I was seventeen years old, when I assisted the local district surgeon. I would open up the bodies in his presence so that he could perform the post-mortem. I remember the body of a young woman who had been beaten to death by her husband. He had hit her very hard on the jaw, causing multiple fractures to the jawbone. The woman had a ring fracture around the foramen magnum, which is the large opening to the spinal cord. The fracture was clearly visible at the base of the skull. In the case of Isaac Miggels, no such examination was carried out the first time round – that was clear.

Poor and inaccurate post-mortems are of critical importance in legal proceedings. In the case of Miggels, not only had the post-mortem not been properly conducted the first time round, but when the pathologist redid it, she came up with a completely different finding – an utterly ridiculous situation!

After the media asked me for an opinion on the quality of the pathology as I saw it and I had responded – I was very outspoken, and will continue to fight this battle until they do things correctly – my comments were challenged by a man called J.J. Dempers, a junior forensic pathologist at Tygerberg Hospital. He wrote a letter to the *Cape Argus* in 2004, in which he referred to the 567 CapeTalk radio interview I had given on the matter. He defended the post-mortem, commenting that I was caught up in the past and should familiarise myself with current developments in forensic science.

I immediately wrote a letter to the *Cape Argus* in response, saying that anyone who does a post-mortem should follow the basic principles, and that the Steve Biko inquest in our recent history is a glaring example of where rules are made as people go along. I also addressed the issue that family representations at post-mortems are discouraged, with which I do not agree. I ended my letter by pointing out that those who do not know history are condemned to repeat it.

As a result of the second post-mortem report, there was a full investigation into the death of Isaac Miggels, and a murder inquiry. His friends later admitted that they had hit him against the head and in the face, as he had been swearing at them. They had taken his unconscious body and dropped it into the dam, where he died.

The battle that rages between private forensic science and state forensic pathology is counterproductive. The two disciplines should instead work hand in glove to investigate crimes. The pathologist should be at the scene of the crime, for example, and in many overseas countries, this is the case. Not so in South Africa. Crime-scene management is appalling in this country, as was the case with the recent investigation into the murder of Inge Lotz (see Chapter 20). Unlike the state pathologists, private pathologists usually involve me in their work. Indeed, it is possible for a family to decide to have a private pathologist perform the post-mortem, but the state usually makes this very difficult.

Essentially, *all* pathologists need to be trained to conduct the full investigation: post-mortems should ideally be a case of teamwork. The enormous risk run by separating forensic science and pathology is that there is potential to overlook critical clues in solving crimes.

||||||||||||||||||||||||||||||||||||||||||||||||||||||||||||||

CHAPTER 17

THE MYSTERY OF FLIGHT 295, THE *HELDERBERG*

'Power tends to corrupt and absolute power corrupts absolutely. Great men are almost always bad men ... There is no worse heresy than the fact that the office sanctifies the holder of it.'

– JOHN DALBERG-ACTON (LORD ACTON),
English historian

Captain Dawie Uys spent the last few terrifying minutes of his life fighting to keep SAA Flight 295 in the air. It was a hopeless task, and at seven minutes past midnight on 28 November 1987, the doomed aircraft crashed into the Indian Ocean 134 nautical miles north-east of Mauritius's Plaisance Airport. On the Boeing 747-244B Combi's final flight, en route from Taipei to Johannesburg, all 140 passengers and nineteen crew members were killed.

South Africans were devastated by the news. This was undoubtedly one of the great air tragedies in the long history of South African Airways (SAA), and it was also one of the great mysteries of all air disasters, leaving far more questions than answers in its wake. Even now, more than two decades later, the *Helderberg* crash is shrouded in mystery. It has become my personal quest to find the answers and to unravel the lies and deceit that surround this tragic event.

A board of inquiry was established shortly after the crash, initiating a process that would take almost three years to complete. Judge Cecil Margo was appointed to head the inquiry, and the final report was addressed to the Honourable Minister of Transport and of Public Works and Land Affairs, Pretoria, on 14 May 1990. In my view, this report stands out as the vilest piece of dishonesty in the history of the South African judicial system, and it is a sad chapter in the long, dark and lamentable catalogue of human crime.

At the time, Margo was a judge of the Supreme Court of Appeal in the Witwatersrand Local Division. During the Second World War, he had been a pilot, flying medium bombers for the South African Air Force. He continued his practice as an advocate after the war and, after some time as a senior advocate at the Johannesburg bar, he was called to the bench, where he served until his death in 2000. Despite occupying the position for many years, he never rose to higher office.

Margo's wartime flying experience, together with the fact that he had acted for SAA in many of their high-profile cases, made him an obvious choice to chair the inquiry. He had headed up investigations into the crash of the *Rietbok* just outside East London in 1967, and the *Pretoria* accident outside Windhoek in 1968. Margo was also the chairman of the inquiry into the loss of Samora Machel's flight to Mozambique on 19 October 1986 – a Tupolev that crashed near the village of Mbuzini in Mpumalanga, some way short of the Mozambican border, killing all on board. Within a year, Margo was appointed chair of the inquiry into the *Helderberg* disaster.

My involvement with the *Helderberg* started when I was consulted after the tragedy by the legal representatives of the Boeing

Company. It had been alleged that the passengers and crew of the *Helderberg* had died from carbon monoxide poisoning, and Boeing had appointed Advocate Fanie Celliers to safeguard their interests. It was of great importance for Boeing that, whatever else had happened, no finger of blame was pointed at them.

Amidst the wreckage of the aircraft, a few mangled bodies had been washed up on the beach. Tests had been conducted on these bodies to determine the levels of carbon monoxide in the blood. Carbon monoxide is a nasty gas that binds very tightly to the haemoglobin inside the red cells in the blood, preventing the haemoglobin from doing what it should – carry oxygen. The unfortunate victims suffocate to death in the very presence of the life-giving oxygen needed to sustain them.

I was asked to determine whether the test results of the health chemical laboratory were accurate. The problem was that the blood had been mixed with sea water and, once diluted in this way, no definitive test results can be obtained. I gave the theoretical material on the measurement of carbon monoxide to Celliers, who used some of it to cross-examine Dr Hein Schroeder, the state expert who had measured the carbon monoxide levels in the deceased.

It rapidly became clear at the inquiry that there were several camps, each of whom was trying to shift responsibility away from themselves. Boeing didn't want any blame, the Pilots' Association didn't want to be held accountable, and SAA certainly did not want to be seen as being at fault. It was as if no one cared about the cause of the crash as long as their noses were clean. My involvement with the Margo Inquiry ended right there. I never gave evidence and my investigations at that stage were limited to the issues that interested Boeing.

Margo's inquiry concluded that there had been an intense fire that had started in the right-hand forward pallet of the aircraft, causing the demise of the aircraft, and that it was impossible to ascribe blame to any person or body. Margo spent an inordinate amount of time on relatively irrelevant issues, like whether there was one debris field or two, and whether the engines were turning when the plane hit the water. He ignored the real questions: namely, the source of the fire, and who had been responsible for loading the material that had caused the fire onto the aircraft.

I suppose the matter would have rested there had it not been for a man called Norman Chandler, who worked under the editorship of David Allen for the *Weekend Star*, one of Johannesburg's newspapers. The journalist initiated a public debate around the *Helderberg* with a series of luridly written articles, which were published in the newspaper. Chandler popularised the notion that the *Helderberg* was carrying red mercury and that this, somehow, was responsible for the fire on board the aircraft. The articles, which began to appear in early 1995, made sensational reading for months. I have included some of the press cuttings to illustrate the fever pitch of the journalism (see Appendix E). In addition to red mercury, Chandler introduced the idea that there had been two fires on board the aeroplane, and that the captain, Dawie Uys, had been reluctant to take off with the dangerous cargo. It was nail-biting reading, but rather poorly researched journalism.

The response was predictable: the *Weekend Star* was hauled before the Press Council of South Africa to face many and varied complaints about this sensational reporting – and this is where the case became intriguing. It would have made sense if these initial objections were brought by SAA, as they seemed to have the most to lose by the reporting. The complaints, however, were lodged by none other than Armscor!

Armscor spent its time creating weapons whose function was to kill other human beings. In the pursuit of these evil ways, it was prepared to stop at nothing, so to defame Armscor would seemingly not be possible, as it had no good reputation to defame in the first place. Yet Armscor saw fit to protest against the newspaper.

Among other things, Armscor complained that certain articles of Chandler's alleged that some of Armscor's procurement officers were 'international criminals'. Well, had Armscor forgotten about the four people who were arrested in England in the early 1980s and detained pending their trial for trying to buy weapons, thereby contravening the arms sanctions? Had they forgotten that the four were returned for some or other reason, with our government having given an assurance to the British and to Margaret Thatcher that they would all return to stand trial? The detainees never went back, as far as I know. Had Armscor forgotten about the arms procurement officials who were caught attempting to steal plans for a submarine? I am reminded of Eva Perón, who, on one of her many trips abroad, complained to her travelling companion – he had been an admiral – that a voice from the crowd had called her a whore. 'Madam,' he reportedly said, 'it is fifteen years since I stood on the deck of a ship and they still call me admiral.'

Then there was the red mercury issue: Armscor also objected to the newspaper's allegation that the plausibility of red mercury being on board the aircraft had been confirmed by Dr Frank Barnaby, 'a top international nuclear scientist'. Barnaby did confirm the *existence* of a substance called red mercury in a conversation with me when I called him while I was doing my research. He referred me to the scientific journal in which the findings of inorganic chemist A.W. Sleight, who had prepared the substance, were published.

Only a single journal article ever appeared about this substance. This usually indicates that it has a military application and is classified information. Barnaby told me that he felt that red mercury was of interest as a neutron-focusing substance – in other words, it could focus a beam of neutrons like a lens. A nuclear reaction is the result of a number of neutrons striking other uranium atoms. If you can focus them, minimising the diffusion of the neutrons, you can get a more intense result for the same amount of effort – in short, more bang for your buck. This is useful if you are making small bombs with a limited amount of radioactive material in them.

Rumours did the rounds furiously, and debate raged as to the existence of red mercury and the possibility of its being the cause of the air disaster. It was even reported in the *Mail & Guardian* by Robert Kirby that *I* had said red mercury was the cause of the fire aboard the *Helderberg*. This is completely untrue – I never made that statement, and I have always maintained that the red mercury issue had nothing to do with the fire on the *Helderberg*.

Apart from Armscor, SAA also saw fit to lay a complaint with the press council against the *Weekend Star*. They objected to the allegations that certain dangerous goods, destined for the use of Armscor, had been part of the cargo of the *Helderberg* aircraft, and that these dangerous goods had ignited during the flight, causing the air disaster. They complained that SAA was falsely made out to be a co-perpetrator (with Armscor), and protested against the suggestion that SAA had either been a part of or had not prevented an instruction being given by a senior government official to the pilot in command, Captain Dawie Uys, before departure of the aircraft from Taipei. (The newspaper report states that Uys had serious misgivings about dangerous cargo on board the aircraft but was instructed against his will and better judgement to proceed with the flight.) Furthermore, they took exception to the newspaper's claim that the then chief executive of SAA, Gert van der Veer, or some senior government person, had instructed Uys not to land the aircraft at some intermediate airport after the first fire broke out because, had the aeroplane been allowed to land, its cargo would have been seized by the authorities, revealing SAA's clandestine involvement in the transportation of dangerous cargo. The scurrilous nature of this allegation was that SAA's highest-ranking official had callously instructed the pilot in command to risk the lives of all aboard the aircraft. Finally, they took issue with the claim that SAA had, in effect, involved itself in defeating the ends of justice by intentionally erasing the so-called ZUR tape recording. This tape recording supposedly contained the criminal instructions that were reported to have been given to the pilot.

These few points illustrate the gravity of the complaints laid by SAA against the *Weekend Star* newspaper. At the same time, they illustrate the essence of some of the accusations that I make against both Armscor and SAA and its senior staff in the case of the *Helderberg*.

At the time, I was completely unaware of the ructions simmering beneath the surface, apart from the sensational reporting, which I read along with the general public.

I was approached by Peter Reynolds, who was a senior partner at the law firm Webber Wentzel Bowens, which specialised in media law. They were acting on behalf of SAA *and* the *Weekend Star* newspaper. I had assisted Reynolds previously in an unrelated matter. He enlisted my help and, after outlining the problems with the *Helderberg* case, sent me off to find whatever I could that related to the loss of the aircraft. I was assisted in this quest by the editor of the *Weekend Star*, David Allen.

I decided on a direct approach and contacted everybody who had the remotest connection with the *Helderberg*. As I spread my net wider and word spread that I was investigating, some interesting things started to happen. People began to approach me with information. I collected every scrap of paper relating to the case and filed it away. I telephonically interviewed most of the major role players, including Roy Downes of the Directorate of Civil Aviation (DCA), forensic expert Greg Southeard, who had conducted the investigation on behalf of Boeing, and Tony Snelgar, the pilot who had been waiting on the island to take over from Dawie Uys. I also contacted Dr T.C.B. (Theuns) Kruger, the financial planning manager (technical) at SAA; John Hare, senior general manager of SAA; and Flippie Look, who was a retired pilot for SAA.

I had some fun when I phoned Look, who was very entertaining. When I spoke to him, he did the old name, rank and number bit with me (he had obviously seen a few war movies). He would not deny or confirm anything and kept referring me back to the airline officials. It was important to talk to him because he had been the pilot in charge of an aircraft parked at Ben Gurion International Airport in Israel when he had allegedly seen a crate drop from the aircraft loading bay and split open to reveal missiles.

Look was at his most obtuse until I said to him, 'They [the SAA staff] say that you don't know the difference between fuel tanks for a Mirage and military ordnance.' Suggesting that he couldn't tell the difference between drop tanks and missiles caused Look to explode. 'Christ!' he cried, outraged. 'I called my co-pilot and said, "Come look here!"' The old pilot's ego had kicked in and he confirmed my allegation without intending to.

During one of my conversations with Hare, who had previously held a senior position at Armscor, it became obvious why Armscor was pursuing the complaint. Hare indicated to me that SAA was incensed about a newspaper report in which they were accused of cremating their passengers. He also mentioned that the airline was probably going to launch a full-scale civil action against the *Weekend Star* to recover damages after the hearing.

Before I interviewed Kruger, I read all eight volumes of the Margo Commission transcript as part of my investigation. This in itself provided some interesting insights into the matter. Of particular interest was a section of the transcript that took place just after tea. The prosecutor was Brian Southwood, who is now a judge in Pretoria. Southwood stood up and said that Captain van Heerden of the Pilots' Association was in the audience and would like to introduce himself. Instead of Van Heerden, however, a certain Viljoen stood up, saying that he represented the Pilots' Association. The discussion between Margo, as chairman, and Viljoen went like this:

Mr Southwood: Mr Chairman I have been informed that Captain van Heerden of the South African Pilots Association is present. He omitted to announce his presence and would like the opportunity to do so.

Captain Viljoen: Thank you, Mr Chairman, I am Tony Viljoen and I represent the International Federation of Airline Pilots Associations, known as IFAPA.

Chairman: We are about to hear an excerpt from the CVR [cockpit voice recorder] tape; not from the tape itself, but from a transcript. Have you any submissions to make about that tape?

Captain Viljoen: Sir, the reading of the tape into record we do not object to.

Chairman: *The whole of the tape?*

Captain Viljoen: As far as the pertinent conversation between the pilot and the air traffic control – as far as it applies to the full accident investigation, we have no objections at this stage.

Chairman: What are you objecting to?

Captain Viljoen: *Nothing at all, not at this point.*

Chairman: Well then can the whole of the cockpit voice recorder be played in open court, because you are objecting to nothing?

Captain Viljoen: Sir, I would agree to that.

Chairman: Yes, but I don't want to encourage you into an objection which you don't want to make, but we will notice now that you will take the point that confidential portions of the conversation should not be played in public.

Captain Viljoen: I would take that point, yes.

Chairman: Well I don't know what point you're taking now. You've told me that you raise no objections to the whole tape being played and now …

Captain Viljoen: You asked me if confidential portions of the tape should be read into the record.

Chairman: Well I have heard the tape in advance. It will have to be played again to the full Board. There is nothing that is particularly confidential, but it's private conversation up to the point where the fire alarm signal sounds. Perhaps you had better consider your position and let us know a little later what you want us to do.

Captain Viljoen: Certainly Sir.

Chairman: Mr Southwood, meanwhile you're going to lead the witness only on that portion of the tape from the time that the alarm signal sounded.

– Margo Commission of Inquiry report, page 55
  (emphasis added)

This entire conversation is bizarre. Margo indicates that there is nothing particularly confidential in the tape recording, and then keeps the first part of the recording from being heard publicly on the basis that it is confidential! He so clearly wanted Viljoen to object to the transcript being read out. What was it that he wanted kept out of the record?

Viljoen was being dense. Margo was evidently expecting or hoping for a prearranged objection to enable him to rule on the first part of the tape. Somewhere along the way the lines must have got crossed, and Viljoen was not bright enough to pick up the ball and run with it: Margo had to do it for him. On page 109 of the Margo transcript – some time after the above-quoted conversation took place – a representative from IFAPA, Van Heerden, made the objection for which Margo had been fishing. This was the Van Heerden to whom Southwood originally referred.

This whole comedy of errors indicates that there was a conspiracy of sorts between Margo and Van Heerden, and that something on that CVR transcript had to be concealed. The transcript was never read out at the inquiry, and I was determined to find out what it was that they were concealing.

My next port of call was Theuns Kruger, who reluctantly let me see the CVR transcript, but would not let me copy it. He left me alone to read it, so I read it aloud into my tape recorder. This particular transcript was produced by Colonel Leendert Jansen, who had worked in the police forensic laboratory on audio tapes in the days of General Lothar Neethling. After leaving civil service, he had gone into the private audio-analysis business.

What I read was a transcript of the recording of the voices in the cockpit. Cockpit voice recordings tape over themselves every thirty minutes, so they always constitute a record of the last thirty minutes of conversation in the cockpit. In the Margo Inquiry, this was said to be the last tape recording of the cockpit voice recorder for the *Helderberg* – the final words recorded of the pilots before the aircraft crashed. This is of particular significance considering what the recording contained.

I suddenly realised what Margo had wanted to keep out of the open court. In the early part of the recording (ten minutes and fifty-eight seconds into the tape), a woman's voice says, '*Kaptein, jy moet toesig hou op vanaand se vlug*' (Captain, you must keep watch on this evening's flight). This comment is of crucial importance, as the accident was supposed to have happened on the top of descent, just outside Mauritius – in other words, near the end of the flight. This remark would have been irrelevant and nonsensical if it had been made at the flight's end – it was clearly made at the beginning of the flight.

Margo stated that the fire had occurred just outside Mauritius. He also said that there was 'nothing that is particularly confidential' on the voice recording, yet he prompted the witness so blatantly in the hearing to suggest that parts of it *were* confidential. The point is that this recording was, in theory, a record of the last thirty minutes of the flight, yet the woman's comment telling the captain to keep watch paints a different picture, as does the subsequent conversation in the cockpit, which is even more revealing (the numbers next to the dialogue refer to the number of minutes into the recording that the words were spoken):

> **11.36** *Hierdie ou word nou honger… Ek wens ons kry nou* dinner …
> **12.00** Joe's got exactly the same …
> **12.06** This is bloody junk food as well …

A male voice then says that he must stay away from something. We know that Captain Uys had an allergy to certain foodstuffs, so there might have been an item on the menu that would not have agreed with him. The word 'dinner' is also used. This is a very specific word: it's not breakfast; it's not lunch – it is the main evening meal. Clearly food was being served at that stage on the flight. Yet food is usually served shortly after take-off, preceded only by drinks, as there is no sense in allowing the food to dry out in the warmers until many hours later. The cockpit crew is typically served just after the first-class passengers have been served, and generally from the same galley. When the *Helderberg* reached its cruising altitude and the activity in the cockpit was not particularly intense, it would have been the appropriate time for the cabin attendants to serve dinner. This is a far more likely scenario than the cockpit crew all eating dinner at the top of descent: just before preparing to land, the atmosphere in the cockpit would have been busy, if not frenetic.

This is why Margo wanted this first part of the tape kept out of the record. If it had been included, it would have raised awkward questions, including why the conversation about the meal and the comments about keeping watch had not been taped over many times before the alleged first fire outside Mauritius.

The rest of the conversation is nothing out of the ordinary – all sorts of banter one would expect in the course of a normal cockpit conversation – men, while on their own, talking about girls' salaries, seniority and a whole host of other trivial matters.

Only the last part of the recording was included at the Margo Inquiry: twenty-eight minutes and thirty-one seconds into the tape recording, the fire alarm sounds and a voice says, 'There is the fire-alarm bell.' This is followed by about ninety seconds of recording while the captain and crew try to make sense of what is happening, and then there is silence. That is the end of the recording.

Reading the full transcript gives the impression that a whole scene in a Shakespearean tragedy has been taken out of context and slapped into another part of the play. At the time, the debate was rife over what the cockpit voice recording contained, as it was of very poor quality – almost as if it had been tampered with and perhaps overlaid with white or pink noise. Boeing would not have put such inferior equipment on their aircraft. It doesn't really matter, though, because Margo had at least had a transcript of the conversation made. It was clear that Margo believed it contained important enough information for it to remain confidential: he made sure that it stayed out of the inquiry.

It is a fact that this was the last thirty minutes of conversation recorded in the cockpit of the *Helderberg*. It also appears that this conversation took place shortly after take-off. So why is it that this is the last recorded conversation? The reason is that the cockpit voice recorder stopped working some time immediately after this conversation – long before the aircraft reached Mauritius and the scene of the supposed first fire.

From the reference to the fire alarm on the cockpit voice recording, and the fact that the CVR suddenly ceased functioning, it was clear that there had been a fire on board the aircraft. Indeed, pieces of the wreckage confirmed burn marks on the crown of the aircraft (a fire burns upwards, so the greatest damage would be to the crown). The voice recorder had ceased to work either because the fire had burnt through the power and input cables that passed along the aircraft's crown, or because the pilots had pulled the circuit breaker so that they could retain the last parts of their conversation, ensuring that it didn't get taped over. We will never know which it was.

If a fire had burnt through these power cables, it must have started in the early part of the flight – round about the time when the crew were discussing dinner – and not at the end of the flight, as Margo wanted us to believe.

Conflicting statements and cover-ups

'Nothing vast enters the life of mortals without a curse.'
— SOPHOCLES

It was clear that Margo wanted the public to believe that there had been only *one* fire on the *Helderberg*, and that it had occurred just outside Mauritius, shortly before the aircraft crashed. Yet, if the transcripts of the cockpit voice recording are to be believed, the fire took place just a few hours after take-off. Why did Uys then not land the aircraft as soon as possible?

His behaviour directly contradicted all the principles of pilot training. If there had been a fire on board the *Helderberg*, the first step would have been to extinguish it and land the aircraft immediately. A pilot in this situation would not know if damage to the skin of the aircraft had occurred, whether the structure and integrity of the aircraft were still intact, whether he would run into a storm or turbulence, or whether there was the potential for another fire – too many unknown factors simply to continue flying. Despite all this, however, Uys flew on. Why did he not do the simple thing and land the aircraft, which would have saved his life and the lives of the remaining passengers and crew, especially since there were several places where this stricken aircraft could have landed?

At the time of the Margo investigation, the flight engineers wrote a dissenting view about the fire and submitted it to Margo. Ray Scott, a flight engineer, told me at a meeting in Midrand on 11 April 1995 that Margo had called the engineers to his private residence on a Sunday and said to them, 'Listen, you don't know what you are doing. This thing has security overtones. If you carry on with this, you will cost the country R400 million. [The insurers wouldn't pay out.] The safety of your future and your families is at risk.'

Over and above calling the flight engineers to his house on a Sunday, Margo had discussed the matter with other engineers in his chambers, without other interested parties and legal representation present. This was grossly improper. Yvonne Bellagarda, wife of the late Joe Bellagarda, the flight engineer who had been on board the *Helderberg*, gave me an affidavit on 27 May 1998, in which she stated that Jimmy Mitton, a close friend of hers, was called in to see Margo during the inquiry.

> During the inquest Jimmy Mitton and I would go to court together to hear the proceedings. I was with Jimmy Mitton on the day that Judge Margo summoned him to his chambers. I was not present in the chambers, but when Jimmy Mitton came back to me, he was visibly upset. He told me that at the time Margo had insisted that he drop his line of inquiry. Furthermore, that Margo said to him that the country could not afford to have him pursue this line of inquiry. It would cost too much and his job and career and safety were on the line.

This, combined with the fact that Margo spent considerable time sending the inquiry in different directions and reached a nonsensical conclusion, points to a cover-up.

So why did Uys fail to land the aircraft after the first fire? The answer is straightforward and obvious: if Uys had landed the *Helderberg*, he would have had to land in an anti-apartheid country.

South Africa was a very different country in 1987 from what it is today. We were deep into the reign of P.W. Botha and the dishonest, paranoid gang called the nationalist government. Our international friends were also numbered among the polecats of the world, and we certainly did not have many political allies in the Indian Ocean area over which the *Helderberg* was flying. Landing the aeroplane would have invited inspection of the hold, and the dangerous cargo would have been discovered. The revelation that the apartheid government was carrying dangerous, even deadly, cargo aboard one of its passenger aircraft would have been the kiss of death for SAA. This, and *this alone*, was a powerful stimulus for Uys to keep flying.

But there is also a more sinister reason: a fire that involves the burning of plastic material produces copious quantities of very toxic substances, such as cyanides and carbon monoxide, which come from the phosphate-containing fire retardants in the plastic. Even more toxic substances than these are also produced – the toxicology of some of these gases is still poorly understood. If there had been a first fire shortly after reaching the cruising altitude, there would certainly have been severe casualties, and even deaths, on board the *Helderberg*.

On 22 August 1985, a fire on board an aircraft on the Manchester airport runway caused numerous severe casualties and some deaths. This aircraft was on the ground, and evacuated within three minutes. The so-called oxygen masks that drop from compartments above the passengers in such emergencies do not actually provide pure oxygen: they emit a source of cabin gas to which oxygen has been added to make the air breathable. If there are any toxic substances in the cabin gas, these will be supplied to passengers together with the oxygen. Death will result not from lack of oxygen, necessarily, but from the toxicity of the smoke and combustion products in the cabin gas.

The injury and probable deaths of an unknown number of

passengers on the *Helderberg* would have caused an international outcry. At the very least, Captain Uys would have been arrested wherever he landed and tried for either murder or culpable homicide. The government and the airline could never have withstood such a happening, and Uys would probably have been disowned by SAA.

After the first fire, which Uys thought he had successfully extinguished, he would have done what all pilots would do in that situation – use his radio to contact home base. The radio system was quite different in those days. Because of our appalling international relations at the time, particularly over Africa, the aircraft of SAA were obliged to fly some unconventional routes. For instance, we did not fly over Africa to Europe, the most direct route; we flew around the bulge instead and landed at out-of-the-way Portuguese islands, such as Isla de Sol, to refuel. Normal flying routes had radio beacons, which an aircraft could tap into to navigate, but we did not have access to these. So to keep in contact with its far-flung fleet, the management of SAA created and maintained a high-frequency shortwave radio station in Johannesburg, at what was then Jan Smuts Airport. This radio station was known as ZUR, and was manned twenty-four hours a day by different shifts of operators. It was, in essence, radio telephony.

There were set schedules for the aircraft to call in. If an aircraft was, for whatever reason, late in calling, there was a method of alerting the crew to the need to report home. This method was called Selcall – selective calling – incidentally, also the name of the pilots' in-house magazine.

The calls were monitored on a continuous basis, and each transmission was recorded on a large reel-to-reel recorder, which had capacity for just over twenty-four hours of conversation. Depending on the air traffic, the reel would be replaced every twenty-four hours or so. As a recorded reel came to its end, it would be lifted out and replaced with a fresh reel, and the recording would be placed at the back of a row of about thirty-five reels in a closed cabinet. It would then slowly work its way along the row until about thirty-five days later, when it would appear at the front of the row again, ready to be reused.

When the *Helderberg* crashed into the sea off Mauritius, this tape would have been a vital piece of information in either eliminating or confirming certain possibilities. Naturally, the men from the DCA would want to hear this tape.

One would have thought that time would be of the essence, but the tapes, strangely, were only collected by the DCA an extended period after the crash. And when they were collected, there were just two tapes available: the recording of the take-off, and the recording of the events of the following day – the search-and-rescue operation. The tape recording of the crucial in-between time, when Uys would have been battling the fire and calling home for help, was missing. Inexplicably, no one knew the whereabouts of that tape.

How does Margo deal with the tape in his report? He says, 'There was no further contact between ZUR and the aircraft' (page 12). Later, he states, 'The ZUR tape recording ran until about 16.34. As the follow-on tape was apparently later mislaid or inadvertently reused *there was no further communication between SA 295 and ZUR on record*' (page 30, emphasis added).

This is very strange. How did the tape get lost? And why was no one questioned or reprimanded for the missing tape? If it was over-taped in error, why was *that* tape not given to Margo? I believe that Margo knew all along where the tape had gone and that it was damning.

Margo concluded that 'The circumstances were investigated in full by the board, which is satisfied that there was no connection between the failure to comply with the instructions and the accident to the *Helderberg*' (page 137). Margo goes on to elaborate on the point that there was no connection between the ZUR tapes and the demise of the *Helderberg*. I totally disagree with Margo on this issue. Margo was being less than honest when he put these remarks in his report, and I will explain why.

Firstly, whatever was on the tape would have been of benefit to the commission. If it had simply been a conversation about taking the cat to the vet, it would have assisted the commission in knowing that there was no foul play during that period. It would have instantly silenced a host of critics – myself included – who maintain that there was dirty dealing at the crossroads.

Secondly, Margo's suggestion that he and the board had investigated the disappearance of the tape does not survive even the most elementary scrutiny. If the tape had been lost, someone would have come to Margo or the investigators and said, 'We have lost the tape.' We know that that didn't happen. The next alternative is that the tape was inadvertently over-taped. This also did not happen: these are huge tapes, each with their own index card and identifying marking. Had the relevant tape been over-taped, someone would have led evidence to that effect and said to Margo or anyone else, 'Look, here is the tape. I messed up and accidentally taped over it.' This never happened. Margo's claim that he and the board had examined the disappearance of the tape thoroughly also does not bear scrutiny on his own records, on the transcript of the court proceedings. So what really happened to that tape?

I was determined to get answers. After asking around, someone suggested that I contact a certain Captain Jimmy Deal, whom I called late one evening in Durban. He had a bad cold and was feeling poorly, but I said to him directly, 'I was told that you took the missing ZUR tape out that evening. What did you do with it?' He admitted that he had given it to Mickey Mitchell, who was the chief pilot for SAA at the time. Then Deal realised what he had said, and tried to backtrack. When I cross-examined him later, he was unsure about whom he had given the tape to, and ended off by saying that the tape never went missing. It was clear that this was a tape recording that SAA wanted hushed up.

I needed to know a little more about what I thought was the first fire. One of the people to whom I spoke was Athol Hardy, who worked for a company that sold fire equipment. The Monday morning after the *Helderberg* accident, which took place early on Saturday morning, he was at Jan Smuts Airport and overheard a conversation, which he repeated to me in a signed statement on 24 February 2001:

> I am at present station officer at Benoni Fire and Emergency Services. I have been a fire officer for about the past 12 years. In 1987 I was working for a company called Harwil engineering (a company belonging to my father) which manufactured aircraft tenders among other fire-fighting equipment. On the Monday after the accident I was at the airport fire station. I had some servicing work to perform. This was at approximately 8.00 a.m. in the morning.
>
> Normally when I get there I would speak to the other officers and chat about this and that. That Monday the only topic of conversation was the *Helderberg*. The conversation between the officers was to the effect that the plane had had a fire plus minus three hours after take-off and that the plane wanted to divert to Singapore. They had used up all the fire extinguishers on board. The captain thought that the fire was out and hence the reason for the diversion.
>
> There had been some talk that if there had been a fire on board that the passengers would have been dead and that essentially they were flying a coffin and the only survivors were the senior steward and the cockpit crew. I got the impression that the senior steward had done the bulk of the fire-fighting.
>
> There were two consequences: 1. the officer said he would put it [the plane] in the drink; 2. there was a second fire and they could not control it.

The people in the office at the room were myself, Tony Cavallier, Vossie Vorster, Blackie Swart (Training Officer) and a man with a large black beard.

They had obtained the evidence from the SAA staff. It appeared that two senior officers were in on a meeting with SAA personnel where the whole issue had been discussed.

Clearly there was radio communication between SAA and the plane (not the tower) earlier in the evening. The officers had been notified earlier in the evening.

According to the officer's discussion the pilot had been refused permission to land the aircraft.

A similar version of events was relayed to me by Lucas Meyer. One of the radio operators, Gavin Dick, had been on duty in the ZUR room the evening of the accident. The next morning he went to visit his father, who worked in the avionics department. In the presence of at least one other person, Dick said that he had been in contact with the aircraft that evening, and that they had asked to land because of a fire but had been refused permission. When I questioned Dick on the issue, he denied having had the conversation – but he had been overheard by Meyer (see Appendix F).

I have a signed, sworn statement dated 16 March 2007 by a third independent person, Christiaan Pieter Hattingh, who had heard about the fire early on the Monday morning.

At the time of the *Helderberg* accident I was Flight Simulator Instructor on the B747 for South African Airways. We were scheduled for a training session that Saturday morning. I cannot remember the exact time of our programme but on a Saturday it was most likely to have started at 0800 in the briefing room and 0900 to 1300 in the simulator. It was only after my arrival that I heard that SA295 had crashed near Mauritius. The information was basically little, and one of the crew members decided to go to ZUR to find out more. He came back with the story that SA295 had reported a fire earlier on but had decided to continue.

That Saturday morning the only information that could have been available was from ZUR and they must have been in contact with the aircraft earlier. Yet, during the investigation and hearing it turned out that they were not in contact with SA295. That cannot be the truth.

I believe I am just one of the few people that knew of the fire earlier in the flight. Like the flight engineers who tried to submit their report.

Jimmy Mitton was a Flight Engineer Instructor on the flight simulator and we often worked together and talked about the *Helderberg* accident.

Three entirely independent sources confirm the theory that there had been a fire on board the doomed aircraft shortly after take-off.

Various people have criticised my view that Uys chose not to land, saying that he was in ultimate control of the flight. There is one fact we cannot ignore: Uys surely knew that he had loaded dangerous cargo. After the first fire, he probably had bodies on board, as some of the passengers would have died from the toxic gases. He realised that if he landed with a cargo of dead bodies and traces of a dangerous substance, he would be dead in the water, as he had risked the lives of innocent people.

During my investigation, I came across an attorney of the Supreme Court by the name of Andrew Kenneth Miller. He was consulted by two clients, Sally Baker and Gina Hart, who wanted to provide certain information regarding the *Helderberg* accident. Miller gave a sworn statement on 20 April 1995, in which he repeated what they had told him. At the time, his clients did not want their names mentioned. In the first statement, which is quite damning, his client states that she was at an aviation conference, where she met Renée van Zyl, who was then the head of the Directorate of Civil Aviation.

> [Van Zyl] stated that, to his knowledge, approximately 2–3 hours after take-off from Taipei a fire occurred in the front right hand pallet of the *Helderberg*. The crew, using fire extinguishers and other available equipment, managed to put out the fire. This fire had apparently melted cabling encased in metal situated along the inside of the body of the aircraft. One of the things that was mentioned was that there was a collapse in communication between the cockpit, cabin crew and fire fighting crew, presumably due to the destruction of the cables. I vaguely recall it being said that the decision was made to bring the plane close to home as opposed to landing it elsewhere … It was said that a second fire broke out during the aircraft's descent into Mauritius and this time the equipment on board had all been utilised and was therefore rendered useless … I also remember hearing that the captain of the plane was not happy about carrying certain items listed (under other names) on the cargo manifest and, at some stage before the plane went down, he stated that he 'had told them this would happen'. I cannot remember clearly from whom I heard this but am totally sure that I heard it on or around the time of the conference. It was also stated to myself and a colleague that the fire was caused by rocket fuel at the front of the holding compartment of the plane.

In the second statement, Miller's client says that she met Captain Eddie Bourhill, chairman of the 'Committee for the Safe Carriage of Dangerous Goods' – the South African Air Safety Council (SAASCO) – in April 1990, during discussions regarding an aviation conference.

Captain Bourhill expressed concern and indignation at reports that the cause of the *Helderberg* fire and subsequent explosion was due to fireworks being carried in the hold … [H]e said that the captain of the *Helderberg*, having noticed certain strange items on the manifest in Taipei, investigated the nature of these items and discovered that they contained rocket fuel but had been listed under code names. Knowing the aircraft was a combi, he registered a complaint and refused to take off with this cargo. Apparently SAA moved very quickly and obtained instructions from as high as President PW Botha and General Magnus Malan. These instructions threatened the captain with instant dismissal without pension if he did not fly the plane. Since this was to have been his last or second to last flight before retirement, he obviously felt he had no choice but to comply. I was also told that the reason for the tapes from the aircraft to Plaisance Airport as the plane was coming down were not available for inspection was because the captain could quite clearly be heard to say 'I told them this would happen'.

These statements point in one direction – the total opposite to the official version of events: that there were two fires on board SAA Flight 295.

The Flying Coffin

I saw a city filled with lust and shame,
Where men, like wolves, slunk through the grim half-light;
And sudden, in the midst of it, there came
One who spoke boldly for the cause of Right.

– JOHN MCCRAE, CANADIAN POET

What substance could the *Helderberg* have been carrying that would have resulted in such a tragedy? Rocket fuel was mentioned a number of times. My theory is that the substance that had caused the *Helderberg* crash was ammonium perchlorate – or possibly one of the other perchlorates – the main component of rocket fuel. A number of clues lead to this conclusion.

At the time, South Africa was fighting a bloody war in Angola. Our air force used ageing Mirages, which were struggling against the Russian MiG 23s being flown by the Angolans. We needed faster rockets to be effective. One of the problems was with the fuel we used: it didn't make our rockets fly fast enough. So we needed a new fuel.

Because South Africa was in the throes of sanctions and arms embargoes, Armscor had perfected the art of replicating weapons and ammunition. One has only to look at the R1 rifle to see that it is a replica of the Belgian FN, just as the Z88 pistol is a replica of the Beretta – so much so that the weapons' parts can be interchanged with ease. It was all-out war in South Africa, so no rules applied.

Ammonium perchlorate is an extremely dangerous chemical. It contains chlorine combined with oxygen and, because it has its own oxygen, it does not need an external source of oxygen to ignite and burn, as most other chemicals do. It can therefore ignite on its own, and it is able to burn under water. Ammonium perchlorate can be used to make rocket fuel or explosives, acting as a base material for these compounds. It also contains many other components that enhance its performance. Replicating this cocktail would take time; Armscor needed a sample to analyse and test before attempting to manufacture it themselves.

The state of the wreckage provided vital clues as to the cause of the fire on the *Helderberg*. It is important to understand that the aeroplane was a Combi: the front half of the middle deck was where the passengers were seated; the back half was where the cargo was stored. The pilots and Business Class passengers were seated above the Economy Class passengers. The fire took place in the front, right-hand pallet of the aircraft, and was so hot that it burnt the outside of the aircraft. A piece of wreckage retrieved from the area of that pallet showed this clearly. At that high altitude, the *Helderberg* would have been flying at temperatures of around −40 °C. It is possible to calculate the rate of heat transfer from the inside of the aircraft to the outside by looking at the damage to the aeroplane's skin and taking into account the airflow, the outside temperature and the speed of the aircraft.

This could not have been a diffusion-flame fire. In an ordinary diffusion-flame fire, such as that of a candle, there is a blue region inside the flame and an orangey incandescent glow in its outer area. The chemical reaction takes place where these two regions meet. Oxygen needed to sustain the flame comes from outside and meets the fuel being vaporised at that boundary. The flame temperature is limited by the rate at which oxygen can diffuse from the outside to the reaction zone. The temperature of the average diffusion fire is limited to burning at just under 1 000 °C, and will very seldom go beyond that. For instance, you rarely find copper melted in a fire, as it needs heat of over 1 000 °C to melt. If copper *has* melted in a fire, it is a clear indication that something more is at play.

In the case of the *Helderberg*, the damage to the skin of the aircraft showed that the temperature of the fire had been well in excess of a diffusion-flame fire. There had to have been something like ammonium perchlorate burning inside, as there was obviously an additional source of oxygen, and, as mentioned, ammonium perchlorate has its own built-in oxygen.

An interesting question is why the substance would have ignited. A chemical compound like ammonium perchlorate will ignite spontaneously if it is agitated enough. The *Helderberg* was late in departing from Taipei, and I believe it encountered a subtropical storm. The turbulence would have been enough to cause the spontaneous combustion of a substance like ammonium perchlorate.

If Uys knew about the cargo he was carrying (and this may not have been the first time he had carried such cargo), one would think his wife would have had some comments to make on this.

A puzzling event took place in this regard. Out of the blue, a reporter from Durban, Paul Kirk, contacted me, saying that he had an affidavit from Johanna Uys, the wife of the pilot, which had been sent to him. Kirk was calling from a public telephone and seemed nervous, saying that he had been sent an affidavit by the security police. He read the affidavit to me over the phone, and then later sent it to me. I immediately doubted the validity of this document – it was suspicious, as it was written in English, and it was also intensely contentious.

Johanna Uys stated that Dawie had called her previously just before leaving Taipei and had told her that he was being forced to carry an extremely dangerous substance containing ammonia. He had been told that if he did not fly the aircraft, he would lose his pension money. Once Johanna was aware of the crash, she threatened to talk about the phone call and was told she would lose her pension if she mentioned it. She decided to keep quiet. She was also apparently told by the security police that she would be 'taken care of for life' if she kept quiet.

I saw this 'statement' as being part of a strategy or game to put me, and others, off the scent. Some people will go to any lengths to discredit you in an investigation. You will be given some accurate information, and some that is pure rubbish. If you swallow it all hook, line and sinker, they can later nail you on the inaccuracies of your findings. I recognised this affidavit as such. Johanna Uys would never have written an affidavit in English and, on top of this, the contents were doubtful.

Johanna Uys *did* actually make a statement to a more trustworthy source, in Afrikaans, her home language. She spoke to Torie Pretorius, chief prosecutor for the National Prosecuting Authority (NPA). She had felt that there were issues being debated on which she had to comment. Pretorius made notes of the discussion, which he shared with me, and which appear in translation below:

I am the widow of Captain Dawie Uys who was the pilot of the fated *Helderberg* aircraft that crashed into the Indian Ocean on 28 November 1987.

This is the first statement that I am making with regards to the death of my husband, the passengers and crew of the *Helderberg*. I have not made a statement to any officially regarding the *Helderberg* prior to this.

I have also not made any statements to the media. My attorney, Mr Willem Bester, has taken care of all my affairs.

I was questioned on 8 August 1997 by Dr Pretorius and Superintendent Venter regarding my husband's habits and his career.

I was an air hostess in the employ of SAA from …. to …. [*sic.*] I flew on numerous domestic and international flights with my deceased husband.

He took his work seriously. He was a careful and experienced pilot. I recall him being unhappy a few years prior to the accident about the cargo he was carrying together with passengers on a flight from London. I am not sure about his exact words, but I recall him saying that he was not happy transporting ammunition on the same flight as passengers. He also said that he was so unhappy about this that he posted a copy of the cargo manifest to his own address in South Africa.

He apparently received an instruction from the station commander to fly the aircraft, despite his misgivings. He received the copy of the manifest later at his home address. He sat for a long time one evening in his study with the manifest.

It should be possible to trace this incident, as a written copy of the report of such an incident should be filed at the Ops Room. Captain Dok Malan headed up the Ops Room at that stage. Another person who can be contacted regarding this is Mr Jan Lategan who currently lives in Smithfield. This was not the only time that he was unhappy about the cargo. The Ops Room is a small building just beneath the Holiday Inn hotel. It is a kind of control room where airplane information is dispatched from. It is not part of the main building.

Jan Lategan went to see someone who has allegedly been set up on a farm in the Cape. This person apparently had something to do with the disappearance of tapes.

After the Margo Enquiry [sic], a certain Piet Taljaard, presumably the chairman of the pilots association, tried to make contact with me. I avoided him because I was not happy with SAA.

I have also tried to trace my deceased husband's logbook which contains detail on all his flights, but I have not had any success.

There was also a senior pilot, a Jimmy Hippert, who was involved in the investigation on behalf of the airline. Just before he was due to testify, he was transferred or sent away to Air Singapore.

I am aware of the contents of this statement and understand the contents.

I have no objection to taking the prescribed oath.

I regard the oath as binding on my conscience.

This made more sense. Clearly Dawie Uys had flown these dangerous missions before, and had voiced his misgivings.

After having her statement typed up, Torrie Pretorius returned it to Johanna Uys, but she refused to sign it, saying that it was not an accurate reflection of what she had said. This is very strange behaviour, to put it mildly. Torie Pretorius swore blind that he had simply recorded what she had told him. She then demanded financial guarantees before she would sign the statement. I have evidence of this: on 27 March 1991, I tape-recorded and made notes from the investigator Mark Whale. The advocate in charge of the special investigation, John Welch, was in contact with Whale and Johanna Uys's lawyers when she stated that she wanted financial guarantees.

What did Johanna Uys mean by 'financial guarantees'? The only financial link that she had to SAA was her husband's pension fund, to which she would have been entitled, as he had died. However, if she was to be paid some kind of money in exchange for her silence, this would have been illegal – *contra bonos mores* – a contract based on immoral considerations.

It defies logic that Johanna Uys would deny making the statement to Torie Pretorius. He was a senior legal professional and had no interest in fabricating a false affidavit. He had his notes from the interview and a witness to confirm what Uys had said.

Johanna Uys has remained silent on this matter all these years, and it is time that she broke her silence. I have also asked the state (in particular John Welch, the advocate who investigated the matter on behalf of Dullah Omar, the then Minister of Justice) why they simply didn't serve a Section 205 of the Criminal Procedure Act subpoena on Johanna Uys. This would have allowed the state to force her to make a statement in front of a magistrate. The reasons for not doing so are unconvincing.

We know that the fire on the aircraft was hot enough to burn the skin, so there was something on board that had its own oxygen, was unstable and would ignite easily if turbulence occurred. A number of comments were made indicating that there had been more than one fire on board the *Helderberg*, yet these were hushed up or denied.

Things were kept quiet because the government could not afford to have that aeroplane land. Contraband cargo was, and still is, frowned upon. I am aware of a cargo manager at the time who was told to report to SAA head office. He found the room full of top military officials, who wanted to know which routes back from the East and Europe had extra capacity in the hold – they were using these routes to bring various things into the country, breaking the embargoes and sanctions against South Africa at the time. Transporting innocuous substances can be forgiven, but certain dangerous materials should never be carried by air, particularly not when passengers and cargo are on the same deck. If the cargo hold is below the passengers, it can be flooded with carbon dioxide to kill the fire. But if this cargo was indeed ammonium pechlorate, it would have made little difference, as ammonium pechlorate does not require oxygen to burn. What happened with the *Helderberg* was grossly irresponsible and detrimental to innocent civilian lives.

At the time, families of the deceased passengers were paid out pittances of around $75 000, as specified by the Warsaw Convention. No challenges were posed to SAA, and most families could not afford to litigate. Transparency was certainly not an issue in the P.W. Botha era in South Africa: the 'official' version of the story was publicised, and everyone had to accept it. It was a frightening time.

The Margo Commission of Inquiry's finding was the definitive word on the *Helderberg* air disaster: a single fire just outside Mauritius was the reason the aircraft had crashed, and the cause of the fire was 'unknown'. I believe that the inquiry was a complete sham – Margo prompted responses from witnesses, threatened others and made absolutely sure that events would progress in a direction that suited SAA.

There are too many 'ifs' and 'what ifs' when it comes to the *Helderberg* – too many unanswered questions. After nearly twenty-three years, I am still dissatisfied with the official explanation given at the Margo Commission of Inquiry. For me, the case has never been closed. Although I have tried over the years to have it officially reopened by government officials, they have not been interested.

Later, there was a special investigation at the TRC into the *Helderberg* crash. It was concluded that more investigation would be necessary before this matter could be laid to rest. I participated in this investigation, and the TRC summary of the Special Investigation into the *Helderberg* crash is attached as Appendix G.

In an interesting twist, in 2004, *Sawubona*, the SAA in-flight magazine, mentioned the *Helderberg* in an article on SAA's seventy years of flying. The article appeared on a website, but never saw the light of day in print, as that issue was destroyed and reprinted without the article, at a cost of more than R800 000. The airline plainly did not want its passengers to read about the *Helderberg*. Yet it is a story that will never go away.

The affidavits and other material I have collected over the years point to one feasible scenario only: that the *Helderberg* was carrying rocket fuel destined to assist a flagging South African Air Force in their Angola campaign. This rocket fuel caught fire, and everything that happened subsequently was a sustained government conspiracy to conceal the truth from the public and the rest of the world.

The journalist Robert Kirby had a field day with me in his column 'Loose Cannon' in the *Mail & Guardian*, lambasting me for suggesting that Uys would have allowed his authority to be overruled by government or SAA officials. Kirby never understood the consequences of landing the aircraft en route with severe casualties and possible deaths on board. Landing would have opened the whole can of worms, with dire consequences for the pilot and South Africa. Uys was a military man, and these consequences were too much for him. So he flew on into the abyss.

||||||||||||||||||||||||||||||||||||||||||||||||||||||||||||||||

CHAPTER 18

THE NAKED TRUTH

'[T]ruth and falsity are uniquely and unequivocally determined by the confrontation of statement with fact.'

– THOMAS KUHN,
American philosopher

Forensic science exposes the frailties of humankind, leaving behind only the naked truth about people. When someone ends up dead or in a situation beyond their control, the veneer of civilisation drops away, social airs and graces evaporate and the reality of life is what is left for the forensic scientist to investigate.

Life is difficult, and people respond to stress in different ways. Some turn to various forms of sexual gratification; others feel cornered and burn down their houses; still others kill themselves or their family members. It makes my line of work fascinating and, while I am sympathetic towards these people and their problems, there but for the grace of God go I, as the expression goes.

In death, there are few secrets. This becomes apparent when one looks at accidental deaths, which occur from time to time. Whether someone has died as a result of suicide or accidental death is often an issue of dispute. I have been involved in an advisory capacity in a few cases of sexual asphyxia, where the victim has gone too far and accidentally hanged him- or herself during sexual play. It is important to understand that, in these cases, if a life assurance policy has a suicide clause, the claims should be paid out, as they are not suicides, but rather accidental deaths.

Sexual asphyxiation is a road not frequently travelled. Some people believe, however, that by partially obstructing the blood flow to the brain during orgasm, they can achieve a heightened orgasm. The majority of the blood flow to the brain is through the carotid arteries, which run up through the neck just behind the jawbone. If someone suspends himself by the neck, the compression of the tissues in the neck cuts off the blood supply to the brain, so that the only blood pumping through is via the vertebral arteries at the back of the neck. This is not sufficient to feed the brain, which then dies: the person becomes unconscious.

So, the trick is to cut off the blood supply just enough – without blocking the blood supply to the brain completely – and, at the right time, to achieve the heightened orgasm. That's the theory, anyway. But every now and then someone misses the cue and ends up unconscious, suspended, and death rapidly supervenes.

These victims are most often men, although women are not excluded. Frequently the men in such cases are cross-dressers or are found with indicators of sexual activity close at hand, such as pornographic material or dildos. They are also usually on their own.

The range of humankind's sexual behaviour and tastes is exceptionally wide. The *American Journal of Forensic Medicine and Pathology* used to be affectionately known as the *Journal of Kinky Sex*, as it contained articles on all sorts of medical complications from interesting and varied sexual practices. One story centred on a woman who had a deer's tongue firmly lodged in her vagina. Another case involved a man who had lost the end of his penis because he was giving himself a blow job with a vacuum cleaner. Strange things are seen in hospital casualty wards – some may need to be seen to be believed!

I recall a case in South Africa years ago involving a man who came into the casualty ward at Johannesburg General Hospital, where I was working while studying trauma proteins in the blood. He was having difficulty walking, and, after an examination, was discovered to have an object stuck in his rectum. The rectal muscles had contracted and gone into spasm, and the object could not be removed. The man was booked into theatre, and the doctors removed a Melrose cheese-spread jar from his rectum. I still remember it was cheese-and-onion flavour!

The next day, of course, everyone wanted to know from him how it had got there. His explanation was that he had been walking across the kitchen floor and had slipped, falling onto the jar. The matter was left at that!

Suicide is always a challenging investigation, as it exposes how people cope with adversity in life. I have acted on behalf of insurance companies in some cases, and also very often on behalf of the family of the deceased. Frequently, the families have put me under immense pressure to come to a finding that is *not* suicide. I was involved in a case a while ago where a young man had financial problems and shot himself in the head. His father would not accept it and desperately wanted me to say that something else had caused his son's death. Failing to accept the facts, however, can lead to anger, bitterness and frustration.

Families battle with the concept that a loved one was so troubled and unhappy that suicide was their only perceived way out. However, from the forensic point of view, there is often no other reasonable explanation: the person was alone and there was a contact shot to the head or inside the mouth, with the weapon found close by.

Contrary to popular belief, most suicide victims do not leave a note. As the forensic investigator, you have to infer what took place from events that transpired before their death, such as changes in behaviour (see Chapter 23, in which I discuss this point in relation to the highly publicised death of a well-known South African businessman).

There are no firm patterns as far as the method of suicide goes, but women tend to use less violent methods, such as drug overdoses, while men are inclined to choose firearms. Suicide by hanging is also quite common. In the case of a man I knew quite well, whom I had seen at a social gathering just a few days before his death, there seemed to be nothing untoward in his behaviour. His son later called me in to investigate his death: he had hanged himself from a beam in his garage. He had been under severe financial strain, and had seen suicide as the only solution to his problems. People reach a point of emotional flatlining and become so desperate that death seems to them to be the only option.

One suicide case stood out for me because of the immense tragedy of it all. It was the death of Jamie Verhoef, son of Gordon Verhoef, who was then the owner and director of Gordon Verhoef & Krause, one of the largest firms of refurbishers and painters in the country. Jamie's father was a very wealthy man, but, sadly, Jamie had a rather mixed outcome in life. The son of divorced parents, he had a chequered career, dropping out of school at the end of Standard 8 before going to the army, where issues arose concerning him and drugs. After his army stint, Jamie was at a loose end; he had no qualifications or skills – all he had was a fabulously wealthy father.

Jamie tried a number of different careers. First, he wanted to be a boat builder, so his father sent him to New Zealand to one of the top boat builders in the world to learn the trade. A few months later, he came home. He then decided that he wanted a career in property management, something that usually requires tertiary education and years of experience. His father sent him to New York to a top firm of property managers to learn the art of managing high-rise buildings. Soon Jamie was home again, unqualified and jobless.

He then decided to be a game ranger and conservationist, which also would require a degree in zoology or something similar. Gordon Verhoef bought a magnificent game farm. Lavish guesthouses were built on the premises with gold-plated taps, broekielace and a chef: no expense was spared. The farm was stocked with the best animals, and guests would stay over and hunt on the farm or view the animals. Jamie managed the operation, and was given a Remington .243-calibre rifle as part of his equipment.

The game farm was located about ten minutes outside of Beaufort West. On entering the gate, it took well over forty minutes to get to the farmstead. The road was atrocious – a 4×4 was needed to navigate it – and there were steep drops along the side of the road: if your wheel went over the edge, you faced a thousand-foot drop. The farm was a very beautiful place, yet it was also desolate and lonely.

Jamie would go into town every now and then. During some of those visits, he struck up a friendship with an attorney, who was part of the elite in Beaufort West. Jamie also met and fell in love with a local girl. There had been rumours that Jamie had also been visiting a girl in the coloured township, and the new object of his desire seemed hesitant to become too involved with him, perhaps because of this fact. This love triangle came to an unpleasant end at a party on the evening of 18 January 1992.

The attorney and his wife played host to the who's who of Beaufort West that evening. Food and drink were laid on, and the event was a highlight of the social calendar. Jamie and his cousin were invited. All went well until the girl Jamie liked had a huge disagreement with him in front of all the guests: she publicly stated that she was no longer interested in seeing him. To add insult to injury, she snuggled up to one of her erstwhile boyfriends at the party. Jamie, mortified, fled outside. It was a major disruption – so much so that the hostess felt she had to halt the proceedings temporarily to console Jamie.

Some time past one o'clock in the morning, Jamie drove back to the farm with his cousin. Despite the fact that they had consumed alcohol and Jamie was visibly upset over the events of the evening, the two of them managed to find their way along the dark, treacherous road. Jamie parked the car and bade his cousin goodnight, saying, 'See you in the morning.' A short while later, his cousin heard a gunshot. He raced to Jamie's cottage, where he found him dead, his brains splattered all over the ceiling and walls. The Remington was on the floor next to him.

There was a large amount of money at stake: Jamie's life was insured for a million rand – the equivalent of roughly ten million rand or more today. The Verhoef family wanted the insurance policy to be paid out. Aegis Insurance Company came to consult me for an opinion on the matter, and I looked at all the facts: a contact wound under Jamie's chin indicated suicide. I advised the insurers that, since Jamie's was a recent policy with a suicide clause, and that the cause of death appeared to be a suicide, they should repudiate the claim. The family then pursued the matter. I thought it wise to have someone other than me in the defendant's corner: it was going to be a tough battle in court and I wanted an expert who could merge the clinical aspects with the findings of the post-mortem. I made some calls and was referred to Vince di Maio, the author of *Gunshot Wounds*. He met with me and we discussed the case.

I had conducted considerable experiments with pigs using the same rifle that killed Jamie Verhoef, and we put the case together. The family's experts contended that Jamie had dropped the rifle and it had gone off, or that Jamie had stumbled and in the course of this the dog had pulled the trigger! I showed that this was possible, but not in such a way that a contact wound would result. The weapon would have to have been within half a millimetre of Jamie's skin in order to tear it the way it did.

The case was heard in Cape Town. I decided to get Di Maio to testify instead of me, and he did well. He showed the court that the fatal shot had to have been a contact shot. He demonstrated that all the reflexes of someone who tripped would not have produced the picture we had in front of us. He was extremely convincing. When I had seen which judge was on the bench and observed her body language and attitude, however, I was filled with foreboding. At the break, within ninety minutes of the start of the case, I said to our counsel, 'You can stand on your head in front of our judge and it won't make any difference. You are going to lose this case.'

The opposing side had in their camp Lionel Smith, former professor of forensic medicine at UCT, and Wollie Wolmarans, former police ballistics expert. All they had were theories, and all that they attempted to do was to disprove our contention that Jamie had put the gun under his chin and pulled the trigger. The judge found that Jamie had picked up the gun to shoot a piet-my-vrou – a red-chested cuckoo – in the pitch-darkness. He had been walking and had tripped. Instead of looking down and stretching his hands out to break his fall, he had clutched the gun to his chest and looked up, and somehow the weapon had accidentally discharged. She seemed to accept the explanation by Wolmarans that the dog could have pulled the trigger by making no comment about this suggestion. Her view was that Jamie Verhoef's death was an accident, not suicide.

The insurance company was at a loss, and I told them that if they didn't fight this to the bitter end, they might as well not have a suicide waiver in their policy documents. The case ended up in the Supreme Court of Appeal, where the judges took a much more rational view, making a few unflattering comments about the previous judge's understanding of ballistics and shootings. We won the case on appeal.

(The death of Jamie Verhoef vividly illustrates the problems with post-mortem reports outlined in Chapter 16: there were two reports written, with conflicting descriptions of the wound. This played a large role in the protracted insurance claim.)

I will never forget that farm in Beaufort West – it felt like the saddest, loneliest place on earth. Sometimes, if you sit in a cemetery, that same spirit of desolation comes over you – the feeling of death. And it was so quiet. The only sound was that of a lone bird. After Jamie killed himself, it would have been a terrible place for his father to go. All the money in the world cannot make up for the tragic loss of his son.

||||||||||||||||||||||||||||||||||||||||||||||||||||||||||||||||||

CHAPTER 19

TILL DEATH US DO PART

*'The entirety of one's adult life is a series of
personal choices, decisions. If we can accept
this totally, then we become free people.
To the extent that we do not accept this
we will forever feel ourselves victims.'*

– M. SCOTT PECK,

American psychiatrist and author, *The Road Less Traveled*

Life does not always go as planned, and the same can be said of relationships. When matters reach breaking point, we as human beings can react in many ways – one of which is resorting to murder, or attempted murder.

Murdering your husband or wife may be a crime of passion, committed in a moment of intense emotion, or it may be well planned and premeditated. That is the work of forensic science – piecing together the left-behind evidence of a murder to arrive at the truth, or as close to the truth as possible.

The 'three-in-a-bed' murder trial in 1987 was a sizzling case that caught the attention and imagination of the public, as it exposed the 'other side' of life behind high walls and manicured lawns.

Thirty-five-year-old Maria Krebs went on trial in March 1989 for the murder of her husband, and the court had to decide whether the murder was as a result of abuse, self-defence or financial motivation. What made it even more sensational was that Maria Krebs was also on trial for the attempted murder of 'Pat' du Preez, a hooker, who was present in the couple's company and bed on the night of the murder.

Ralf and Maria Krebs lived a comfortable life in Bedfordview, Johannesburg, with their children, aged three and five at the time. Ralf Krebs was no saint – a week before the murder, he confessed to his wife that he was having an affair. Maria testified that he had, in fact, contracted pubic lice from this encounter.

The day of 21 October 1987 was rather uneventful. According to the evidence presented in court, at around 8 p.m. the children were put to bed and the couple made love, Ralf telling Maria how much he loved her and that he never wanted to hurt her. According to Maria, once they were finished, at around 10 p.m., Ralf informed her that he wanted her to get over her hang-ups about him having sex with other women. According to him, it was just sex, not love. He said that he would like to share this experience with her. This was not the first time Ralf had wanted another woman in their bed. Some time after Maria's hysterectomy, he'd wanted to have sex with her and she had said it was too painful, so he told her to provide an alternative. While holding a gun to her head, he made her call an escort agency to get a girl brought over. Maria was so distressed after this incident that she went to see a psychiatrist, who then wanted to see Ralf. He never went.

Maria was petrified of Ralf, as he had used physical violence against her previously, when he had been drinking. That October evening, as Ralf looked in the newspaper for an escort agency, Maria reluctantly agreed to make the call. He dialled the number of Playmates Escort Agency and gave his wife the receiver so that she could speak to them. She identified herself and requested that a 'lady' be sent over. A short while later, the doorbell rang and 'Pat' du Preez arrived.

Maria was still in bed, naked, and Ralf asked her if she had money in her purse. She replied that she did, and Ralf took out about forty rand. He went downstairs and paid George, the driver, before coming back upstairs with Pat. Maria lay under the covers, still naked, and perplexed as to what would happen next, while Ralf poured wine for everyone and took off his dressing gown.

Pat came towards Maria, who pushed her away in fear, screaming that she didn't want to be touched. Ralf grabbed her and tried to pry her legs apart. When Maria looked again, Ralf was on top of Pat. She grabbed a vase and smashed it over Ralf's shoulder, then took the wine bottle out of the cooler and hit him on the head with it.

Ralf was furious, and Maria jumped off the bed and fled the room in terror. A violent argument ensued, and Maria ran through the house with Ralf chasing her, brandishing a .38 revolver. Between two bedrooms of the house was a shared shower cubicle that had Georgian wire glass on each side, and it was here that Maria fled, locking herself in. As she cowered on the shower floor, Ralf tried to break the glass with the revolver. He was unable to make much of a hole in the strong glass, but he damaged it severely. He left that side of the shower, thinking that he could get to her from the other side, from the adjacent bedroom. But he made the fatal mistake of leaving the revolver behind. As Maria saw him leave, she left the safety of the shower and reached for the weapon.

Maria sat on the bed and tried to open the revolver to remove the bullets. As she was holding the revolver, Pat came into the room, saw Maria with the revolver and left immediately. Pat ran next door to a neighbour, Mr Chudleigh, begging him to call the police and telling him that the lady next door was going to shoot her husband.

Maria, terrified, ran out of the main bedroom, along the passage and down the stairs. She saw that the front door was closed and, when she looked up, Ralf was at the top of the staircase. She shouted for him not to come any closer to her. A shot was fired, and Ralf fell to the floor.

I was appointed by Maria's defence team and proceeded to investigate the evidence to establish whether there was a forensic basis for her version of events. When I examined the house, I saw the broken glass shower door. The bullet was found in Ralf's shirt – it had passed right through his body into the back of his shirt.

The bullet told a story. As Ralf had pounded on the glass door with the revolver, tiny glass fragments had become entrapped in the barrel of the weapon. When the shot was fired, the bullet picked up these glass fragments. I could still see them on the bullet under the microscope, where they had remained during the bullet's passage through Ralf's body. This was direct evidence that Maria's version of events was accurate. It played a role in her case, and my report was accepted into evidence.

Mr Justice Vermooten was on the bench. He seemed riveted by the evidence of 'Pat' the hooker, particularly by the fact that she wore her high heels to bed. I have often wondered if Mrs Vermooten came in for a few surprises after that trial! The lurid details of the evening of 21 October 1987 provided the public with much insight into the world of call-girls and sex in the suburbs.

Maria Krebs was found not guilty of murder, but guilty of culpable homicide – a mere slap on the wrist. She was also fined R2 000 and sentenced to a further three years' imprisonment, which was suspended for five years. The court rejected for the most part the evidence of 'Pat' du Preez, saying it was full of contradictions. 'Pat' later sold her story to *Scope* magazine and was interviewed on M-Net's *Carte Blanche*, where she said that she was full of regret and had turned her life around. For me, this case was a clear illustration of a man's brutality towards his wife, and of the potentially terrifying consequences of a person being pushed to the limit.

I was involved in another murder case, this time in Standerton, where a woman was pushed too far by her husband, and she shot him. A wonderful, charming man is how he was described in court – until he had a drink or two. Then he would turn into a monster, locking his wife in a cupboard and terrifying her by emptying a magazine of bullets into the cupboard door, or chasing her down the road, brandishing a pistol, threatening to kill her. Of course, once he sobered up, he would be full of regret and apologise most profusely. Then all would go well – until the next time.

One fateful day, he was holding his wife by the ears and literally hitting her head against the wall. She felt around for her husband's pistol and, when she found it, she emptied it into his chest.

I believe that this man was a latent homosexual. Many of these abusive cases have a sexual component: some such men cannot satisfy themselves with their wives, and their frustration builds up to a level where it becomes debilitating. This theory of mine was corroborated by the deceased's brother-in-law, who testified in court about how the deceased had tried to sodomise him.

We were also able to demonstrate that the woman had been on antidepressants as a result of the pressure of her marriage. Indeed, at the time of her husband's death, she had been tranquillised so heavily by her doctor that she couldn't have formulated the intention to commit a crime.

In this case, I gathered facts and provided the lawyers with information that they could use in court. This role – one more akin to that of private investigator or police detective than a forensic scientist – is one I often find myself playing. This was one of the quickest court cases I have ever seen: the defendant was acquitted before lunch time.

The bloody hand does not inherit. This was the burning issue in a case that took place about ten years ago, when a husband and wife were found dead in their home. Both had been shot, and it was a mystery as to who had shot whom. It was the second marriage for both the husband and the wife, and they each had children from their previous marriages. The order in which they died became very important in determining the disposition of the estate – if the wife had pulled the trigger first, her husband's children would inherit the estate; if the husband had shot his wife first, her children would inherit. South African law states, '*de bloedige hand erf niet*' – the bloody hand cannot inherit from the crime.

From the blood-splash analysis, I was able to determine that the wife had shot her husband first, and had then turned the gun on herself. The case was held before Judge Peter Schutz, and its ending was controversial, with much unhappiness from the deceased wife's children.

Murder cases involving intimate relations can sometimes leave more questions than answers for me, as happened with the Kobrin matter. This case also highlighted blatant flaws in police procedure, which seems to be a thread running through so many of the cases in which I have been involved.

Raymond Kobrin was a medical doctor who was murdered in the early 1990s. His wife was charged with organising a hit on her husband. I was called in by her defence team to assist with the investigation.

Janet and Raymond lived in Bedfordview, Johannesburg, and had several children. Raymond ran a successful GP practice in Benoni, after having trained at the University of Pretoria – in fact, he and I had been at school together. Strangely, he seemed to have all sorts of contacts outside the world of medicine that were both disturbing and unusual. There were rumours of connections with military intelligence, and these ghosts seemed to haunt the investigation from time to time, although they were never fully explored.

The Kobrin marriage was far from happy, and Raymond was not the faithful husband he should have been. At the time of his death, he had a girlfriend, whom he stayed with on occasion. It was a stressful time, and there was talk of divorce.

The car in which anti-apartheid activists were murdered on 8 June 1988 in the Piet Retief massacre. The police fired all sorts of shots from the left-hand side of the car

The other side of the same vehicle used by the activists in the Piet Retief matter. The police claimed to have fired the shots during a shoot-out, but this could never have happened: the policemen on the right-hand side of the car would have been firing shots directly at the policemen standing on the left-hand side of the car

The lonely stretch of road just outside Piet Retief where the murders took place. The police had been hiding in the woods on the left-hand side of the road when the driver of the car had got out on the pretence of needing to relieve himself. The security force from Vlakplaas had then moved in and murdered the activists in the car

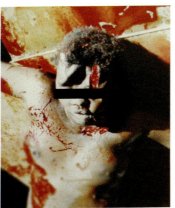

The effect of the fusillade of shots on one of the victims of the Piet Retief massacre

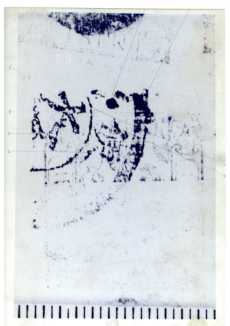

The so-called Japanese stamps in the 1987 matter of *Abrahams v Barclays Bank*, where the identical nature of the cancellation mark on the two stamps can be seen. This was crucial in proving that the stamps were not forgeries but were the original stamps handed in by Cyril Abrahams to Barclays Bank as security

The pavement in Eleanor Street where David Webster fell after being assassinated on 1 May 1989. Webster and his partner had just returned in their Ford truck from buying plants at the nursery when Ferdi Barnard had driven up alongside Webster and fired a shot into his chest

The police tried to keep David Webster's bloodied T-shirt away from me to prevent the truth from emerging. I had spent hours searching for the bullet that I believed to have passed through Webster's body, but as soon as I saw the shirt, I knew that a shotgun had been used and that the pellets would never have exited the body

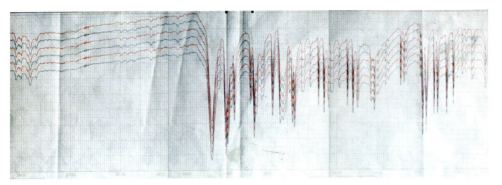

This set of infrared graphs, produced by an infrared spectrometer in a drug-related case I worked on in 1988, indicates that the police repeatedly analysed the same laboratory reference sample rather than analysing actual samples of Mandrax: the results of the analysis of the drug are identical in their peaks and the noise on the baseline is also identical. The top line represents the lab reference sample

The arrows point to specks of blood found on the seat of the car in the 1986 Henry Burt necklacing investigation. It is impossible that two crystalline spots of blood could have been left on the seat after it had been thoroughly washed, as alleged by the police. It is my belief that they were planted by the police to advance their case

A map showing the route of the SA *Helderberg* on its last, ill-fated flight from Taipei across the Indian Ocean to its final resting place just north-east of Mauritius

The committee of the Truth and Reconciliation Commission Special Investigation into the *Helderberg* Crash with a number of people who lost family members in the crash. I am standing to the extreme right in the photograph

The damaged Astra revolver used in the infamous 1987 'three-in-a-bed' murder case involving Ralf and Maria Krebs. Glass fragments were embedded in the gun's barrel when Ralf Krebs tried to smash the glass shower door to get to his wife, who was hiding there. This evidence played a role in the outcome of the case

Fred van der Vyver, who was accused of murdering his girlfriend, Inge Lotz, in March 2005

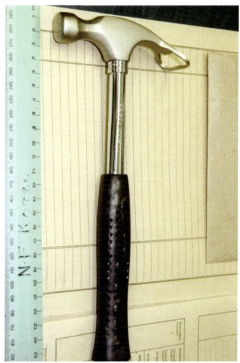

The hammer that the police accused Fred van der Vyver of using to batter Inge Lotz to death. They never found any blood on the hammer, and their final experiments using the hammer were a parody of what constitutes true forensic science

The bloodstain made by Fred van der Vyver's shoe, according to the police. The stain bears no resemblance to prints that would be made by the shoes Van der Vyver was wearing that day and is testimony to the incompetence of the police footprint expert in this matter

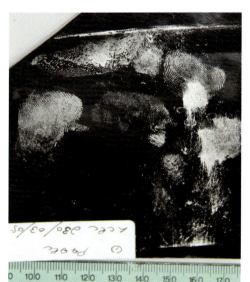

The fingerprint that allegedly placed Fred van der Vyver at the scene of the crime

The scene of Brett Kebble's shooting, which took place in Johannesburg on 27 September 2005. Before the shooting, Kebble's car was parked on the left-hand side of this lonely stretch of road. The car later moved up the hill and came to rest against the railing of the bridge over the M1

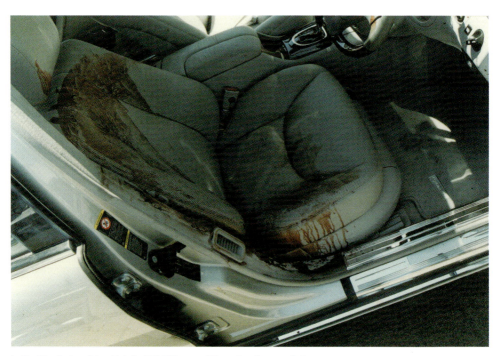

The bloodied seat in which Brett Kebble was sitting when he was shot

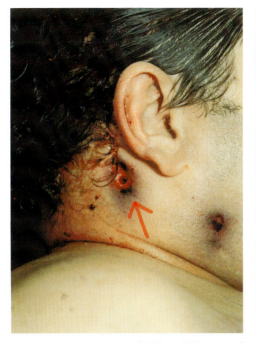

The close-range wound behind Brett Kebble's ear. The bullet from this final shot came to rest against his spinal column. Note the blackening, which indicates that the pistol was very close when the shot was fired

Peter George (left) and Brett Kebble during Kebble's baptism in George's swimming pool a short while before his death

'Inspection in Loco': The magistrate and me (left) in the 2003 Kraaifontein train-crash matter examining a similar type of locomotive to the one driven by the defendant at the time of the accident

The mouse that became the cause célèbre in the early 2003 'Mouse in the Coke' case. The field mouse was later found not guilty, as it showed no sign whatsoever of decomposition

The process whereby we canned the mice in order to examine the effect of Coca-Cola on a mouse in a can over six weeks. Note that we used different cans at a Coke bottling plant in order to make certain that we did not release a mouse-infested Coke into the general circulation

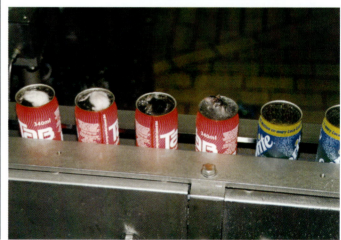

At work in my laboratory, 2010

One afternoon, Janet and the children went out to a movie and the family's staff had the afternoon off. Raymond came to the house, the reason for which was never quite clear – perhaps he was there to fetch some clothes or talk to the family. He suddenly disappeared. When his girlfriend didn't hear from him, she became worried and frantically started calling around. These were pre-cellphone days, and Raymond, being a doctor, carried a pager. She called the paging company and left a message for him to call her.

Two and a half weeks later, someone noticed a nasty smell coming from a car parked at the airport. When the locks were forced open, they found Raymond's body in an advanced state of decomposition, with a single small-calibre bullet hole in the back of his head.

Janet Kobrin was the main suspect. The police investigated, and I was appointed by Janet Kobrin's attorney, Graham Edwards, to conduct a forensic investigation. I went to the house in Bedfordview and was met by Warrant Officer Holmes, the investigating officer. I still recall thinking that he was like Sherlock Holmes, but he turned out to be anything but. I put my hand out to greet him and he ignored it, asking me, 'Who are you?'

I introduced myself. 'I have heard of you,' he replied, saying that he had learnt of me while at police college. I asked what they had said, and he answered, 'They told me that if that guy comes to your crime scene, you tell him fuck all!' I saw this as one of the few genuine compliments about my abilities from the police!

I started investigating the case. Raymond's girlfriend provided one of the key pieces of information: she had called Janet in the late afternoon of the day that Raymond had disappeared to ask her if she knew where he was. Just before she called Janet, she paged Raymond. A distinctive 'bleeping' sound was made every time a message came through. The girlfriend swore blind that she heard the 'bleep' as she was talking on the phone to Janet, which meant that Raymond's pager must have still been there when she phoned.

Janet was adamant that the pager had not been there when the girlfriend called. Something else must have gone off that sounded similar, I thought. There were blood stains on the carpet, so Raymond had been at the house when he was killed.

I spent quite a bit of time trying to find something that sounded similar to the pager sound that the girlfriend had heard. I tried the alarm clock, the kitchen timers – everything and anything in the house that made a noise.

It subsequently transpired that it *was* Raymond's pager that had gone off, and that Janet had known that but had let me waste time on a wild-goose chase. I have a very firm belief: if a client lies to me, I withdraw from the case. It is simply too dangerous to get sucked into a potential web of lies. My job is to find the truth using scientific investigation, which is impossible to do if untruths are at play. As a result, I withdrew from the case, yet I continued to follow its progress.

The police did appallingly sloppy work. They tried to get Janet's son to make a confession by assaulting him while in custody, which led to a court application being made and cast doubt on the police's abilities. The police, a bunch of hoodlums, thought they could get away with anything: many crimes in those days were solved by a confession, which was often obtained by assaulting the accused or a witness.

A strange aspect to this case was the murder weapon. It was found much later in the incinerator at the nursing home where Raymond worked. Someone found the carbonised remains of a frame of a pistol. Who would have known to hide it there?

At the end of a long case, in which no conclusive evidence came to light, Janet was acquitted on the charge of murder.

Honesty, for me, is always paramount, and its benefit was brought home to me by another case of husband–wife murder. A man had shot his wife. He said that he had found her in the arms of another man and had murdered her in a crime of passion. I was asked to do a reconstruction of the crime scene.

We knew where the cartridge cases had been found – on the right-hand side of the room – and also that an automatic pistol ejects the cartridges in a particular way. The man's version of the story was completely at odds with the way the crime scene looked, taking into account the trajectories, wounds and other elements of the scene. I told him that his explanation was improbable, and he said, 'I think I had better tell you the truth.' He gave me another account, which was much closer to the truth and which was believed in court. He had actually committed cold-blooded murder, but the fact that he opened up in court was an extremely important component in his not receiving the death sentence. Honesty does pay, in the long run.

Poisoning your intimate partner may be seen as a 'clean' way of eliminating him or her, and every thirty or forty years arsenic seems to raise its head in popularity. I have had a number of clients approach me over the years on the suspicion that they were being poisoned by their partner. Ninety per cent of the time there are innocent explanations for the symptoms they are experiencing – arsenic produces symptoms very similar to those of gastro-enteritis – but, once in a while, poison is a reality. (In the famous 1932 case of Daisy de Melker, the pathologists were fooled into thinking that her first two husbands had died of gastro-enteritis. It was only when her son died and his body was later exhumed, together with the husbands' bodies, that traces of arsenic and strychnine were found.)

A few years back, a dentist in Swellendam became very ill after eating poisoned chocolates. At around that time, I was visited by a woman who was convinced that her boyfriend was trying to poison her. He had given her a beautiful box of chocolates and had encouraged her to eat them all herself. She became desperately ill afterwards and came to see me.

I took a statement from her and, from what she described, I

suspected that it was a case of arsenic poisoning. I was not sure what I was dealing with here because of arsenic poisoning's mimicking of gastro-enteritis. This poison is easily identifiable in a person's hair, so I took hair samples from the woman and analysed them – she was loaded with arsenic! I called her and asked her to come in and see me. I told her my findings, and she looked visibly shocked. She then asked me if I thought she should go back to him. I looked at her in disbelief and said, 'Madam, that is a no-brainer!'

People do strange things in relationships. One fellow came to see me, suspecting that he was being poisoned. He had seen his girlfriend sprinkling something over his curry one evening and, after he ate it, he fell violently ill. He had managed to get hold of the bottle and brought it with him, wanting to know if the contents were toxic.

One of the problems with analysis of this sort is that there are about four million organic compounds, and a significant number of those are toxic. Many of these substances are used in herbal remedies that are readily available.

There was a minute amount of the substance used by the girl-friend left in the bottle, and I was at a loss as to where to start, so I placed it under a microscope and had a look. In the corner I found a tiny pair of insect wings, so I put the contents back in the bottle and went to see Dr Zumph, a medical entomologist at the South African Institute for Medical Research. He identified it as a wing from the cantharides beetle, otherwise known as the Spanish fly. Among other medical uses, this beetle is ground up and used as an aphrodisiac, but it contains a corrosive substance called cantharidin. The dosage should be minuscule; a harmful dose can cause painful urination, fever and sometimes a bloody discharge. In some cases, it can prove fatal. This man had clearly been given too much of this substance, which caused his illness. Whether his girlfriend had administered it by accident or purposefully, I will never know!

The truth, it has been said, is often stranger than fiction, and I recall a rather amusing case where a woman came to see me with a problem. She drank Johnnie Walker whisky, and couldn't understand why the first few drinks always tasted fine, but then started to taste terrible. She suspected that her husband was trying to poison her, and brought the bottle of whisky for me to analyse.

I ran extensive tests and could find nothing. I then heated a small sample and the strong smell of a urinal began to emanate from it. I took a sample and tested it, and I found it to be full of urine! Her husband waited each time until she had had a few drinks, and then urinated in the bottle – probably just to irritate her! I told her that she was unlikely to die.

I see all kinds of people and all manner of things in my practice. The veneer of civilisation drops away so easily; all that is left is the plain truth about people and how they deal with life and relationship problems. Mine has been a varied practice – it has certainly never been boring!

CHAPTER 20

BENT COPPERS?:
THE MURDER OF INGE LOTZ

*'There are those state agencies who are so blind
to the possibility of innocence that they ignore or
withhold evidence consistent with it as irrelevant.'*

– GEOFFREY ROBERTSON,
human rights lawyer, author and broadcaster

Around 10 p.m. on the evening of 16 March 2005, the Lotzes
received the message that all parents dread: their daughter, Inge,
had been found brutally murdered in her flat in Stellenbosch. The
tragedy of this beautiful young woman's death is impossible to
quantify. Even more tragic, however, is that the subsequent criminal
investigation stands out as one of the worst police investigations
ever to have taken place in South Africa, leaving her killer roaming
free. Whether it was stupidity, dishonesty or a combination of both
on the part of the police we will never know for certain, but every
mistake that could have been made was made in this case.

Inge's boyfriend, Fred van der Vyver, was arrested for the murder, and I was called in by his family to investigate on behalf of the
defence team.

The story starts with a young couple, Frederik Barend van der Vyver and Inge Lotz, who started dating at Stellenbosch University in 2004. Inge was highly intelligent, making strides through the academic world with her studies towards a master's degree in mathematics. She had the world at her fingertips: not only was she bright, but she was attractive and likeable.

Fred was also mathematically gifted, having obtained a scholarship to study actuarial science from Old Mutual. He was working for the financial services company at the time of Inge's murder. It was their common interest in mathematics that had brought Fred and Inge together: they had met through the Department of Mathematics at Stellenbosch, and a relationship had developed between them. Inge's parents knew Fred well, and the relationship had all the hallmarks of one that could have ended in marriage. Unfortunately, it was not meant to be.

With a staunch Dutch Reformed background, Fred was a highly religious person. He was an active member of His People Christian Church, a charismatic church with a strong belief that the Bible is the undiluted word of God, and he took his religion seriously, living his life accordingly. I was led to understand that he never had a conventional sexual relationship with Inge in the form of full penetrative sexual intercourse, but that there had been significant petting between them.

Like any couple, Fred and Inge had their ups and downs. It appeared that, prior to Inge's murder, there had been some kind of lover's tiff between them: Inge had written a letter to Fred in which she apologised for the argument, yet they appear to have parted amicably on the morning of the fateful day on which Inge was killed. Fred left her flat that day and proceeded to a second-hand furniture shop to purchase a bookshelf for a friend. Since Fred drove a light pick-up van, he was able to transport the bookshelf, and he was going to deliver it to his friend later.

Unaware of the horrific events that would ensue, Fred then

drove to work in Pinelands, where he clocked in at Old Mutual at 11.05 a.m. The advanced access-control system – the only way to enter or exit the building – monitors staff's photographs as they move through the turnstiles: these records proved that Fred was in the Old Mutual building from the late morning onwards. He was in meetings for the rest of the day, finishing somewhere between 5 p.m. and 5.10 p.m. Fred then logged on to his computer at 5.14 p.m., and technical evidence indicated that he sent and read emails at this time. The access-control system showed that he left the building at 6.11 p.m.

Leaving work, Fred went home to his flat in Pinelands, where he had supper before delivering the bookshelf to his friend, who lived in the same block of flats as him. At 7.10 p.m. he received a call from Bennie Schoeman. The call, which registered at the Old Mutual 1 tower serving the area around Fred's flat, lasted for more than eight minutes.

While delivering the bookshelf to his friend that evening, Fred parked in a no-parking zone and his wheel was clamped. This event, as irritating as it must have been for him at the time, ultimately played a critical role in his defence, as there was a record of his having spoken to the security staff at around 7.45 p.m., when he requested that they unclamp his wheel.

Fred simply could not have had enough time to drive the roughly thirty-kilometre trip from Pinelands to Stellenbosch to murder Inge. If Fred had left work just after 6 p.m., as the access-control system at Old Mutual indicated, he would have had to drive in peak-hour traffic to Stellenbosch, have words with Inge, murder her, clean up the blood splatters on himself and get back to Pinelands in time for his phone to register at Old Mutual 1 at 7.10 p.m. and to have his wheel clamped at around 7.30 p.m. Considering these time frames, this simply isn't possible.

Fred knew that Inge was planning to stay at home to study that evening. They SMSed frequently; the last message he received from her was at 1.36 p.m. Fred SMSed Inge a few times that evening and couldn't understand why she was not replying. He became increasingly anxious, and at around 9 p.m. he called Mrs Lotz, SMSing her a short while later. Fred's flatmate, Marius Botha, then arranged for another friend, Christo Pretorius, who lived close to Inge, to go and investigate while Fred departed for the Lotz home to get the keys to Inge's apartment.

Fred collected the keys and left the Lotz house, heading for Inge's flat. Just after he left, however, he received a call from Marius asking him to turn back and wait at the Lotzes' house, as Marius wanted to speak to them. Fred and Mrs Lotz then waited for Marius, who arrived just before 11 p.m. to break the devastating news: Inge's body had been found lying bloodied and lifeless on the couch in her flat.

The police arrived on the crime scene shortly afterwards. There followed a series of events that can best be described as a catalogue of blunders.

It is sacrosanct in forensic science that the scene of the crime is cordoned off immediately. Anyone entering the scene must be properly clothed with footgear, overalls and other kit so that they do not contaminate any crucial trace evidence that could be the sole basis on which to build a case. The first mistake made in the Lotz investigation was that the crime scene was not cordoned off properly. Policemen traipsed in and out of the flat so freely that when a blood-stained print was discovered, the investigating officer had to take all his men to one side to see if one of their shoes had made the footprint. That is appalling, and should never have been allowed: the very basic principles of forensic investigation were broken at the outset.

Inge's flat was not broken into and nothing had been stolen, and she was skimpily dressed in shorts and a T-shirt. It appeared from these factors that she knew her killer. Later, at the trial, it became obvious that Fred had been the main – and sole – suspect from the beginning. In all fairness to the police, the people closest to a murder victim should always be on the list of suspects: many murders are committed by people intimately involved with their victims, as their emotions overwhelm the normal social rules governing human behaviour. It is therefore quite acceptable that Fred was placed in the frame of suspects, but he should not have been the only one. The police should have examined the evidence and decided whether it incriminated or eliminated him. It appears that this did not occur.

As Fred was the one and only suspect, the police investigators believed that he had to be lying, for whatever reason. Once a crime investigator makes up his or her mind in a forensic investigation without looking at the facts, he or she is liable to make every mistake in the book. That's exactly what happened.

After Fred had left her flat earlier that day, Inge had gone out at around 3 p.m. and bought a hamburger and chips from the local Steers. She had also rented a DVD, *The Stepford Wives* – a sadly ironic choice in the light of what was about to happen to her – but we will never know whether or not she watched the film before she was murdered. She was last seen alive by tilers arriving at her complex at around 4 p.m.

The DVD and a fingerprint became the centre of a heated debate. Fred's alibi was always that he had been nowhere near Inge's flat that afternoon: he had been at Old Mutual from eleven o'clock in the morning until just after six in the evening. The police claimed to have found a fingerprint on the DVD cover that belonged to Fred's left index finger, implying that he had been at Inge's flat after 3 p.m., precisely when he professed to have been at work. Had this been true, it would have blown his alibi right out of the water.

When the other fingerprint expert and I examined the fingerprint, there appeared to be a number of irregularities. The first was that it appeared not to have been taken off a flat rectangular surface. Folene, a type of sticky tape, is used to lift a fingerprint. When you pick up a fingerprint, you also pick up the background

– the substratum behind it. If a print comes off a wooden surface, for example, you will pick up the wood grain as well; if the surface has curved edges, these will be seen on the lifted print too.

There were curved lines on the folene lift of the fingerprint we examined in the Lotz case. It could not have come off a DVD cover, which is flat and has only straight edges on the outer surface where the print was found. It is impossible to lift a curved line off a straight-edged surface. When I spoke to the police about the fact that this fingerprint had clearly been lifted from a curved surface, they were defensive.

One would also have expected other fingerprints – Inge's, for example, and those of the shop assistant – to be present on the DVD cover, but only one person's print was lifted, and it belonged to Fred. This pointed to another strange, but obvious, fact: there was only Fred's fingerprint present. There should have been additional prints on the underside of the DVD cover, as it is impossible to hold a DVD box with only one finger.

To make matters worse, the police returned the DVD to the DVD shop, failing to retain it as a vital piece of evidence. The DVD cover should also have been photographed where it was found, as should the actual fingerprint before the cover was moved. In addition, the DVD container should also have been photographed *in situ* after it was dusted for prints. These are the most elementary of forensic procedures, yet they were simply not carried out. A policeman merely pointed out where he had found the cover. Handled correctly, this piece of evidence alone could have convicted the murderer.

The fingerprint blunder doesn't end there. After the police's approach had come under severe attack by the defence, the police took the print to their central lab for examination by Roger Dixon, the control forensic analyst at the police's forensic science laboratory. He came to the same conclusion as us: that the print came from a curved surface. This certainly suggests that this evidence was tendered by the police in bad faith – how could they have made such an elementary mistake, and one of such enormous proportion?

Another piece of 'damning' evidence was raised against Fred – a bloodstained mark on the bathroom floor in Inge's flat. It would certainly have been damning had it been justified. The police employed in-house footprint 'expert' Bruce Bartholomew to examine the mark. He found it to be a mark made by Fred's shoe, and the police were adamant that this was indeed the case.

One has to understand how this type of comparison – between the sole of a shoe and a print – is done. Before you compare two marks, they have to have the same class characteristics. There are thousands of Hi-Tec trainers (or Caterpillar boots, or whatever the case may be) with the same pattern on the underside – this is called the 'class characteristic'. Marks that do not share class characteristics escape comparison. Thus, a mark made by a shoe with a diamond pattern cannot be compared to a shoe with a club-shaped pattern on the underside, as the print clearly could not have been made by that shoe.

Fred's shoe had a specific pattern on the sole that, according to the police, seemed to match that of the bloodstained mark. Given that there are many thousands of shoes sharing the same pattern on the underside, there has to be a match in 'individual characteristics' between the print and the shoe. These come about through individual wear – a piece of glass that may have cut the sole at a given spot, or damage from treading on a nail in a specific place or way. The chance of two people making the same marks on the soles of their shoes is so minuscule that it can be accepted as being impossible. It follows that, if the individual characteristics are identical, one can accept that as proof positive that the marks match.

In the case of Fred van der Vyver's alleged footprint, there were no individual characteristics on the print. The police hinged their allegation on the fact that there were purportedly three specks of dust on the shoe sole, which, they said, made a specific imprint that showed up in the print.

This was further complicated by the unsatisfactory way in which the mark was compared to Fred's shoe. When you lift a fingerprint (or footprint, or any other kind of print) from a surface, you get a mirror image of the actual print. You need to compare the lifted print to an inverted image of the actual print, which is obtained by inking the suspect's finger and taking a print. You cannot compare the finger to the lifted fingerprint.

For some reason, the police didn't make an inked print of Fred's shoe. Their argument was that they didn't want to disturb the three specks of dust that they alleged were present on the sole of the shoe. These three or four specks of dust were critical to their argument that this was Fred's shoe. Bartholomew merely compared the photo of the blood mark on the floor to a photo of the surface of the shoe. This is not the way to do it.

Inge's attack and murder were frenzied. She had been assaulted with at least two separate weapons and had been violently stabbed – there was blood everywhere. Whoever had carried out this terrible act would have been covered in minuscule specks of blood. Forensic science is very good at identifying tiny spots of blood, even if they have been washed off the surface in question. Considerable scrubbing is required to remove blood from clothing completely, particularly from shoes, which have many nooks and crannies in which blood can lodge and stick.

Yet no blood was found on Fred's shoe. If he was the killer, he would have had to have washed the shoe over and over again. Yet three or four little specks of dust had remained on the shoe, despite Fred's alleged scrubbing. Why, then, would the dust have been dislodged if Bartholomew had done an inking? The approach of the police investigators fails in logic.

Because the police had been seriously attacked on the fingerprint issue, they were becoming edgy with their evidence on the shoe. They decided to send Bruce Bartholomew to meet with an FBI expert on footprinting, William Bodziak, who has also written a book on the subject. Bodziak took one look at Bartholomew's efforts and declared that it was not even worth commenting on them. Bartholomew sent a message back saying that Bodziak had agreed with his assertion that it was a good match. No one in the police or prosecution questioned Bodziak; Bartholomew's statement was accepted without question.

The defence team came to hear of this and called Bodziak, who made short shrift of Bartholomew's statement promoting the idea that it was Fred's shoe that had made the mark. The FBI expert eventually became a witness for the defence. Despite this, Bartholomew doggedly stuck to his unscientific and improbable version of events.

How can forensic investigators make such serious mistakes? Did they in their hearts believe Fred was so guilty that they were willing to ignore scientific principles – or the truth? The fingerprint and footmark were two crucial pieces of evidence that were so flawed that there was no hope of success for the police investigators in court.

The manner in which evidence relating to the murder weapon was handled is also laughable. The hammer that was allegedly used by Fred to bludgeon Inge to death was an ornamental hammer that had been a gift to Fred from Inge. He kept it in his car, under the seat. If it had been used to murder the girl, there would have been blood on it – it would have been very difficult to remove all traces of blood from the murder weapon. Yet the police found no blood on the hammer. They also decided to keep their blood expert away from the defence.

The police investigators decided to compare the wounds on Inge's skull to the wounds that would be made by such a hammer. They bought an identical hammer, and on the first blow to a pig's head, the hammer bent. That should have been the end of the experiment, as that hammer could not have been responsible for a blow of that nature.

Not so in this case. The police went out and obtained a similar hammer, but one that was substantially thicker in the places where the original hammer had bent. They repeated the experiment, ignoring the basic scientific principle that you cannot alter the test to get the results you want. The police presented the results of the second test in court, and Frans Maritz, the police ballistics expert, concealed from the court the fact that he had replaced the original hammer with a second, stronger hammer.

The defence enlarged a photograph that appeared in Maritz's report, and noticed that the hammer, buried in the pig's skull, was not like Fred's hammer. Only in cross-examination was the swapping of the hammer revealed, and Maritz then admitted in court that he had replaced the first, ornamental hammer because it had bent during the experiment – this after having stated under oath that he had used an identical hammer.

At one point, Fred's father, who had employed me to act in his son's defence, wanted me to write a report to the prosecution to get them to drop the case. I refused, trying to explain to him that they would never drop it, as the prosecution was under pressure to find someone guilty. I was not prepared to write a report that would put me under huge pressure were I to be placed in the witness box – there was no obligation for the defence team to produce a report, and my report would just have provided the state with ammunition in court. We parted ways over this, but because of my mounting horror at the police's conduct and their determination to prosecute a man who appeared to be innocent, I remained involved in the case in an advisory and consultative capacity.

Judge Deon van Zyl was on the bench, and we were all astounded when he did not grant us an acquittal at the end of the state case. The defence team proceeded to fly in experts from all over the world, including Holland and America. This international team eventually annihilated the state case. The costs were enormous, finally amounting to around R9 million.

The Lotz family decided to file a civil suit against Fred van der Vyver à la O.J. Simpson, who had been acquitted of murder in a state case but found guilty in a civil case. In a criminal case, a person needs to be proven guilty beyond reasonable doubt, so there is a much higher onus on the state to prove its case than there is for a plaintiff in a civil case to prove theirs. In civil cases, a person has to be found guilty on a balance of probabilities.

At the end of the day, there was no evidence to find Fred guilty of the murder. O.J. had been acquitted in the state case on a technicality, but there was no such similarity here – it would have been a complete waste of money to pursue the civil case against Fred van der Vyver. Fortunately, the Lotz family dropped the case. The police had also probably encouraged the Lotz family to go ahead with the civil case in an effort to vindicate themselves somehow. They were so convinced that Fred had committed the crime and had managed to wangle his way out of it that they did not even investigate the murder further, despite the fact that he was acquitted in a court of law.

I feel immensely sorry for the Lotzes, in that they have been let down by the whole criminal justice system, ranging from the police investigation to the entire legal system. What do you say to people in their position? They have no answers to their daughter's death and no closure; one cannot even begin to understand their pain.

This case illustrates so clearly that you cannot set off on a scientific quest with preconceived ideas. My quest is to find the truth: if a client of mine is innocent, I will do my utmost to make certain that the evidence is put to the ultimate test. By the same token, if my client is guilty, they may be hanged, so to speak, by their own witness if they make use of my services.

The investigators' zeal to convict Fred backfired horribly on the police, resulting in a massive civil trial the Van der Vyvers instituted against the SAPS to recover damages from them as a result of their dishonesty. Blinded by their own preconceived ideas, the police had been completely distracted by the 'noise' around them. Forensic science is about searching for that elusive creature called the truth, to which we try to get as close as possible through experimentation and understanding. A skilled forensic scientist has the ability to tell the difference, metaphorically speaking, between diamonds and pieces of glass. In the investigation into the murder of Inge Lotz, the little glass chips on which the entire case was built translated into an utter waste of time and money, yielding no answers or closure for anyone.

Sadly, the killer of Inge Lotz is still walking free today, a happy person with their guilty secret intact.

||||||||||||||||||||||||||||||||||||||||||||||||||||||||||||||||||

CHAPTER 21

SMOKE AND MIRRORS:
THE DEATH OF BRETT KEBBLE

*'[Lawyers are a] passive and enervate race,
ready to swallow any thing, and to acquiesce
in any thing ... obsequious only to the
whisper of interest, and to the beck of power.'*

– JEREMY BENTHAM,
English jurist, philosopher and social reformer

Brett Kebble, mining magnate, philanthropist and illustrious South
African businessman, reached the end of his road on 27 September
2005, when he was shot and killed at the age of forty-one. His life
was steeped in controversy, and his death was no different. It was
the hot topic of conversation at dinner tables for many months,
and the debate around the exact circumstances of his mysterious
death still rages today.

Initially, the Kebble family stated that they were satisfied with
the police investigation into the death, but later they expressed dissatisfaction: there seemed to be mixed messages emerging from
the Kebble stable. A few days after the shooting, I was approached
by Judge Willem Heath, who had been a judge in one of the home-

lands and had led the Heath Commission of Inquiry into malad-ministration and corruption under Nelson Mandela. Heath asked me if I would investigate the matter.

I flew up to Johannesburg and met him at a hotel, where he briefed me. According to him, he was acting on behalf of Roger Kebble, Brett's father. The next morning, on 30 September, I was collected at the hotel and we proceeded to the scene of the shoot-ing in Melrose.

Kebble was shot on a deserted stretch of road that leads out of Rosebank and follows a long downhill path, passing the old Melrose Bird Sanctuary. At one point, the road crosses a river, and at the bottom is a gate and waste-disposal yard, where people dump their garden refuse. It is a lonely place and, as it is badly lit, it would be dark and deserted at night.

Something seemed out of place in this investigation. At the scene of the shooting, I was met by Major Leonie Ras from the forensics laboratory of the South African Police. As fellow forensic investi-gators, Leonie and I knew each other and I regarded her highly. As we chatted, we were joined by a man called Botha, a forensic pathologist from Bloemfontein. He refused to speak to me.

A crime scene is always reconstructed, using all the evidence at hand. When key evidence is tampered with, as in this case, all one can do is to reconstruct a reconstruction in an effort to figure out vaguely what happened. This compromises the effective pursuit of justice and is unacceptable in an official forensic investigation.

The investigating officer who had first arrived on the scene had picked up all the cartridge cases – a major blunder. Cartridge cases are a crucial component of a crime scene: when a firearm dis-charges a cartridge case, you can trace the position of the shooter based on where the cartridge case lands. The cases will discharge in a similar direction, most often to the right of the shooter. While some weapons will discharge at short range, others will do so at a longer range, but knowing the weapon and seeing where the cartridge case falls provides a good start in reconstructing the scene of the crime. This particular policeman had simply picked up the cartridges and put them in his pocket. He had even failed to mark where they had fallen.

In addition, cartridge cases are vital pieces of evidence for the fingerprints they can provide. When a firearm is loaded, the cartridge is pushed into the magazine with the thumb, which means that there will often be a partial thumbprint on the cartridge case. The moment people start picking up the cases, that kind of evidence is lost.

As I stood there that morning talking to Leonie Ras, I asked her what she had found in the car. She replied that she hadn't seen the car yet. The alarm bells started ringing – it was dismaying to me that, three days after Kebble's death, the state forensic department had not yet examined the car, a prime piece of evidence that ought to have been checked for fingerprints and any other clues immediately. I then heard via a contact that the car had been released to Clinton Nassif, Kebble's former security boss, with orders that it be cleaned.

I suggested to Leonie that we immediately leave to see the car, and we raced off to Danmar Autobody, where the car was being kept – it had been released from the police yard and was waiting to be cleaned. On examining the car, it was interesting to note that it was completely empty. Kebble was known to have carried two or three phones with him at all times, yet there was not even a cellphone in the car. Even more worrying was that the mark resembling a bloodstain on the bonnet of the car, which I had noticed on TV footage, appeared to no longer be present. Other bloodstains were visible, but the evidence had already been compromised. The car could not render us as much information as it might have had it been left untouched, so I turned my investigation in another direction.

Kebble had been shot by a total of seven bullets, but only one of these had exited his body – the bullet that had entered through the thick piece of muscle between the fleshy part above his shoulder and neck. On exit, it had broken a back window of the car. This was the only window that was broken, so Kebble had to have been shot with the driver's window wound down. This was an unusual situation: a businessman in an expensive car drives into an exceptionally dangerous, lonely part of town at night, with his window open, and stops there.

I also realised that, most unusually, Kebble had been shot in an almost straight line along the right-hand side of his body. One shot was lodged in his neck. The bullet had entered the right side of his neck, just below his ear, travelled until it had hit his vertebral column, and slammed against the first and second vertebrae, cracking them. It had done no further damage. We knew that the bullets had been fired by a 9-mm Parabellum, which is a substantial weapon. A bullet from such a weapon should have gone right through the vertebrae – it would have slowed down slightly, but would certainly have travelled right out the other side. I then examined the car: none of the other bullets had exited.

This became of particular interest. Since a 9-mm Parabellum bullet will generally go straight through a person, particularly when it hits a fairly slender structure like the neck, there should have been extensive damage to the vertebrae. I realised that this was an unusual weapon – a weapon that fired 9-mm Parabellum bullets, but firing a reduced-power round. The workings of the weapon are simple: when a shot is fired, the recoil pushes the slide back with the force of the bullet and then reloads it. If you were to load this weapon with reduced-power bullets, it would fire one shot and jam, because the force of the bullet slamming back against the slide would not be sufficient to cycle the weapon – the gun is designed for full-power bullets.

There are certain circumstances where the full power of the weapon is not desired, such as in cases of anti-hijacking, dealing with a person in a crowd, and so on. It is bad practice to fire a shot that goes through your victim and proceeds to hit an innocent person. Because these kinds of weapons have to be modified – the tension of the springs has to be reduced – ordinary people do not usually have access to them. Generally, only those in the security industry could have their weapons modified to fire like this one.

Kebble did not die after the first shots were fired. Using eye-witness reports and my knowledge of anatomy and physiology, as well as the forensic detail regarding the shots, I could reconstruct the last minutes of Kebble's life. He left home and drove down a deserted road. He stopped the car in the dip of the road and was shot whilst stationary, probably with six shots. The theory at the time was that he was hijacked. Kebble drove the short way up a hill and around a slight bend (about 400 metres) after having been shot. His car then left the road and gently rammed its nose into the balustrade where the bridge crosses the M1 motorway. There was very little damage to the front of his vehicle and to the railing into which the car had bumped.

A bullet that slams into your spinal column will generally result in immediate flaccid paralysis. This means that Kebble would not have been able to drive or steer the car after the shot into his neck was fired, as all the nerves that controlled his arm and leg muscles would have been paralysed by the force of the bullet hitting the spinal column. So this shot couldn't have been one of the first shots fired in the dip of the road: it must have been the final shot. A dying Kebble had driven up the hill and someone had followed him there, where he had finished him off – a kind of coup de grâce.

As I stood at the scene of the shooting, I did what any competent investigator should do – I looked around me. I noticed a whole row of houses some 200 to 300 metres away, so I walked up the road and started knocking on doors. At the second house, someone had seen the shooting. I inquired if anyone had taken a statement from them, and they said no.

On the evening of Kebble's death, the domestic worker who worked at this house had been standing talking outside in the garden and had seen a big car drive slowly down the hill. This was unusual, as Kebble was known to be a man who had only two driving speeds: 'flat out' and 'stop'. She saw the car rolling down the hill and come to a stop before she heard a succession of shots. Helpfully, she described the shots as 'bang, bang, bang', which told me that the weapon was cycling – firing one shot after another – as opposed to 'bang, reload, bang, reload'. As a result of this evidence, I knew that the weapon was automatic and cycling properly. This narrowed down the field of who could have committed the shooting: it would have been someone in the security industry or someone with a guarding or anti-hijacking interest. The eyewitness saw nothing further. She ran inside the moment the shots were fired, fearing for her life. I was starting to put some of the pieces together.

How was it that Clinton Nassif had instructed the police to release the car even before the forensic team had had a chance to look at it? Nassif was part of the Kebble inner circle, and also had connections to Glen Agliotti. A rank-and-file police officer would never have authorised the release of the car, as it would have been a career-limiting move. I felt that someone in a very senior position of authority must have given the go-ahead for the car to be released. I put a spanner in the works and started asking questions, which led to a renewed effort to have the car released from Danmar Autobody, where it had still not been cleaned.

Suddenly, the police were non-cooperative and Leonie Ras stopped talking to me. The investigating officer, Charles Johnson, also clammed up on me. I was told that I was not allowed to examine the car and that I should leave the investigation.

I decided to pay a visit to the Kebble household, situated in Illovo, where I met with Kebble's butler, Andrew Minnaar. He gave me a rundown of the events that had taken place in the hours prior to Kebble's death.

At about 7 p.m., Kebble had met with a man called Dominic Ntsele, a spin doctor and Washington-trained lobbyist. Kebble had told Minnaar that he was planning to go out for dinner with a man called Sello Rasethaba, chief executive of Matodzi Resources Limited, Kebble's BEE 'flagship'. He also told Minnaar that he had a letter for Pahad – it could have been either Essop Pahad or his brother – and that Ntsele was in possession of this letter. Although he had said that he was going out for dinner, Kebble asked Minnaar to prepare a meal for him, which he and Ntsele ate around 7.40 p.m. By 8.15 p.m., the dinner was finished. Kebble called Minnaar over and asked him for an envelope, saying that he was going to deliver the letter to Rasethaba, who would give it to Pahad. Minnaar provided him with an envelope and Ntsele departed about ten minutes later. Kebble left while Minnaar tidied up the dinner dishes. When he had finished, Minnaar left for the evening.

There are three interesting aspects to Kebble's behaviour that night. Firstly, Kebble never went anywhere without a jacket, yet that night he left without wearing or carrying one. Secondly, Minnaar noticed that Kebble had been preoccupied and had seemed agitated the whole evening. Thirdly, whenever Kebble went to visit someone, he was known always to take a good bottle of wine or Scotch with him. That evening he left with nothing.

What is the significance of these minute details? Cases are about little things; about the detail. People are creatures of habit, and everyone has their routine. When these habits are broken or the routine changes, there is a reason for it – and I want to know why. That evening, Kebble was doing things differently: he said he was going out for dinner, then changed his mind; he went out without a jacket; he was agitated; he left without a gift for his host; he drove slowly; and he stopped in a dark and dangerous place. As Minnaar had driven out the gate on his way home, about 100 metres down the road he had seen Kebble just sitting in his car, parked at the side of the road. Minnaar didn't stop to ask questions – he did not want to pry – instead, he went on his way. That was the last time Andrew Minnaar saw Brett Kebble. From there, Kebble proceeded to his assignation with death, a mere two or three kilometres away.

A couple of days into the investigation, there were suggestions that Kebble's death had been the result of a hijacking. Yet things didn't add up. Why would someone open their window for a hijacker, and how would that explain his drastic changes in routine and behaviour?

I then received a phone call from Alfred Koch, a forensic investigator for Liberty Life. He wanted to know if I was aware of the fact that Kebble had taken out two large life-cover policies a few months prior to his death, well within the suicide waiver period on all life insurance policies. This was the first I had heard of this. Koch wanted to know if anything seemed suspicious to me, but since I had not yet seen the post-mortem results, things appeared normal at that point. Warning lights were starting to flicker in my mind, however, and the events of the next few days brought the matter into focus.

I received a call from forensic accountant Danny Sabbagh, who asked me if I knew that a photograph of Kebble being baptised had been taken shortly before all of this happened (see photo). I discovered that Kebble had found the Lord in Peter George's swimming pool a short while before his death.

Kebble's business dealings had often been quite unorthodox, even dubious. I contacted Peter Skeat, a very successful mining engineer who had sold Kebble some shares in a coal-mining venture, for which Kebble never paid. There was a very large sum of money involved – hundreds of millions of rands – and Skeat took Kebble to court. Kebble lost on the first round. The case went to the Supreme Court of Appeal, and Kebble lost on the second round. It then ended up in court again. In the run-up to the court date, Kebble told Skeat to back off or he would make Skeat's life a misery.

Skeat ignored the threat and told Kebble he would see him in court. Peter Skeat returned from an overseas business trip shortly afterwards, and found a warrant for his arrest as he landed back on South African soil. He was arrested and locked up, despite the fact that no charge was brought against him. He was released shortly afterwards. Kebble must have arranged, possibly through Agliotti and Jackie Selebi, for Skeat to be 'roughed up' a bit so that he would be more amenable to doing business. But even more fascinating is that, shortly before his death, Kebble had called Skeat to make amends and seek forgiveness.

The picture suddenly started to slip into focus: Kebble had been taking out insurance policies – both for the here and for the here-after. For the here, he took out two insurance policies, with his wife appointed as beneficiary. The joint proceeds of the policies were R30 million. For the hereafter, Kebble's policy took the form of a baptism and attempts at making peace in his life on earth for the day when he had to answer for it.

I called Alfred Koch, asking him to disregard my comments to him previously, as I now believed Kebble's death to have been an assisted suicide. All the hallmarks were there: Kebble knew people who could easily access the type of weapon that had been used, Clinton Nassif was involved, Selebi, perhaps, too – all facts pointing to a possible assisted suicide.

I then received a call from former High Court prosecutor Piet-man Mostert, who had insight into the state matters. He asked me if I knew that there had been a warrant issued for Kebble's arrest shortly before his death. I hadn't known this. All the pieces now slotted into place: Kebble had run into debt problems of many billions of rands. He had been disempowered, in that he no longer had any influence in Durban Roodepoort Deep and the various other mining operations in which he had been involved – part of the rescue package of Investec to these businesses was conditional upon Kebble's complete removal from any position of power.

So he was isolated, finding himself in a position where he had no money and few friends. I found out that he had been trying to sell some of his properties, but the market was down and times were tough. It was obvious: if he was arrested, the whole pack of cards that was the Kebble empire would fall apart. There was no more room to manoeuvre – it is very difficult to act from a jail cell, or even to find an attorney to represent you if you do not have a substantial amount of money to offer. It would have been a high-profile case, and no attorney would have represented him without cash upfront. Suddenly all the attorneys who had surrounded Kebble when he had money would be nowhere to be found.

If Kebble went down, he would leave nothing but disgrace and poverty for his family. He had a wife and children to consider, for whom he needed to provide financially. Any money that came in would go into his estate, and his creditors would get first pickings. The only way to avoid this was to ensure that money was paid directly to his wife, bypassing the estate and creditors. In order for this to happen, she had to be listed as the beneficiary on his insurance policies. In the lead-up to his death, Kebble seems to have had good intentions and demonstrated some family values.

It astounded me that, despite my manifest warnings, Liberty Life and Discovery Life paid out the claims. If the case had concerned an ordinary person, they would most certainly have waited for the inquest. They would also not have paid if there was a hint of suicide in the air.

I went to see Judge Heath and his son, Marius, who listened intently to what I had to say about Kebble's death. I told them that Clinton Nassif was right in the middle of this mess, and that the death was probably an assisted suicide; I didn't think it was a hijacking, I said to them. I believed that higher authority was involved. Interestingly, Judge Heath just raised his eyebrows.

I finished my report and then received a call from Marius Heath, who informed me that Jackie Selebi wanted Judge Heath and me off the case. I agreed, saying that I would submit my report, but that I wanted my account settled first – until then, the report stayed with me. It was about a month later, in early December 2005, when Willem Heath called me, wanting to meet. We met, and he told me that I could laugh off any chance of being paid for my work.

I never quite understood what Judge Heath's involvement was in this whole matter. It later emerged that he, who worked for the Kebbles, was deeply involved in the Kebble–Agliotti–Selebi saga.

Since I hadn't been paid for my work, I decided to talk about it – there was no confidentiality clause binding me – and I was interviewed extensively. A reporter for e.tv, in editing, called me a mad conspiracy theorist. I was a little taken aback by this, to put it mildly.

I contacted Liberty Life to see if they were interested in my report and any further investigation. They jumped at the opportunity, and I continued investigating on the insurer's behalf. I obtained access to the affidavit submitted by Agliotti, in which he stated that Kebble's death had been an assisted suicide. A man by the name of Mikey Schultz, as well as other characters, were named as having been involved in the plan. This affidavit confirmed exactly what I had said in my television interviews a year earlier – the e.tv producer had to eat his words.[*]

The story of Brett Kebble's death leaves many unanswered questions. What was Willem Heath's role exactly? In what way was Agliotti connected? Why was the involvement of these men not clarified? Why did Agliotti phone Selebi on the night of Kebble's death? Was Selebi involved in the decision to release the car to Nassif?

Brett Kebble's death was clearly his last great financial scam. His business deals were all smoke and mirrors: just about every law firm in Johannesburg was involved in his shady deals in one way

---

[*]　See Appendix H for the 2010 revelations regarding Mickey Schultz.

or another, yet none of them saw through the fraud and facade. And then Brett Kebble died just as he had lived – in a cloud of smoke and mirrors.

|||||||||||||||||||||||||||||||||||||||||||||||||||||||||||||||||||||

CHAPTER 22

THE DYNAMIC INVESTMENT THAT SHRANK

'[P]rediction of the unknown and unknowable is
a cherished and often well-rewarded occupation.'

– JOHN KENNETH GALBRAITH,
Canadian-American economist and author

What is a retired couple to do when they invest their life savings, only to find a few years later that some of their money has 'disappeared'? If these funds are their sole source of income, it can cause more than a mild panic, particularly if there are no straight answers forthcoming from the company with which they invested. This was the problem facing Mr and Mrs Wentzel.

I have found myself in later life being more active in assisting people with claim settlements as opposed to investigating on behalf of insurance companies. Big business, and insurance companies in particular, spew forth wonderful advertising messages, but seem so reticent in delivering on these promises when push comes to shove.

The Wentzels were schoolteachers who had retired to Cape Agulhas. When they retired, they had invested their money with Sanlam, who had offered to guarantee their capital and pay them a reasonable income every month. They were happy with this arrangement, and after five years they had received their capital back. They wanted to reinvest with Sanlam, but were told that the same product was no longer available, as market conditions had changed.

The Wentzels shopped around and met a broker, Leon Coetzee, who represented Dynamic Wealth, an offshoot of a company that used to be called De Witt Morgan. A few years earlier, Morgan, the senior partner, had made the strange decision to invest in maize futures, which had lost the Johannesburg City Council R1.8 billion of their pension fund.

Coetzee convinced the Wentzels to invest with Dynamic Wealth. He arrived at their home with Johan Strydom, one of the directors of the company, and they promised the Wentzels an income of R3 500 per month, saying that their capital of R450 000 would be preserved. They were sold a policy from the Dublin-based Scottish Mutual International, a company not registered as a life insurer in South Africa, so the Wentzels had no protection under the Long-Term Insurance Act. This product should not, therefore, have been marketed in South Africa in the first place.

All went well, until the Wentzels started receiving a fairly irregular and slightly lower monthly income of R3 100. They were not too perturbed, however, as they felt safe in the knowledge that their capital would be preserved.

Then, in 2008, a shock came: R210 000 of their capital was paid back to them at the end of the term – less than half of what they had invested. They tried in vain to get some kind of explanation from Dynamic Wealth, but could not get hold of anyone from the company. Messages were not returned, and the Wentzels' mood changed from disappointment to anger. In desperation, they approached me to see if I could help them.

I called Dynamic Wealth and was initially referred to their compliance officer, Willem Lecante. He skilfully evaded my questions and openly taunted me, questioning my involvement in the matter, as I would not be paid for the work. I then received a letter stating that I could talk to the company's attorneys. I informed them that I do not deal with attorneys, and that I would talk to them in another way.

I called Bruce Cameron, editor of *Personal Finance*, and sent him my file to look at. He then wrote to Dynamic Wealth, asking them what they were going to do about this situation. When Lecante unpleasantly tried to evade Cameron's queries, as he'd done to me, he received an even stronger reaction. At long last there was some action, and two of the company's directors came to see me. They asked me what I'd like them to do.

I replied that I wanted to speak to Strydom, the broker. I received a visit from Strydom, who told me how anxious the Wentzels had been to invest with them and how hungry they had been for risk. He had warned them, he said, of the potential risks involved in investing offshore.

It was clear that we were not going to make headway on our own, so we agreed to take the matter to arbitration. Since I am not a lawyer, I prepared my documents as well as I could, and simply stated the facts and the particulars of our claim. We exchanged papers with the other side, and I received a multipage document from them, filled with legal jargon.

As prepared as we could be, the Wentzels and I flew up to Pretoria the day before the arbitration was due to start. It was comforting to know that the retired Judge President of what was the Transvaal, Judge Frikkie Eloff, a man of high standards and integrity, was to preside over the matter.

The next morning, as we were waiting for Judge Eloff to arrive, the advocate representing Dynamic Wealth came to introduce herself. Observing this, Mrs Wentzel anxiously called me aside to check whether they were really using an advocate to defend themselves in this matter. I told her that they were. She then asked me if I had any legal qualifications, and I had to tell her that I didn't. She looked me straight in the eye and said, '*O, fok!*'

As the plaintiff, we started the proceedings. I was in full swing, outlining the case as well as I could, when Judge Eloff stopped me mid-sentence. 'Doctor, have you read this contract?' he asked.

'Yes, I have, my lord,' I replied.

'Have you understood this contract?'

'I think I have,' I said.

'Proceed.'

We all breathed a collective sigh of relief.

I was a little rattled by all of this, but I continued, and proceeded to call my first witness, Mr Wentzel, asking him if he had signed the contract. When he responded in the affirmative, I asked him if he had read the contract. He replied that he had not. Why not, I asked, to which he replied that it was because he had listened to the man who came to see him, and pointed to Johan Strydom. 'We trusted him,' Wentzel added.

The advocate then had her chance at cross-examination, and she grilled Wentzel, telling him that ignorance of the law is no excuse and referring to specific clauses in the contract, amidst all kinds of other legal jargon. Wentzel was quite overwhelmed by this, and left the witness box visibly shaken.

I then questioned Mrs Wentzel, and she was a little more forceful. She told the court that she and her husband could never get hold of the company to find out where their money had gone. She spiced up the proceedings a little by saying that she had left a few messages with explosive expletives on voicemail out of sheer frustration because no one ever returned their calls!

These were ordinary people who wanted straight answers. Eventually we found out where their monthly income was coming from: it was being taken out of their capital, which is why the capital had reduced to such an extent.

It was then the advocate's turn to present her case. As she was about to start her argument, Eloff interrupted, asking her if she was planning to call a witness. She was – Johan Strydom. The broker, Coetzee, had left the company to become a pastor. It transpired that he was being pursued by the Receiver of Revenue and had some judgments against him, which tells a story in itself.

As Strydom was testifying, it became apparent that Judge Eloff was rather taken with him – he started chatting to Strydom about financial matters. Strydom came across very well in his testimony, but said something very interesting – that he could remember more or less what he had told the Wentzels about the risk. I bided my time.

In cross-examination, I asked Strydom if he considered himself a professional. 'Yes,' he replied. I went on further, asking if that meant that all the detail in the contract and pleadings was accurate and thoroughly checked. He agreed with this, and said that he had read the contract and the pleading document. Seeing as this was a brokered deal, I said, there would be no vicarious liability to the company, and that our remedy, if any, must be sought from the broker. Strydom concurred. In theory, I knew that we had little recourse because Coetzee was nowhere to be found.

I then referred Strydom to page three of the contract, asking him to tell the court whose name was written down as the broker. There was dead silence. I knew whose name had been noted as the broker, of course – Johan Strydom. There was no need even to mention Coetzee's name in the arbitration. The whole basis on which Dynamic Wealth's case rested was cut away with that simple question. They had been so confident that they had not even read their own contract properly.

I referred back to the discussion that had taken place in my office in Cape Town previously, and asked him if he could recall exactly what he had said to me on that occasion. At the time, he had said that he could remember the exact words he had used when he spoke to the Wentzels five years earlier. I asked if he could remember that I had questioned his infallible memory of a discussion that had taken place five years previously, even though he dealt with many of these contracts. He had stood by this fact at our meeting in Cape Town. Now he was telling the court that he could remember *more or less* what he had told the Wentzels. I wanted to know from him on which occasion it was that he was lying – then or now. It was downhill from there.

The advocate was looking a little green around the gills, and Judge Eloff suggested that the parties spend more time preparing closing arguments. I objected, saying that my clients had no more money to travel back to Pretoria again, and that we should proceed. So we did.

I launched into my closing argument, throwing in a few legal terms. Judge Eloff stopped me again, when I was in mid-flow. 'Doctor,' he said, 'what is your case?'

'What do you mean?' I asked him, my heart skipping a beat.

'Are you coming to me in contract or in delict?' he wanted to know.

Slightly flustered, I replied, 'Neither, my lord; it's a sort of mixture.'

He raised an eyebrow at me, and I rattled on. 'It's mainly delict, and about the way in which these people were lied to. It's also about equity, and we are arguing this matter in terms of the SAFEX Rules, as this allows your lordship a wide scope in terms of equity.'

'Well, yes, that is so,' he replied, hauling out the SAFEX book, in which he already had some pages flagged. After reading from some of the pages, Judge Eloff announced that he would not give his judgment that day.

The Wentzels were unhappy, as they wanted an answer, having waited so long. I pointed out to them that if Judge Eloff had wanted to rule against them, he would have done so immediately. The fact that he wanted time to think about his ruling was a positive sign.

A week later, on 25 April 2008, the judgment was faxed through to my office. Judge Eloff had blown the delictual basis of my argument right out of the water, but he found for the Wentzels in the contract. The verbal contract had overridden the written contract. Irrespective of what the Wentzels had signed, the verbal discussion that they had had with Strydom took preference and was binding. This meant that there was no contributory negligence on their part. The Wentzels were to be paid back R244 557.71, plus interest at 15.5 per cent per annum, and all costs were to be paid by the defendant, Dynamic Wealth.

Judge Eloff is a man of great fairness, with the highest degree of integrity, and this case serves as a warning to investment companies.

Interestingly, because this was a legal issue and I was acting as an imitation lawyer, I could not charge a fee for my services. For me, the case had been great fun, and I learnt something new. Lawyers often get so wrapped up in their own jargon that they forget they are dealing with real people with straightforward needs. And everything has a simple answer at the end of the day if you cut through the clutter.

In yet another example of the arrogance of big business, I challenged Sanlam in the case of Leonard Louw, an unfortunate client who found that his investment had mysteriously 'shrunk'.

When Louw, a mining engineer, left his employer in 2001, he invested his pension payout – R613 000 – with Sanlam. He was advised by his broker, Eugene van Eeden, to invest 80 per cent in gilt funds and the balance in a Sanlam Money Market account.

Initially, Louw was very happy with the progress of his investment. He received regular updates from Van Eeden, and at one point his investment had apparently grown to R793 000.

Some time later, Louw and his wife divorced. Finding that he owed her half of his pension payout, in April 2003 he notified Sanlam to make the payment to his ex-wife, expecting the sum to be around R400 000.

The letter that he received came as a huge blow: Louw's invest-ment was now worth only R306 711, roughly half of what he had originally invested. He tried in vain to obtain explanations from Sanlam, but felt as if he were running into a stone wall. The company's call centres were not able to give him any explanation and nobody returned his calls. His wife became suspicious of him, so he approached me to ask me to investigate.

I called Sanlam and eventually managed to get through to one of the senior members of the investment fund in question. 'Look,' I said to her, 'you've got twenty-four hours to find me somebody who carries the can and is answerable to the public on this par-ticular issue.'

I subsequently received a phone call from a Mr de Villiers. 'Does the buck stop with you?' I asked him.

'Ja,' he said, 'it stops with me. In fact, it lives on my desk!'

I wrote a letter to Sanlam on behalf of Louw, in which I asked some rather cheeky questions. The letter appeared in *Noseweek* magazine in September 2004, in an article ironically titled 'Happily Ever After'.

> *How is it that a company of your size and reputed expertise, of which I am constantly reminded in the media, can manage to lose half this client's money in so short a time?... Who advised the client to invest his money in this way?... Why is it that your company, despite the disastrous advice given to this client, still debits the man with a fee? I have come across some shameful acts, but this one must surely take the cake.*

I received a letter back from Sanlam reprimanding me for the tone of my letter, but also informing me that Louw's investment had been switched four times within a month in mid-2002. This, they wrote, probably explained the sad state of affairs, particularly because of the 'switch fee' and broker's commission, which would have been deducted on each occasion. According to them, Louw had authorised these switches. They enclosed copies of each of the signed mandates.

I examined these documents, and it soon became apparent that they were all forged: all the signatures were identical – they were merely photocopies of each other. So I wrote another cheeky letter to Mr de Villiers, in which I alleged that the signed mandates were all forgeries and that they clearly were not signed by my client.

This naturally created a small panic within Sanlam, and they rushed off to find another handwriting expert, hoping to prove me wrong. Their expert was a retired brigadier from the police force's handwriting division. As I expected, he reached exactly the same conclusion that I had reached. The principles of forensic science are rigorous and unbending: again they proved that, by challenging information and cutting through the confusion, the truth can be ascertained.

Mr Louw was a happy man – Sanlam injected R343 961 into his investment, placing him in the same position in which he would have been had these fraudulent switches not taken place.

Also interesting was that I found out during my investigation that the broker who had sold Louw the investment, Van Eeden, had been arrested for fraud at a South African airport in April 2003 while trying to flee the country with his family. Sanlam did not disclose this to me when I called them the first time.

It is the dirty dealings in the above cases that I find so interesting. Certain companies happily seem to gamble with people's money, dressing their business up with fancy advertisements, smartly clothed employees and, often, false promises. One needs reminding of what Ambrose Bierce, a famous American columnist, wrote about business: 'The gambling known as business looks with austere disfavour upon the business known as gambling.' You have to be careful when dealing with these big companies, especially when it comes to your money. They are quick to take your savings but very slow to rectify any damage they do, even if it loses you money. My approach does not make me a favourite among these large companies – but then again, you can't make friends with everybody in the world.

|||||||||||||||||||||||||||||||||||||||||||||||||||||||||||||

CHAPTER 23
TOO GOOD TO BE TRUE

*'The time will therefore come when
the sun will shine only on free men who
know no other master but their reason.'*

– MARQUIS DE CONDORCET,
French philosopher, mathematician and political scientist

There are times when the facts seem to be too obvious. It is easy
to jump to conclusions based on incorrect data or the sway of a
specific context. On occasion, people's lives hang in the balance,
thus the correct investigation and interpretation of facts is impera-
tive. One such case in which I was involved was the matter of the
insecticide and the sangoma.

In the late 1990s I was enlisted by Legal Aid, which was acting
on behalf of a sangoma who lived in the then Western Transvaal.
The sangoma was about to be found guilty of murder, and, to the
attorney's credit, he felt that something might be amiss.

An elderly man had been ill and went to consult a doctor. He was
diagnosed with pneumonia and prescribed tetracycline, a broad-
spectrum antibiotic, which he duly took. Not feeling any better, he
decided to consult the local sangoma, who mixed him a potion that,
she said, would heal him. On his way out, the man said that he was

thirsty and asked the sangoma for something to drink. She filled an empty two-litre Coca-Cola bottle with water and gave it to him, and he drank it. The old man died later that afternoon.

His family was very distressed. They contacted the police, who took possession of the Coke bottle for analysis. At the post-mortem, they found minute quantities of organophosphate insecticide both in the Coke bottle and in the body. The sangoma was charged with murder. By the time I was called in, the state and defence had already closed their cases and were awaiting judgment and sentencing.

I looked at the facts and realised that the organophosphates could never have been the cause of death. We knew that in order to be lethal, a gram of that particular organophosphate would have to be consumed, and also that the chemical has a foul smell. If the old man had consumed a whole gram, he definitely would have noticed the odour. Calculating the amount of the substance found in his body, we realised that it was at least 5 000 times less than what would have been needed to kill him. We went to court just as sentence was about to be passed.

The magistrate was grumpy, as he wanted the case closed. The sangoma's attorney argued the matter, however, and persuaded the magistrate to reopen the case. After I'd presented my evidence, the prosecutor stood up to cross-examine me. As luck would have it, both the prosecutor and the magistrate were keen gardeners, so as soon as I mentioned the trade name of the organophosphate, they recognised it, and were aware of the foul smell that it emits. They knew that one could never make a man drink enough of it to kill him. The case turned around by 180 degrees, and the sangoma walked out a free woman.

The truth was that the old man had died of pneumonia, which can kill old and young people very quickly if not properly treated. He had had fluid in his lungs, which is symptomatic of organophosphates, but also of pneumonia. During the post-mortem, the state had jumped to a conclusion without examining any further.

Ironically, one of the problems with modern forensic science is that the equipment is so sensitive that it can detect traces of elements that could not possibly have a physiological affect, yet they are nevertheless present.

This is often a problem in the horse-racing industry, where, every now and then, a horse tests positive for a drug that could have been obtained naturally. Stinkblaar (*Datura stramonium*), for example, is a big problem, as it contains scopolamine, an alkaloid drug. It is sometimes found in animal feed. If a horse inadvertently eats a few leaves, the drug can be detected in the horse's system and the owner will be charged.

Another problem can occur in athletics, where all kinds of drugs can be detected in quantities far below their ability to affect sporting performance. If you eat a roll with poppy seeds sprinkled on top, for instance, the instruments will detect the opiates in these seeds despite the fact that they cannot affect you in any way. Because of the sensitivity of today's equipment, the *interpretation* of results is critical.

The importance of the accurate interpretation of test results was illustrated in another case on which I worked, in Willowmore, in 1998. A farmer's house had burnt down, and the attorney representing the farmer called me in. Finding my fee to be too high, he sourced another forensic scientist to work on the matter. The scientist concluded that it was a case of arson and switched sides to work for the insurance company.

The farmer then employed me, and with a new legal team, we sued the insurance company in an effort to get them to pay the claim. I examined the facts and concluded that the problem was that the analyst working for the insurance company had seen a run mark outside the window. Analysis showed the substance to contain toluene, which is present in petrol. Based on this, he came to the conclusion that the farmer had doused the house with petrol and set it alight.

Petrol, however, contains toluene as well as many other substances. The sample contained *only* toluene. What the analyst hadn't realised was that there were a number of foam mattresses in the house, and that when these burnt, toluene was produced. The reason for this is that the mattresses were made of polyurethane, which is a combination of toluene and isocyanurate, among other things. When the mattresses burnt, they produced toluene in a thick, gooey consistency. This is what had run out of the windows.

In this case, the full impact of the chemistry results and fire patterns were not taken into account, and quick – incorrect – conclusions were reached. The use of analytical tools is wonderful, but they must be used with care when interpreting results. If the forensic scientist fails to do so, he or she creates scope for glaring errors.

Many years ago, I worked on a case involving Mandrax, in which the analysis of the samples was just too good to be true – all seven samples were identical. I have conducted many analyses over the years, so experience taught me to question the result – most people would simply have accepted it. It turned out that the analyst had run the laboratory test seven times on the same sample instead of testing seven different samples (see graphs).

Sometimes, even the most innocent of comments can lead to people reaching the wrong conclusions. In 1997, I worked on a pyroforensics case near Kimberley. One night, the owner of a hotel woke up to flames and smoke – his hotel was ablaze. He called the fire brigade, and they excitedly rushed to the scene – they were operating on a voluntary basis and were thrilled to have a real-life fire to put out.

At some point, for reasons unknown, the owner of the hotel went to the head of the fire brigade and said, 'Listen, chaps, here's R1 000 each, now bugger off home.' The head of the fire brigade was offended that he should be asked to give up the one good opportunity of putting out a fire. Instead of taking the R1 000, he refused it and reported the incident to the insurance company, who promptly repudiated the hotel owner's claim.

My involvement came some two years later, when I acted on behalf of the hotel owner. An analytical chemist with very limited expertise in forensic chemistry had been called in to investigate the fire. On analysis, he had found traces of lead in the samples he had scratched out of the flooring, off the walls and from underneath the skirting boards. He drew the conclusion that, since petrol contains lead, the presence of lead in the sample meant that petrol must have been used to start the fire. He failed to understand that the lead in petrol is a very specific, organic kind of lead: it is either tetraethyl or tetramethyl lead rather than plain lead. Petrol was only one of the possibilities that would give rise to the presence of lead in the debris of this particular fire.

I was briefed to appear as a witness for the plaintiff, but this was not ultimately necessary, as counsel cross-examined the expert to such an extent that he conceded the point that there were twenty or thirty different sources to which the lead found in the debris could be attributed – for instance pewter, solder, some printing inks or even paint, which, in the old days, contained an oxide of lead. The expert failed to demonstrate that the lead he had identified was tetraethyl or tetramethyl lead, which meant that he could not say whether or not the lead in the fire had come from petrol. His conclusion, therefore, was erroneous.

Just before counsel posed the last question to the witness, court proceedings closed for the day. The next morning, as we started in court at nine o'clock, counsel posed the final question to the witness: 'Sir, of the thirteen conclusions that you drew yesterday in your expert summary, are there any to which you wish to adhere?'

'No,' replied the expert. (Counsel in this matter was Henri Viljoen, who will appear later in this book.)

The insurance claim was paid out and the owner of the hotel left court without a blemish on his character.

Whether it is a case of life or death, or something less dramatic, it is vital to make sure that your results are seen in the right context. Jumping to easy conclusions can prevent you from getting as close to the truth as possible and can seriously pervert the course of justice.

Justice was well served in a case on which I worked a few years ago, in which I acted as an assessor. In January 2003, a train collision occurred between the Muldersvlei and Kraaifontein train stations in the Western Cape, resulting in the death of ten commuters. The train driver, Mervyn Matthee, was charged with culpable homicide. It was a frightening accident: it was alleged that Matthee had been negligent, as he had not stopped at three red-light signals between the two stations. The brakes on the train had been in perfect working order.

The magistrate wanted someone to assist her with the technical aspects of the case, and I was approached to fill that role.

Matthee was a man in his sixties whose wife had died from cancer some eighteen months previously. He had never really recovered from her death, and was having regressions and blackouts. It transpired at the trial that he was depressed and had sought help from his employer, but they had offered little sympathy or support. In fact, their approach to him had been uncaring and callous.

It was a fact that Matthee had driven the train and caused the accident. I wanted to know more about his state of mind, however, so I posed a number of questions relating to this from the bench. The state brought in a psychiatrist, and I asked him whether it was possible that Matthee could have serious disassociative conditions resulting from the loss of his wife – in other words, times when he could be cognitively disassociated from the reality around him. The psychiatrist replied in the affirmative, saying that this was common. I also wanted to find out if it was possible for Matthee to be unaware of this condition. According to the psychiatrist, the train driver could have been completely oblivious to it.

In order to commit a crime, a person must have been negligent or must have *mens rea* – the guilty mind, or the knowledge of wrongdoing that constitutes part of a crime. If you are unaware of your state of mind and the consequent danger in operating machinery, you cannot be held liable. The state was not happy with this line of questioning, and a second psychiatrist, who was even easier to question, was brought in.

Matthee was acquitted largely because the case was founded in sand. He was not a well person, and justice was served.

Since the answers are not always obvious or easy to establish in my line of work, an innovative approach is sometimes needed. This was key in a case I handled in 2010, when a badly burnt-out car and body were found. An insurance claim of around R20 million was at stake, and I was called in to determine whether the body belonged to the person whose life was insured.

The fire had been so intense that the body was burnt beyond recognition. A petrol fire will burn at just under 1 000 °C and will leave only ashes in its wake. When the paramedics had tried to remove the body from the car, it had crumbled to dust. The pathologist could estimate only that it was a male body, based on the shape of the pelvis. There was no further way of identifying the body, which was of course vital if the insurers were going to pay out the life insurance.

I took the car to a concrete surface and started sifting through the remaining ashes, using a fine sieve similar to a kitchen sieve to look for clues. After four days of sifting, I found something resembling an amalgam filling. I placed it under an electron microscope, where I identified that the chief elements of this item were silver and mercury – also the main elements of amalgam. In this way, I confirmed that it was indeed an amalgam filling.

By finding the amalgam, I knew that the body belonged to someone who could afford restorative dentistry. Occasionally insurance companies find themselves in situations where an unidentifiable body is found. In such cases, these bodies have been planted deliberately; they are unclaimed bodies – John Does – used fraudulently to obtain insurance payouts. Basic dentistry involves removing rather than restoring teeth, and unclaimed bodies seldom have restorative dentistry.

The next step was to approach the insured man's dentist and to examine the man's dental records and any available X-rays. By comparing the amalgam to dental X-rays belonging to the insured man, I could show that the body did, in fact, belong to him. The petrol fire had been hot enough to destroy a human body, but not to destroy amalgam, which melts at a much higher temperature of around 1 500 °C.

Patience, innovation and some menial work paid off in this case. Looking beyond the obvious, I was able to do what was necessary to put together the jigsaw pieces left behind by nature.

|||||||||||||||||||||||||||||||||||||||||||||||||||||||||||||||||||

CHAPTER 24
CREATIVITY KNOWS NO BOUNDS

'Different people of different times and places have fundamentally different realities.'

– GIAMBATTISTA VICO,

Italian philosopher, rhetorician and jurist

It has never ceased to amaze me how people attempt to fool the system; their levels of creativity are sometimes impressive. The lure of money, whether through an insurance claim or through some form of 'compensation', is a strong driving force in many people's language.

Several years ago, a shopkeeper in Holmdene in the Eastern Transvaal thought that a threatening letter, coupled with a devastating fire that destroyed his business premises, would guarantee him sympathy and some extra cash. I was called in to investigate the fire on behalf of the insurance company.

Arriving at the remains of the building, the very agitated owner told me that his business had burnt down and that it was dreadful. After some careful investigation, I realised that the place had clearly been deliberately torched. I asked the fellow, 'Can you think of anybody who might have wanted to do this to you?'

His response was immediate: 'Yes,' he said, 'it was the UDF.' I asked him how he knew this, and he replied, 'Well, they sent me a threatening letter.'

'Oh,' I said. 'What did they say in the threatening letter?' He still had the letter, which he produced for me to scrutinise. The spelling and grammar were atrocious. The letter started out with 'Dear Kullie' and went on in graphic terms to describe what they were going to do to him, including burning down his business (see Appendix I). It appeared to have been written by someone almost illiterate.

I sat him down and dictated a statement for him to write, interspersing various words that had been misspelt in the letter. It was a no-brainer: in the same handwriting as that which appeared in the letter, he misspelt the words in exactly the same way. Needless to say, his claim was not paid.

Claimants who exaggerate the extent of their loss are also not uncommon. In the late 1990s, a farmer in Vereeniging, near Johannesburg, suffered a great loss of teff – a type of grass for feeding cattle – when the building in which it was stored burnt down. I was called in by IGI Insurance, an insurance company that later went bankrupt, to investigate.

I made the trip to the farm and was intrigued by the fact that there was very little residual ash left, meaning that there had to have been far less teff than the many hundreds of tons for which the farmer was claiming. 'How much teff was here originally?' I asked him. In response, he gave me a detailed description of the vast amount of teff that had been lost.

After doing my homework, I asked why other farmers could get a maximum growth of three to three and a half tons of teff per hectare, while he was getting six to seven tons per hectare. Smiling, the farmer said to me, 'Well, you see, the reason is that I irrigate day and night. I'm on a big dolomitic dome; there is a vast amount of water underground here and we've got big pumps. The secret to this is irrigation!'

I asked to see his electricity bills so that I could check that he had, in fact, been running these pumps. 'Well,' the farmer said, 'unfortunately I had a farmhouse fire a year and a half ago and all my records were burnt.'

'Oh, okay,' I replied. 'That's not a problem. Take me down to the poles that supply the electricity. You've got a transformer up the pole and that transformer has a number. I can go to Eskom with that number and they'll give me your bills.' I wanted to read the power ratings from the pumps so that I could work out how much electricity the farmer had used and for how long the pumps had been running.

He was a bit put out by this and said that he could not take me to the poles then because he had to go to church. I returned to Johannesburg, planning to go back to the farm the next day to have a look at the electricity poles. Before I could return, however, the farmer phoned the insurance company and told them that he was unhappy about my presence on his farm. His words were, '*Jy kry daai fokken Dokter Quincy van my plaas af!*' Quincy was a popular TV programme at the time that revolved around a medical examiner who single-handedly solved gruesome murders and other forensic cases, so I took this as an inadvertent compliment!

Based on my calculations of the size of the farmer's crop and the amount of ash that was left, as well as the farmer's fraudulent misrepresentation of the claim, the insurance claim was repudiated successfully. (As an interesting aside, the farmer was charged with fraud of a political nature at around the same time.)

Human frailty is a strange business, and people do strange things. I examined a house in the late 1990s that had allegedly been burgled. On closer inspection, it appeared that the burglars had not broken in, but broken *out*: the window, which had been forced, had clearly been forced from the inside – the bruising of the wood that was visible on the inside could never have been inflicted from the outside.

There had been no need to break out because there had been a key in the door. If anybody had been inside in the first place, they simply would not have had to break out. After some investigating, I managed to get hold of the owner's wife to ask her whether she had any tools. She hauled out what appeared to be the family tool box and gave it to me, and inside I found a fairly substantial screwdriver. I looked at the screwdriver and saw paint that seemed to match the paint of the window on its end. I took the paint from the screwdriver and some paint from the window and could easily show that it was one and the same. In addition, the dimensions of the screwdriver fitted the marks on the bruised wood. The criminal had managed to use and return the tools that belonged to the household in order to escape from the burgled premises. I think not!

Quenching your thirst on a hot summer's day could hold some surprises – or at least that's what Hilton April of the Strand claimed when he allegedly found a mouse in his can of Coca-Cola.

April purchased a 450 ml can of Coke on 31 January 2003, opening it as he was leaving the shop. As he took the first sip, something didn't taste right. After the second sip, he felt a 'slimy tail' on his tongue. On investigation, he saw a mouse inside the can, which he removed with a pair of tweezers.

April then contacted Coca-Cola, claiming that he was ill because of the incident and saying that he wanted financial compensation for future pain and suffering. Coke approached me, as this type of claim is not uncommon.

The mouse was still completely intact and in reasonable shape (see photo). It seemed to have been recently deceased, and there were no signs of decomposition. The manufacture date on the underside of the can showed that it had been left in the factory for six weeks before April had bought it.

I conducted an experiment: I went out and bought six mice and took them to the production line at the factory. After euthanising the mice with chloroform, I took six tins – Sprite and Tab cans, so as not to cause confusion – and inserted a mouse into each one. I then allowed each can to be filled with Coke and had the cans sealed. I marked each one with the production date.

After six weeks had passed, I opened the cans. There was no trace of the mice: they had all completely dissolved. The contents of the cans consisted of a thick, sludgy mess. The reason for this is quite simple: Coke contains phosphoric acid, which had dissolved the mice in their entirety. I was able to prove that there was no way a whole mouse could have ended up in the Coke can at production and been whole a full six weeks later.

Unfortunately for Hilton April, he was charged with fraud and received a five-year suspended sentence. Frequently people try to make a fast buck with a trumped-up story, but science shows up the truth each and every time.

Some of the fire investigations in which I have been involved have demonstrated a quirky side of human nature – one that ensures the protection of their pets at all costs. One such case involved the burning down of a haberdashery shop in Edenvale, Gauteng. Candles had been placed in saucers full of petrol around the shop, so it was quite clear that this had been a deliberate fire. The interesting aspect to the case was that the shop was well known for the parrot that lived on the premises.

On the day before the fire, the owner had taken the parrot to have its nails clipped. He arrived at the veterinary surgeon's rooms, and the vet offered to do the job immediately. 'No, no, I can't take him back with me now,' the owner said. 'Please make certain that I can come back tomorrow and pick him up. Will you keep him overnight?' That was the very night that the fire took place and the property burnt to the ground! Needless to say, the outcome of the case was not in favour of the shop owner.

A second, similar case involved a very 'motivated' parrot. A farmer's house in the then Eastern Free State had been completely destroyed in a blaze. During my investigation, I discovered that the parrot that normally lived in the living room in the house had been found safe and sound the next morning on the front lawn. I remember saying to the farmer, 'Did you lock up?'

'Yes,' he replied.

'And what happened about the parrot? Was the parrot left where it was normally left?'

'Yes,' he said. 'I put the sheet over the parrot cage in the normal way, and I put the parrot to bed.'

'And that was in the front lounge?'

'Yes,' he nodded.

'Well,' I asked, 'can you explain to me how the parrot got out onto the front lawn and escaped the fire?'

The farmer said, 'Well, that parrot must have been very motivated.'

Despite the fact that they are prepared to cheat their insurance companies, very seldom will people murder their pets in cold blood. In the midst of fraud, there is a little corner of the human heart that cannot bring itself to murder a pet that has been a friend for many years.

||||||||||||||||||||||||||||||||||||||||||||||||||||||||||||||||||

CHAPTER 25

OPINIONS, LIES AND SIMPLE TRUTH

'Science is founded on the conviction that experience, effort and reason are valid; magic on the belief that hope cannot fail nor desire deceive.'

– BRONISLAW MALINOWSKI,
British anthropologist

I am not here to win favour, and I have never been afraid to speak my mind. I have always believed in honesty and in the truth, and in saying things that others think but are too afraid to say openly, perhaps. There are always two or more opposing versions of the facts: I believe in slicing through all the confusion and evaluating the evidence from a purely scientific point of view. In some cases this is easy; in others, not so. Whatever the situation, however, I will investigate and present the facts as I find them.

The media has not always been kind to me, and in the early 2000s I crossed swords with Robert Kirby, the playwright and columnist. The battle started out innocently enough, with Kirby writing a few articles about my interest in the *Helderberg* plane crash in the *Mail & Guardian*. I replied to his allegations, and the war became personal. He took great pleasure in lampooning my name and labelling me a conspiracy theorist. In one particular article, which related to the tsunami tragedy of 2004, he blatantly made fun of me, referring to me as 'David Glutzow' (see Appendix J).

I was not afraid to speak my mind in the race debate over blood donation, something that drew even more negative press my way. The incident occurred a few years ago, in 2004, when Thabo Mbeki donated blood but failed to complete the relevant blood-donation questionnaire. As a result, a full unit of blood was not drawn, and that which was taken was discarded. Manto Tshabalala-Msimang, who was Minister of Health at the time, became distressed, saying that the non-use of the blood amounted to racism. This sparked a heated political debate over whether the South African National Blood Transfusion Service (SANBS) should be classifying blood from black donors as high-risk blood, which it was doing at the time.

In the *South African Medical Journal* (*SAMJ*) of April 2004, it was reported that the chief executive officer of SANBS said that the average risk of a black South African being HIV-positive was at least 100 times greater than that of a white compatriot. This is fact, not fiction. Because black donors were such a high-risk group, the race question was asked in a questionnaire prior to donation to protect the recipients of donated blood. This is not a situation unique to South Africa: the officials at the French Blood Transfusion Service were prosecuted at one point for allowing high-risk groups to donate blood.

I made the points publicly that race had nothing to do with this issue, and that while around 15 to 20 per cent of blood donors are black, the vast majority of recipients are also black. We know that the overwhelming majority of people infected with HIV are found in sub-Saharan Africa, an area that comprises 17 per cent of the world's population. To put the whole population at risk for a political gesture is plainly irresponsible.

The onus is on the medical profession to ensure that the blood given to recipients is as safe as possible – from a medical rather than a political standpoint. At that stage, the RNA fingerprinting technique – a complex process that had to be conducted on an individual basis – was not available in an automated form. SANBS was simply acting in the best medical interests of its patients.

What really upset me at the time was that nobody would support me. The *SAMJ* article stated that asking for the race of blood donors had nothing to do with racial stereotyping. Many of my colleagues supported the article off the record, but would not do so openly. I took a lot of criticism over this issue at the time, as did the head of SANBS, Anton Heyns, but it was necessary to say what needed to be said, despite the consequences.

Another matter about which I have always been outspoken is the government's interference with medicine. I would venture to say that the ANC-led government has managed to damage the state of medicine in this country significantly. It has interfered with the forensic science laboratories to the point that they have become non-functional. There are very few handwriting experts in South Africa today, and few people are skilled in fire investigations. I know of no other independent forensic practices that operate like mine in bringing together a number of branches of science and basic medical knowledge of anatomy and physiology.

The state forensic laboratories are now largely defunct as a result of the increasingly poor training of analysts. As an upshot of this, the backlogs in analyses are having a massive negative effect on the work of the law courts. Delays become so excessive that the state is often forced to drop charges – many judges are expressing concern over this situation.

One of the main problematic issues in the field of medicine is that admission to study medicine is based on demographics. The secondary and tertiary education systems are so flawed that many of the graduates do not receive a decent education. Standards, in my opinion, have dropped, and I would not feel comfortable with anyone who graduated from medical school post 1994 treating me. (Similarly, I have seen attorneys who have graduated in recent years who are functionally illiterate – they cannot string a coherent sentence together. The level of university education is poor, to put it mildly.)

A solution to our shortage of doctors has been the 'importing' of foreign doctors. I recently heard from a very reliable source – a surgeon and good friend – of a Cuban doctor in South Africa who had performed a tonsillectomy through the front of the patient's throat. What is normally a minor routine procedure was turned into a major operation with huge risks and a lengthy recovery time. This is but one example of the type of medical care that patients are receiving in South Africa at present. The state-run medical services have had to pay out billions, literally, in compensation for botched medical procedures.

Political interference in the medical system extends beyond issues of admission to the study of medicine. Once students graduate, they are sent to areas often fraught with problems and where there is little equipment. I have been outspoken about the amount of damage to which this is giving rise, as well as the harm being caused by the HIV/AIDS situation (provoked, in part, by Thabo Mbeki's incorrect views on HIV/AIDS).

The result of all of this is that young doctors, once qualified, seem to be leaving the country in droves. There is no motivation for them to stay, and this has a sad impact on health care in our country.

What really bothers me is the tragedy of all of this. Thirty or forty years ago, the education system was not good at all and needed improving, but the medical system was not bad. As I mentioned in Chapter 1, I was mentored as a young man by a district surgeon in Standerton. He was a rampant National Party supporter, but a good doctor nevertheless. I accompanied him on many of his rounds late at night to treat the sick, most of whom were farm workers.

This level of mentoring and education for prospective doctors is simply not available today.

Our problems arise from the fact that there has been political tampering with systems that work. I do not condone the idea of a central system that controls every aspect of state functioning, including police stations, hospitals and district administration. As mentioned in Chapter 4, central government control is never a good thing, whether it is over medicine, commerce or forensic matters. Some clients of mine have tried to control the outcome of my investigations by either inferring or directly requesting that I alter my reports, but this is a practice that I will not follow.

In 2002, a large blue-chip company found that someone was imitating their products and packaging and selling them off as the real thing. They were losing a significant amount of money, and they called me in to investigate.

I was provided with samples of the imitation products to analyse and compare to the original products. I requested the company's records of the exact ingredients contained in the original products, including the perfumes, so that I could compare the samples.

The company had no records of the exact organic compounds used in their original products. All I could compare the imitations to were the current products of the company, which may have differed from the original products in make-up. I explained to the attorney who had briefed me that my test results would not help very much, as I could not compare the imitations to the originals.

The attorney handling the case was from a well-known law firm that dealt primarily with copyright issues. He was not happy with the fact that I could not vouch for the samples being significantly different, and suggested that I omit that particular piece of information from my report.

If I did this, I would be misleading the court. I remember saying to him, 'So you want me to give a false report under oath?' He replied, 'Yes, because it's not going to go to court. You won't be cross-examined.'

This was not the point at all. There was always a possibility in the future that this report may be referred to in another case and that my credibility would be at stake. I refused to omit the information. He was not impressed, and the company concerned was angry that I was not prepared to perjure myself. They were paying me, and they expected me to follow their 'suggestions', regardless of the fact that that would compromise the practice of ethically sound forensic science.

I found myself in a similar situation in 2004, when I was working on a case involving a baby who had been born brain damaged at a private hospital in Hermanus, in the Western Cape. The highly distressed parents wanted some recourse, as they felt that the hospital was to blame for the baby's medical condition. It was not a straightforward matter at all, and I was called in on behalf of the hospital's insurance company.

The mother had gone into labour, and the staff, it was alleged, had allowed the labour to go on until the uterine membranes ruptured. As a result, pressure had been placed on the baby, which caused foetal distress. The baby was born brain damaged, and the parents were naturally devastated and angry. Their first path of recourse was the gynaecologist and the nurses. The gynaecologist said that he had instructed the nurses to administer a drug that causes increased contractions to the uterus. This drug was a synthetic version of the pituitary gland, hormone oxytocin, which makes the uterus contract faster and harder. The problem was that there was no fluid in the uterus, so it pressed against the baby's head and affected the heartbeat. The real question came down to whether the increased uterine contractions and the brain damage to the baby were a direct result of the administration of this drug.

I was called in to calculate how long it would take for the drug to get from the saline bag through the tube and into the patient. That sounds easy, but it proved not to be. The drug is put either into the bag or into the drip itself via a drip port – I didn't know which it had been. The solution then drips into a drop counter, a small transparent reservoir, and affects the concentration of the solution in the drop counter. Each drop that runs through the tube mixes with the other fluid in the tube, and the walls of the tube affect the rate of the flow, making it a complicated calculation.

A number of elements influence the calculation, including how the nurse administers the drug, how long it takes for him or her to get it into the patient, and how the nurse mixes it in the bag – some give the bag two squeezes, others take the bag off and mix it properly, and so on. The actual process of drug administration therefore makes a vast difference to the calculation. I couldn't get an answer for the length of time it would take for the drug to reach the patient until I had answers about how the drug had been administered.

With the knowledge of the advocate and the instructing attorney, I went to the hospital to observe how all of this is done. I then did the calculations, and concluded that the expert for the plantiff was right in his calculations: the drug had caused faster contractions and given rise to foetal distress. The advocate was furious and said to me, 'I don't want you to go out there and do all that *Quincy* stuff,' once again a referral to the popular TV programme from many years ago.

He was unhappy with the factors that I had taken into account in my calculations. I asked him if he wanted me to get into the witness box and say that I had performed the calculation based on the limited number of factors *he* wanted me to use. Had I done so, I would have undermined my integrity and credibility as a professional forensic scientist.

I have been in many situations in which lawyers have said to me, 'Thank you, this is a nice report, but will you alter it, please?' My reply to them is always an emphatic *no*, and consistently they respond with astonishment: 'We're paying your bill; why won't you do this?' My answer is very simple: if they bring me new evidence that will motivate me to change my view legitimately or recant on something I've said, I will put it in my report as an addendum. That way, whoever evaluates the report can follow my path of reasoning and, in particular, the reasons for my change of mind.

Were I to modify a report for a client, that client would be in possession of two differing reports of mine. If there hadn't been a good reason for my altering them and that client one day ends up on the opposing side in another matter in which I am involved, they could discredit me with one question: 'Have you, Dr Klatzow, ever altered a report at the behest of your client?' If I say no, I am immediately discredited for being dishonest – they have the reports as evidence. If I reply that I *have* revised reports in the past, that in itself destroys my credibility in front of the judge.

In the tragic case of the brain-damaged baby, as in so many others, the client wanted me to find only what would benefit their case. I am not prepared to do that. Instead, I will do all the '*Quincy*' work until I am satisfied with the answer: I will forever remain true to my craft.

||||||||||||||||||||||||||||||||||||||||||||||||||||||||||||

CHAPTER 26

CONDEMNED TO REPEAT HISTORY

'If the law has made you a witness, remain a man of science. You have no victim to avenge or guilty or innocent person to ruin or save. You must bear testimony within the limits of science.'

– PAUL C. BROUARDEL,

nineteenth-century French medico-legalist*

Forensic science has no master but the truth. Failure to understand this often creates difficulty for the scientist, who endeavours to get as close to the truth as humanly possible using scientific methods.

Many people believe that evidence will favour the side for which the forensic expert is acting, yet this is not the case: the forensic scientist is a witness to truth itself. Irrespective of whether it is the plaintiff or the defendant, the prosecution or the accused, that has called you as a witness, your duty is to give fair and unbiased

---

*   As reproduced in *Forensic Radiology* by B.G. Brogdon. This quote also appears in *The American Journal of Forensic Science and Pathology* 20 (1) 1999, where it is attributed to Paul H. Broussard, Chair of Forensic Medicine, Sorbonne, 1897.

evidence, and never to pervert or change your evidence or slant your findings. Forensic science is not about being a hired gun, either for political or for business interests (see Chapters 2 and 24). Occasionally, clients have to be warned that you will sink them with your evidence if they place you in a witness box. Many forensic experts fall into the trap of thinking that they are acting for one side or the other, but this is never the case: the role of the expert is to be completely impartial.

Impartiality was a constant battle in the apartheid years. The police laboratories were run along party political lines, and the justice system was no different. Judges were often handpicked by the Nationalist government, which successively deployed the party faithful to positions of judicial power to assist the government by toeing the party line. Certainly, there was a great deal of that in the Magistrates' Courts – magistrates were selected by the government in order to produce judgments that suited the state. In the cases in which I was involved in those years, I experienced first hand the magistrates' extreme reluctance to find the security forces responsible for any of the hideous crimes committed in the name of the government.

During my investigations I frequently found myself up against one particular magistrate who would never find against the police. He went out of his way to be gentle towards the state: he would ignore the most damning evidence, glossing over it in order to find that the police were not culpable. This happened in the cases of the Gugulethu Seven and Ashley Kriel, among many others (see Chapters 8 and 10). It was disheartening giving evidence in front of such judicial officers knowing that they would find a way to discredit you and ignore your evidence. Eventually, though, the truth came out with the revelations at the Truth and Reconciliation Commission.

After the long, hard-fought road to democracy, one would have hoped to see a very different picture today. Our history is littered with fallen heroes and brave men and women who paved the way for freedom and equality for all. In the words of Robert F. Kennedy, 'It is from numberless diverse acts of courage and belief that human history is shaped. Each time a man stands up for an ideal, or acts to improve the lot of others, or strikes out against injustice, he sends forth a tiny ripple of hope.'

Tragically, however, I see some of the ways of the old South Africa starting to develop in our democratically elected government. Certain judges have been selected as a matter of cadre deployment, and some judges are clearly unfit for the bench.

A few years ago an advocate told me about an incident involving the Judge President of the Cape, Judge John Hlophe. Judge Hlophe appointed an acting judge to hear a high-profile murder trial, and the judge found the accused guilty. As Joshua Greeff, the attorney acting for the defence, left the court, he was besieged by the press, who wanted his opinion on the judgment. He criticised it, saying that he thought the judge was wrong and that he was going to advise his client to appeal.

Greeff was quite entitled to say this: he had the right to respectfully disagree with the judge and he could tell the press that he was intending to inform his client to appeal. His response was in no way contemptuous.

When the accused appeared in court for sentencing some months later, the judge sentenced the accused to the maximum sentence possible. The counsel for the matter, Dirk Uys, stood up and asked for leave to appeal. The judge was not interested, and swept out of court in a judicial huff, leaving Uys standing there open-mouthed.

Uys and the instructing attorney, Joshua Greeff, were busy packing up their books when the judge's registrar arrived and said, 'The Judge President wants to see you now.'

Greeff and Uys went up to the judge's chambers, where they were met by Judge Hlophe, who proceeded to tear a stinging strip off Greeff for his remarks, allegedly ending his commentary by saying to Greeff, 'You're nothing but a piece of white shit who should go back to the Netherlands.'

I was outraged that a member of the judiciary, especially one who occupied such a prestigious office, could express these improper sentiments in such vulgar language. I phoned Joshua Greeff, who was reluctant to confirm the event, but when I spoke to Dirk Uys, he verified the whole squalid business. I then phoned Martin Welz, who published the article in *Noseweek* magazine. The incident became a cause célèbre in Cape Town, and it was a severe embarrassment to Judge Hlophe.

Judge Hlophe went on to deny the affair on national television, but later allowed the appointment of Uys as acting judge in his division. One is left with the uncomfortable conclusion that either Hlophe was happy to have a perjurer who had defamed him on the bench, or this was a hatchet-burying job. What was particularly telling was the fact that, in the midst of the denials by Judge Hlophe, he never called the prosecutor, Christhénus van der Vijver, or the judge, Judge Tandaswa Ndita AJ in the matter, both of whom had been present during the encounter, to confirm his avowal that he had not said the unfortunate words to Greeff.

Judge Hlophe didn't stop there: his later remarks about Judge Wilfred Thring are a particular indictment on him. While discussing a case with one of the parties and his counsel at a cricket match, he allegedly told them that he was going to refer the matter to Judge Thring so that he could 'fuck it up' and it could be remedied on appeal. Unfortunately for Judge Hlophe, this information leaked out and I made certain that it was publicised. The comment was irresponsible, improper and an insult to a man who deserved no insult whatsoever. Judge Thring, in my experience, is a scholarly gentleman of great temperance, and a man worthy of respect. Because of his judicial position, Judge Thring was unable to respond publicly to the nasty saga.

When Judge Thring failed to get permission from then Chief

Justice Chaskalson (and later, his successor, Chief Justice Langa) to publish his response to an earlier, widely publicised attack of racism that had been launched against him by Judge Hlophe, he took his entire dossier and deposited it with the national archives in Roeland Street. Inexplicably, the curator placed a twenty-year embargo on it and catalogued it as confidential material, which it was not.

When I heard this, I was outraged. Judge Thring had obviously intended his side of the story to be heard, but he was being muzzled by the state machine. With copies of Judge Thring's papers in hand, I called a press meeting, where I made them available to the press. I believe that this is what democracy is about – openness and transparency. It is not about allowing an improper statement and unacceptable behaviour by one judge, directed against another judge, to be kept out of the public eye. We need to know who is holding our future in their hands when they are making a judgment from the bench.

In my view, Judge Hlophe has been a most unsuitable candidate; a great pity, because he started off with such high hopes from all. He was regarded as a man of great promise by the other judges, but it seems that the power went to his head.

Judge Hlophe went on to accuse, unjustly, other senior advocates at the Cape Bar, as well as a former judge president, of racism. The charge of racism against Henri Viljoen SC arose from a meeting in Judge Hlophe's chambers. Requested by Viljoen, the conference had been called to discuss a case due to come before the court. Judge Hlophe had invited Deputy Judge President Jeanette Traverso to be present. In a letter to the Minister of Justice in 2004, Judge Hlophe complained that Viljoen had greeted Judge Hlophe and then addressed Judge Traverso in Afrikaans. Judge Hlophe does not speak Afrikaans, and was allegedly ignored from that point on.

Details of when this incident took place and who exactly was involved were requested by the Cape Bar Council, but the facts were never supplied. Viljoen categorically denied that the incident ever occurred and pointed out that, in his experience of the judge president, the latter would never have sat through the humiliating experience described by him.

The upshot of all of this was a paper titled 'Report on Racism in the Cape Provincial Division', which Judge Hlophe prepared and sent to the Minister of Justice instead of to the Chief Justice, outlining his complaints about racism on the bench and at the Cape Bar. Despite the fact that the allegations were refuted, Judge Hlophe did not retract the report or publicly apologise to those he falsely accused of racism. It all proved to be just a damp squib, and the affair's lasting legacy is a Zapiro cartoon, which is included as Appendix K.

As I hope to have demonstrated in this book, the purpose of a forensic investigation is to get to the truth. The facts should then be presented in an impartial court of law in order for the correct legal findings to be made. Courts are about justice, and should never be tainted by money or politics. As a forensic scientist who has been involved in the criminal and political life of South Africa for many years, I have a role to play in this regard, and I will speak out whenever I feel it necessary.

In the old South Africa, the police force and judicial system were rampantly politicised. Our police forensic laboratories also failed the test. As discussed in Chapter 9, General Lothar Neethling established a fine laboratory for the police, yet his attitude and injunctions were allowed to contaminate the laboratory and cast a shadow over the work of even the better forensic scientists working there.

I fear that we may be moving in that direction again. This thought is frightening, and it is painfully ironic, after all we have been through in our country, and after all I have seen in my independent forensic work over the years. Yet the wheel seems to be making a complete revolution. Those who do not know history are condemned to repeat it.

APPENDICES

ST. MARTIN'S SCHOOL

NAME _David Klatzow._   English.   REPORT

1/3   SET

At present sloppy and idle.

	TERM		EXAM.	
OUT OF	400	PLACE	%	PLACE
MARK	234	16	36	17
		in standard		41/50

INITIALS _J.R.-_

ALLIANCE. P.E. 41909-809

ST. MARTIN'S SCHOOL

NAME _David Klatzow._   Arithmetic   REPORT

1B. SET

Bad. must learn to ask
questions without distracting
the class: interrupts before he
has thought. A nuisance to his
set at present.

	TERM		EXAM.	
OUT OF	200	PLACE	%	PLACE
MARK	68	19.	22	17=
in stand?	48			45=

INITIALS _E·A._

ALLIANCE. P.E. 41909-809

CHARLES JOHNSON MEMORIAL HOSPITAL
(CHURCH OF THE PROVINCE OF SOUTH AFRICA)

MEDICAL SUPERINTENDENT
E. A. BARKER, M.D., F.R.C.S., (ENG.)

12 July 71

NQUTU
ZULULAND, VIA DUNDEE.
PHONE: NQUTU 8.

Dear David,

like yourself, I found it wonderfully stimulating to meet again, & I hope the next gap in our acquaintance will not be so long — please do come up & see us one day; you will find many agreeable changes & yet much that is familiar here also.

I have just been down at NUSAS congress lecturing there on the "homelands" in the place of Cosmas Desmond who could not give his lecture.

Stay well; keep in touch!

Affectionately,

Anthony

THE BANNED STRIKES UP HIS OWN TUNE BY DAVID KLATZOW

Your article about the secret deals banks do to keep attorneys on a tight lead is redolent of my experience with those other pillars of virtue, insurance companies.

I have always accepted briefs according to the good old 'taxi rank' principle of 'first come first served'. The name of my operation was Independent Forensic Consultants — and that is the way I wanted to be.

Shortly after I handled a case against one of the insurance giants, an attorney at Deneys Reitz, John Neaves, took it upon himself to give me some advice: 'Don't take work from the insured, only from the insurers.'

Why so? 'The insurers won't like it,' he confided.

He was right. It seems they don't want independent consultants, they want mercenaries. I reckoned that if that was what they wanted, they should go to Mike Hoare.

I continued to take work from clients in dispute with their insurers, and, sure enough, my work from the insurers dropped off, until only SA Eagle was left.

One day I took on a case *against* them where they had clearly screwed up badly and were attempting to dream up ways of repudiating a claim from a man in the Western Transvaal. Piet Sandberg's house had burned down and he was left figuratively standing in his underwear for some months, on the profit-driven whim of the claims manager of Eagle at the time, one Wynand van Vuuren. [See *noses* 61 & 62 about him.]

As a result, the semi-head honcho of Eagle, Dennis Burton, banned me from ever again being employed by the company.

But then, some months later, Eagle's attorney in a matter where I had been the expert investigator, asked me to appear for Eagle in the case.

I called the local claims manager, Marius Kuhn, and told him, 'Marius old darling, you have banned me and now you want to have me stand up as an independent witness at a trial for you.

'I think not. I think I will stay banned.'

Faced with his apparent incomprehension, I presented him with an analogy. 'Marius,' I said, 'You lot at Eagle remind me of the young man who for no good reason divorced his comely wife and shortly afterwards found himself in town alone and palely loitering. So he decided to call on the object of his late affections.

'He knocked on the door and when the ex-wife opened, he asked her for a fuck. 'Sure' she said, 'Fuck off'.'

Independence is the most valuable tool in the drawer. Let the attorneys be warned: The bank's patronage is a poisoned chalice. Drink from it at your peril.

Banks and insurers, too, will soon enough discover that acting the bully on the block has only short term benefits. Long term it's going to cost them bigtime. Ask Hitler.

Meanwhile, being banned is not so bad. In fact I've come to like it.

David Klatzow
Rondebosch

— *Noseweek*, February 2008

MISREPRESENTATION OF FORENSIC INFORMATION

53 Forensic information was misused in various ways. Some forensic pathologists omitted crucial information or falsified *post mortem* reports to cover
up the cause of death. There were many cases where doctors misrepresented
forensic evidence and findings in court in order to absolve the state of
allegations of abuse or criminal activity. This required the collusion of police,
lawyers, forensic experts, district surgeons and other health professionals
and magistrates and judges. The misuse and manipulation of specialised
knowledge is illustrated in a number of case studies selected from submissions to the Commission.

ACCIDENTAL OR DELIBERATE?

*Ashley Kriel was shot in 1987 while allegedly resisting arrest and engaging
in a scuffle with a security policeman. The police version of events was that, in
the course of the arrest, Kriel produced a small .22 pistol. Captain Jeffrey
Benzien, the senior police officer involved in the arrest, tried to take the gun
away from him. A scuffle ensued during which Ashley Kriel was fatally injured
by a bullet wound in the back, fired from his own pistol. The evidence presented
by the state forensic experts supported this version of events.*

*On an examination of the facts, however, numerous inconsistencies are evident.
These were not presented to the magistrate by the state witnesses, but were
highlighted by the expert forensic witness testifying on behalf of Ashley Kriel's
family. The two assessors sitting with the magistrate, both of whom were
forensic experts, also failed to point out the inconsistencies or take them into
consideration. The outcome of the inquest was a 'no blame' verdict.*

Some of the inconsistencies were:

- *The marks around both of Ashley's wrists indicated that he had been hand-cuffed before his death. If the handcuffs were removed, why was this done? If they were not, how could Ashley have engaged in a fight with Benzien, and how could he have shot himself in the back?*
- *The size and nature of the entrance wound in Ashley's back was consistent with a direct contact wound; in fact, stigmata around the entrance to the wound indicated that the muzzle of the revolver was held directly against the skin. However, the size and nature of the holes in the clothing that he was wearing at the time (a T-shirt and track suit top) were inconsistent with a contact shot.*

54 There are some well-known examples of cases where doctors reported false causes of death. These include the numerous detainees who supposedly died from such causes as slipping on a bar of soap, dying of an epileptic seizure where no prior history of epilepsy existed, having a heart attack without a history of heart disease, choking on food or suffocating or committing suicide. In addition, doctors were known to give expert advice on the mental health of deceased prisoners, or to conclude that someone had committed suicide because of mental instability, without ever having met the person involved. This type of evidence was advanced at the inquest into the death of Neil Aggett.

55 Expert forensic evidence of gun shot wounds was also used to determine the distance between the victim and the killer.

DETERMINING SHOOTING DISTANCE

In 1986, seven young men were killed in a police ambush in Gugulethu. The police evidence was that all seven were shot from some distance. No contrary evidence was produced by the state experts. Independent forensic experts, however, found evidence of very close range 'finishing-off' shots on the bodies of many of the seven victims. One of the victims had, in fact, been shot in the jaw at such close range that there was almost no dispersal of the shotgun pellets, and the felt wad (which contains the pellets) was embedded in this brain. This evidence was presented at the second inquest into the deaths.

Hence, the police version that this person was shot from a distance of a few metres cannot be true. Again, however, a collusion of silence and a tacit agreement to turn a blind eye by lawyers, state forensic experts, police and the magistrate resulted in a 'no blame' verdict.

– Truth and Reconciliation of South Africa Report, Volume Four

COCKPIT TAPE REVEALS SECRET OF DOOMED HELDERBERG

'MADNESS' OF DEADLY CARGO

Startling evidence comes to light as new scientific technique assesses crew's voices on flight recording

By Matthew Burbidge and Marvin Meintjies

Ghosts of the dead apparently speak about 'the madness' that allowed a 'deadly cargo' aboard the doomed Helderberg plane. They are heard in newly reconstructed flight recordings.

The Helderberg crashed into the Indian Ocean just 160km from Mauritius in 1987, killing all 159 passengers and crew.

The captain of the Helderberg was apparently aware that a 'deadly cargo was being transported on the airplane', before the worst air disaster in South Africa's history unfolded, *Beeld* newspaper reports today.

These startling allegations have come to light following the reconstruction, by the American Forensic Audio Laboratory, of nine minutes of previously inaudible tape of the flight recorder. On it the voice of Captain Dawie Uys is resurrected to shed further light on the mystery that has surrounded the disaster.

Uys is heard to be telling his flight crew that a 'dodelike vrag agter in die vliegtuig vervoer word' (a deadly cargo is being transported in the back of the plane), while a member of the crew complains of 'die gekheid' (the madness) of the deadly cargo being transported on the SAA passenger jet.

Trevor Abrahams, chief executive officer of South Africa's Civil Aviation Authority, said he received an e-mail yesterday from a South African [text missing]. An enhanced copy of the audio recording from the Helderberg's voice recorder.

Abrahams said Van Wyk told him the M-Net magazine programme *Carte Blanche* had been supplied with a copy of the recording.

The CAA picked up the recording yesterday from *Carte Blanche* and then copied it on to a compact disc.

Abrahams said the recording on the CD was 'very indistinct' and he believed *Carte Blanche* staffers had also battled to make head or tail of it.

Abrahams said Van Wyk had transcribed the cockpit conversation, but there was no indication of where the aircraft was when it took place.

'We now have to ascertain the authenticity of the CD, and try to link it to what we were given in the transcript.'

Abrahams said Van Wyk had apparently been given a copy of the cockpit recording by a former CAA investigator, Rennie van Zyl, who now works for the International Civil Aviation Organisation in Toronto. This was taken by Van Wyk to be enhanced by the American Forensic Audio Laboratory.

Abrahams said Van Wyk had apparently written to the former minister of transport, Mac Maharaj, requesting funds to undertake the enhancement.

Beeld said the enhancement of the tape was funded by a British business-man, Richard Price in exchange for film and book rights ...

– *Star*, 17 May 2000

HELDERBERG: 'IT'S TIME FOR TRUTH'

Defence procurement agency Armscor's desperation to help sustain apartheid led to the Helderberg air disaster, a closed inquiry into the crash heard in evidence released yesterday.

This was the real story behind the accident that claimed 159 lives in 1987, expert witness David Klatzow told the Truth and Reconciliation Commission in 1998.

'Armscor begged, borrowed and stole if necessary, any technology it deemed necessary to the continuation of their holy war.'

Klatzow contended that rocket fuel carried illegally by the Helderberg for Armscor spontaneously ignited, causing the aircraft to crash into the sea off the coast of Mauritius in November 1987.

Armscor, far from being the innovative giant that it claimed to have been, was on the level of petty criminals when it came to stealing intellectual property.'

An inquiry headed by Mr Justice Cecil Margo found that there had been a fire in the forward hold of the aircraft. But he concluded there was no evidence of an illegal cargo on the plane.

The TRC in 1998 conducted a closed hearing in the accident at the request of relatives of those who died.

Releasing the 523-page transcript of the hearing, Transport Minister Dullah Omar told reporters in Pretoria: 'It is in the best interests of our country … that the veil of secrecy be lifted.'

According to the document, Klatzow, a forensics expert and consultant, told the TRC that information on the accident pointed to an 'untoward incident' on the Helderberg.

'More importantly, it points inexorably in the direction of a major cover-up on the part of the (Margo) commission, or at best stunning incompetency.' …

– Sapa, 22 August 2000

I Lucas Johannes Meyer a male IDXXXXXXX, residing at 25 Sintra court, Horizon view, Cell XXXXXXX.

Declare under oath that a few days after the Helderberg crashed a few of my fellow workers and I stood in the smoke room of the Avionics building on the 1st floor. The point of discussion was the Helderberg. Colin Dick, who worked with us, introduced us to his son who just joined us. During the discussion Gavin Dick mentioned that they (ZUR the company frequency) were the last people to talk to the Helderberg. At that stage we only new that the Helderberg reported a smoke problem and then went down. Everybody was very eager to find out what happened and we then asked Gavin to tell us what happened. He told us that the Helderberg reported fire to them not long after they left Taiwan. I found this strange because it is the Captains decision to turn back or not. Gavin then said that they were instructed to tell the Helderberg to continue on course till they get permission from higher authority to turn back. He never said who the higher authority was.

Gavin said that a while later the Helderberg were told that permission has been denied to turn back and that they should continue to Mauritius. He did not give any more details about why the decision was made.

A few days later Gavin Dick again visited his father and again the discussion was around the Helderberg. I and some of the other people asked him about the previous comment about them talking to the Helderberg. He then denied that they talked to the Helderberg and said the Helderberg missed its compulsory contact and that they never spoke to them. He denied that he said that they were the last people to speak to the Helderberg.

SPECIAL INVESTIGATION INTO THE *HELDERBERG* CRASH

INTRODUCTION

1   On 28 October 1987, the SAA *Helderberg*, a Boeing 747, crashed into the sea off the coast of Mauritius. All 159 people on board died. Almost immediately after the incident, allegations of foul play were made. A year later, in January 1989, the South African government established a commission of enquiry headed by Justice Cecil Margo to determine the cause of the crash.

2   The Margo Commission found that the crash was caused by a fire on board, but that the cause of the fire was undetermined. Many people rejected this finding, including investigative journalists who insisted that there were strong indications that the fire was caused by dangerous substances on board. Allegations were made that South African Airways (SAA) passenger flights were used to courier arms components and explosives in sanctions-busting activities by the parastatal Armscor.

3   Whilst no hard evidence was provided to back these claims, journalists continued to find circumstantial evidence to suggest that the *Helderberg* could have been carrying such dangerous substances, and that these might have caused the fire on board, leading to the crash.

4   Former SAA employees came forward, often anonymously, to support the allegation that it was not unusual for passenger flights to carry dubious parcels destined, they presumed, for Armscor. Moreover, members of the Flight Engineers Association indicated that the Margo Commission had overlooked important information when investigating the incident. There were allegations of cover-ups by the Margo Commission and experts suggested that the fire might have been 'self-promoted' (with a self-generated oxygen source).

5   The allegations of a cover-up and uncertainty about the cause of the fire prevented families of victims from putting the matter to rest. Individual submissions were made to this Commission by Mr Peter Wills, twin brother of John Wills who was killed in the crash, Mr Rod Cramb, brother of a crew member; Mr Pieter Strijdom, whose wife died on board; and Ms Michelline Daniels, who lost her brother. The Commission also received a submission from Friends of the Victims of the *Helderberg*, urging the Commission to find the cause of the destruction of the plane.

6   The Commission began an investigation in late 1997 despite the fact that it was unclear whether the crash was politically motivated, a criterion for an enquiry by the Commission. Although extensive enquiries were conducted and circumstantial evidence collected, the Commission was unable to determine the cause of the fire. It is hoped, however, that the Commission's efforts will assist any future investigations into the matter.

METHODOLOGY

7   An enormous amount of documentation about the incident was made available to the commission by an investigative journalist. Documents included cargo manifests, submissions to the Margo Commission, newspaper reports, reports by independent scientists and engineers and a report by the Flight Engineers Association, amongst others.

8   Investigators analysed the documentation and identified individuals who could provide additional information to the Commission. These included families of victims and former SAA employees. Once these individuals had been interviewed, the Commission decided to approach a further group of people. Many of these represented the interests of the implicated parties, such as SAA and Armscor. It was decided that the Commission should utilise its section 29 powers to hold an *in camera* investigative enquiry to canvass the views of these people. This would provide them with an opportunity to answer questions in the presence of their legal representatives and would

enable a panel of Commissioners to evaluate the information gained at first hand. The following people appeared as witnesses at the hearing:

- Mr Joseph Braizblatt, SAA cargo manager at Ben Gurion airport, Tel Aviv, Israel;
- Dr David Klatzow, an independent forensic scientist;
- Mr Richard Steyl, an Armscor employee in the shipping department;
- Dr J Steyn, a former Armscor employee and MD of Altech Electronic Systems, which had two loads of cargo on the *Helderberg*;
- Mr John David Hare, a former Armscor employee who joined SAA;
- Mr Brian Watching, a former SAA employee;
- Mr Tinie Willemse, a lawyer who was chief director : international relations of SAA at the time of the incident;
- Mr Gerrit Dirk van der Veer, chief executive officer of SAA at the time of the incident;
- Mr Thinus Jacobs, manager of SAA in Taipei between 1987 and 1991;
- Mr Mickey Mitchell, chief of operations for SAA at Jan Smuts (incorporating Springbok Radio Tower) at the time of the incident;
- Dr André Buys, Armscor general manager: planning

9 Others who were interviewed included:

- Mr Japie Smit, director of civil aviation;
- Mr Leslie Stokoe, an expert on dangerous goods;
- Mr Vernon Nadel, duty officer at the Springbok Radio centre on the night of the incident;
- Mr Rennie van Zyl, current chief director of civil aviation;
- Mr Jimmy Mouton, SAA flight engineer and friend of the flight engineer killed in the crash.

INVESTIGATIVE RESULTS

The cause of the fire

10 Nothing in the cargo inventory could have resulted in a 'self-promoted' fire. However, the original cargo manifests were not part of the record of the Margo Commission, and it is uncertain whether those in the possession of the Commission are authentic. There is therefore no reliable list of what cargo was being transported by the *Helderberg* when it crashed.

11 It was suggested to the Commission that Armscor may have had a goods consignment on the *Helderberg* that could have been responsible for causing the fire. Armscor conducted an internal investigation after the incident and denies having had any items on the flight.

12 The Commission believed that two Armscor employees from the company Somchem, which was producing rockets and missiles during the apartheid years, could provide important information. Armscor could not assist the Commission in locating either Dr JJ Dekker, who was the MD of Somchem, or Mr François Humphries, who was procurement officer at the time.

13 Interviews with SAA pilots indicated that there was a belief amongst pilots that passenger flights were frequently used to transport armaments and components for Armscor.

The timing of the fire

14 Much time has been spent attempting to determine the exact time the fire broke out. The conclusion reached by the Margo Commission was that the fire started just before the descent to land in Mauritius.

15 This conclusion is questionable because of the fact that there is no overlap between the conversation of the cockpit voice recorder (CVR, commonly

known as the black box) and the conversations between the *Helderberg* and Mauritius air control an hour before the crash and again four minutes before the crash. This could indicate that the CVR stopped recording before the descent for landing, and the recorded conversation could therefore have taken place at any time on the nine-hour flight from Taipei.

16 The conversation on the CVR was analysed by the Flight Engineers Association, which concluded that the discussion was likely to have taken place within three hours of the flight leaving Taipei. This would indicate that something stopped the recording at this early stage of the flight. The flight engineers presented the Margo Commission with a submission indicating that they believed there had been two fires on board.

17 The Margo Commission ruled most of the CVR recording inadmissible because it was irrelevant and too personal. Analysts have argued that this decision by Justice Margo prevented his commission from accurately placing the conversation and may therefore have led to incorrect conclusions.

18 The theory of two fires on board was impossible to test adequately, since the recording of the conversations between the *Helderberg* and South African air traffic control went missing shortly after the incident and was never recovered.

In a letter to the Commission, a United States marine said that the CIA had a recording of this conversation. The Commission wrote to the director of the CIA asking him to confirm this and to make a copy available. No response was received.

The fire

19 The Margo Commission did not find a cause for the fire on board the *Helderberg*, but said that it might have been caused by 'ordinary packaging material'. This Commission's investigation indicates that ordinary

packaging material is unlikely to have been the cause, for the following reasons:

- The fire was contained, and burnt fiercely at a high temperature.
- A packaging material fire causes a great deal of smoke, which would have set off the smoke alarms before the fire threatened the structure of the plane. The indications are that the smoke detectors were not activated until the fire had reached dangerous proportions.
- A promoted fire could reach very high temperatures (far in excess of 1000 degrees Celsius) without setting off smoke alarms.
- A promoted fire could cause packaging materials to catch alight if they were to be exposed to the flames.

20 The possibility of a 'self-promoted' fire is raised in a submission to the Margo Commission by Mr Greg Southeard, a chemist working for Burgoyne and Partners of the United Kingdom. Southeard indicated that he believed that the fire could have been caused by an incendiary device or a hazardous substance.

21 The director of civil aviation, Mr Japie Smit, told this Commission that most of such fires the world over are caused by illegal substances on board, and said that, when they simulated the fire, they were unable to put it out without the assistance of the fire brigade.

22 A letter from a Somchem employee to a journalist working on the matter stated that:

South Africa's ammonium perchlorate (APC) production facility was set up in the 1970s at Somchem. Around the time of the Helderberg *crash, South Africa was involved in military operations in Angola, Namibia and on the home front. The operational demand for solid rocket fuels was high. Somchem was not keeping up with the demand. A decision was made to double the capacity. This involved shutting down the plant for the duration of the extensions. Because of the ongoing demand, it was impossible to stockpile APC prior to the shut-down. Obviously a large quantity of APC had to be sourced outside the country for a period of several months in defiance of prevailing military sanctions. This was difficult and expensive, and I believe that initially the necessary APC was sourced from America and that it was brought in on SAA passenger planes as an integral part of the necessary deception (Commission's summary).*

23 Ammonium perchlorate is used mainly in military Class One applications, and as such is forbidden on all aircraft. Class Five, for commercial/technical application, could be carried by air in limited quantities depending on the type of aircraft (passenger or cargo) and packaging instruction. Supplier countries include the United States, China, Japan and France.

The investigation

24 Questions raised throughout the investigation process indicated that the investigators of the Margo Commission had not followed correct procedures. The matters raised are summarised in the finding below.

CONCLUSION

25 This Commission's investigation into the *Helderberg* crash raised significant questions about the incident itself as well as the subsequent investigations that were conducted.

26 The matter is still under investigation by the special investigation team of the Gauteng Attorney-General.

THIS COMMISSION'S INVESTIGATION INTO THE CRASH OF THE *HELDERBERG* ON 28 OCTOBER 1987 SHOWED THAT MANY QUESTIONS AND CONCERNS REMAIN UNANSWERED, INCLUDING THE FOLLOWING:

- THE DIRECTOR OF CIVIL AVIATION (DCA) NEGLECTED TO SECURE ALL DOCU-MENTATION AND RECORDINGS AS REQUIRED BY THE FLIGHT ENGINEERS ASSOCIATION (FEA) REGULATIONS:
- THE CARGO MANIFESTS WERE MISSING
- MR JIMMY MOUTON OF THE FEA ALLEGES THAT THE FEA WAS REQUESTED BY THE LAWYER ACTING FOR THE DCA, AS WELL AS BY JUSTICE MARGO HIMSELF AT A LATER STAGE, TO WITHDRAW ITS SUBMISSION INDICATING THAT THERE MAY HAVE BEEN TWO FIRES ON BOARD.
- THE TAPE WHICH WOULD HAVE RECORDED CONTACT BETWEEN THE *HELDER-BERG* AND SPRINGBOK RADIO CONTROL REMAINS MISSING.
- EYEWITNESSES OF THE CRASH WERE NOT CALLED TO GIVE EVIDENCE BEFORE THE MARGO COMMISSION.
- THE MARGO COMMISSION DID NOT CALL MEMBERS OF ARMSCOR TO GIVE EVIDENCE.

27 It is clear that further investigation is necessary before this matter can be laid to rest.

– Truth and Reconciliation Commission of South Africa Special Investigation: *Helderberg* Crash, Volume Two, Chapter Six

HITMAN TELLS HOW HE BOTCHED 'ASSISTED SUICIDE' TWICE BEFORE SUCCEEDING

'HOW I KILLED KEBBLE'

Natasha Marrian
Sapa

Johannesburg: Boxer Michael Schultz yesterday told the South Gauteng High Court here how he twice botched mining magnate Brett Kebble's 'assisted suicide'.

Schultz, the State's first witness, called by Gauteng deputy director of public prosecutions Dan Dakana, described how he shot and killed Kebble.

'I leaned out the car window, pointing the firearm at him. He just lifted his shoulder, his right shoulder, and looked in front. I aimed at his head and pulled the trigger, but the weapon did not discharge,' Schultz said, describing the night of September 27, 2005. He was testifying as State witness in the trial of convicted drug trafficker Glenn Agliotti, who faced four charges, two related to Kebble's murder.

After the gun failed to discharge the first time, he and accomplices-turned-State-witnesses Faizel Smith and Nigel McGurk drove off. After inspecting the weapon they returned and found Kebble in his vehicle. 'I leaned out of the window and pointed the firearm. Once again the gun did not discharge.'

Schultz said he then told Kebble to wait for him. The trio drove away for the second time. He inspected the gun. They made a U-turn and returned to where they had left Kebble.

However, Kebble had driven off. They stopped their car and saw him coming towards them. They flashed their headlights at him. He made a U-turn and 'stopped hard' next to them.

'I could see the disappointment in his face; he gave me a look like to say 'get this over with, you're putting me through hell',' Schultz said.

He leaned out of the window and aimed for Kebble's body. 'I pulled the trigger – this time the gun fired. I kept firing.'

Schultz could not remember how many times he shot, but said he had been instructed Kebble should not suffer. The three then drove away. Schultz looked back and saw Kebble's car rolling forward and hitting the pavement. They sped from the scene in Melrose Street in Johannesburg to Smith's panel-beating business, where Smith cut the gun into pieces and said he would dispose of it.

The next morning Schultz got up and went to gym.

During cross-examination, Agliotti's lawyer Laurence Hodes SC put it to Schultz that his client 'never ever conspired with you to aid the murder of Roger Brett Kebble'. To which Schultz replied: 'No, he didn't.'

Hodes then asked Schultz whether he agreed that Agliotti had not 'in any manner' killed the mining magnate. To which Schultz replied: 'I agree.'

He asked Schultz whether Agliotti had received part of the R2 million offered by Kebble to help him die. 'Not from the R2 million, no, not to my knowledge,' he replied.

The only time Schultz was contacted by Agliotti about the murder was on September 22 when Kebble was to have been killed. Schultz was phoned by (Kebble's former security head) Clinton Nassif's wife with a message from him that the 'meeting' was off. He received a call from Agliotti to 'call the boys off'.

According to the indictment, John Stratton, Kebble's associate, and Agliotti enlisted Nassif to aid Kebble's suicide after Kebble was forced to resign as chief executive of Western Areas Limited, JCI and Randgold and Exploration. Schultz told the court Nassif knew he was a 'loyal and honourable guy' and 'wouldn't say anything about it'.

'All my instructions came from Mr Nassif,' he said, as did all his payments. He went through with the killing after an assurance from Nassif that Kebble 'would look after us'.

Schultz could gain indemnity from prosecution for his role in the murder if the court finds his testimony truthful.

Agliotti faces two counts of conspiracy to commit murder, a charge of attempted murder and one of murder. The first count is conspiracy to commit the murders of Mark Bristow, Jean Daniel Nortier, Mark Wellesley-Woods and

Stephen Mildenhall. The second count is the attempted murder of Stephen Mildenhall. The last two are conspiracy to murder Kebble and Kebble's murder.

Judge Frans Kgomo adjourned the matter until this morning. – Sapa

– *Cape Times*, 27 July 2010

Dear Kullie

Die eerie en die laste wat ons vir jou moet se is om laat jy pasop vir die vier op jou gat en op jou besegheid — ons het gehoor van jou roper besegheid by onse mense. Ons maak reg, jy maak kaak jou kullie. maar moenie bang wees nie jy moet net bid ons is op pat na jou. Ons weet nie of jy gehoor ons kan vier maak met 'n mens soos jy sonder houde en sonder papier. net wat 'n kaar gabreik is beter vir jou om te brand. ons sal met 'n biekie petrol kom. en jy sal ons ok biekie van jou gee. of nie so. pak weg van die plek af. as jy jou lewe liefhet. Saam met jou famielie want baie mense kom huil hier by ons van jou. ONS IS OP PAD.

We are there while you stay and dance. look at as by any time. Your name is death with petrol.

      WE ARE the WORLD
        We are the children

THE HELDERBERG STRIKES AGAIN

To the true forensically scientific mind the real cause of the recent tragic tsunamis in South East Asia is painfully obvious.

My own recent research has revealed that in its fateful last flight in 1987, the SAA Boeing 747, *Helderberg*, was diverted from its usual flight routing on instructions personally telephoned to the *Helderberg*'s drivers by General Magnus Malan.

The crew were instructed to abandon their route path, turn southwards and fly close to Sumatra, where the ocean depth is known to be in excess of 40 sea-miles. Once there they were instructed to jettison a nuclear device the aircraft was carrying in blatant violation of international air-transport signed agreements.

It was hoped the nuclear device would sink to the bottom and never be found in such deep water. The device had been supplied to South Africa's apartheid government's defence force by North Korea in return for a guaranteed future supply of raw nuclear fuel and red mercury.

The nuclear device jettisoned by the *Helderberg* has lain on the sea floor for all of the 17 years since the 'accident' and on Boxing Day detonated spontaneously after sea water eventually caused a short-circuit in its trigger-system. The tsunamis were caused by this massive underwater explosion.

Please let us have no more of this rubbish about shifting teutonic plates. This tragic tragedy was yet another relic of apartheid.

Anyone wishing to sue either SAA or the apartheid government for enormous damages over this matter is invited to contact me at my usual addresses. Very reasonable consultation and retainer fees will be charged. Special group rates for relatives of victims and pensioners. All credit cards recognised. Normal cellphone rates apply. – *Dr David Glutzow, Johannesburg*

– *Mail & Guardian*, 7–15 January 2005

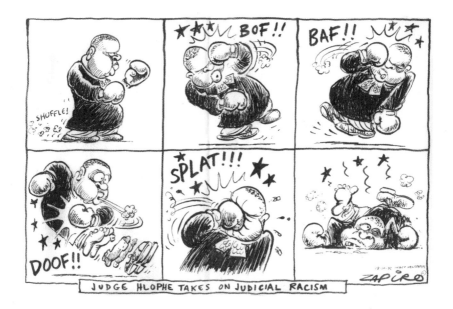

BIBLIOGRAPHY

Books

Bentham, Jeremy. *A Fragment on Government: And an Introduction to the Principles and Morals of Legislation*. Oxford: Basil Blackwell, 1948

Berlin, Isaiah. 'Post Modernism', in Walter Truett Anderson (ed.), *Fontana Postmodern Reader*. London: Fontana Press, 1996

Brogdon, B.G. *Forensic Radiology*. United States: CRC Press, 1998

Malinowski, Bronislaw. *Magic, Science and Religion*. Garden City, New York: Anchor Books, Doubleday, 1954

Marsh, Rob. *Famous South African Crimes*. Cape Town: Struik Timmins, 1991

Peck, M. Scott. *The Road Less Traveled*. London: Arrow Books, 1978

Wilson, Edward O. *Consilience: The Unity of Knowledge*. New York: Vintage Books, 1999

Articles

Breytenbach, Karen. 'Heritage Day Pays Homage to Trojan Horse Three', *Cape Times*, 26 September 2005

Burbridge, Matthew, and Marvin Meintjies. 'Madness of deadly cargo', *The Star*, 17 May 2000

Editor. 'Happily ever after', *Noseweek*, September 2004

Eggington, Shanaaz. 'Help! Daar's 'n muis in my Coke', *Die Son*, 9 January 2004

Khuzwayo, Wiseman. 'Helderberg hello; adios Sawubona', *Business Report*, 4 April 2004

'Lies and deceit in death of 9 activists', *The Star*, 30 July 1999

Moya, Fikile-Ntsikelelo. 'Arendse: I'm being used', *Mail & Guardian*, 14 October 2005

South African Press Association. 'Explosion recalls Cosatu sabotage', *The Star*, 31 August 1988

South African Press Association. 'Ferdi Barnard killed David Webster, amnesty commission told', 15 April 1997

South African Press Association. 'Goniwe murder hearing may be reopened: TRC', 28 May 1999

Lee, N.C. *South African Medical Journal*, 'Murder most foul', Volume 81, January 1992

Stagg, Cathy. 'Three in a Bed evidence at Krebs Murder Trial', *The Star*, 1 March 1989

Truth and Reconciliation Commission of South Africa Report. Special Investigation: The *Helderberg* crash', Volume 2, Chapter 6, Truth and Reconciliation Commission: October 1998

Truth and Reconciliation Commission of South Africa Report. 'Institutional Hearing: The Health Sector', Volume 4, Chapter 5, Truth and Reconciliation Commission: October 1998

'Ultimately it's up to you to watch your own back', *Personal Finance*, 8 March 2008

United Nations Programme on HIV/AIDS, *Global Report 2006*, Fact Sheet 06

Websites

http://www.africancrime-mystery.co.za/books/fsac/chp26.htm

http://www.anc.org.za/ancdocs/misc/trc04.html

http://www.athlone.co.za/heritage/history/0604200601_history.php

http://aviation-safety.net/database/record.php?id=19850822-0his-
tory.org.za/pages/people/bios/webster-d.htm

http://www.capetimes.co.za/index.php?fSectionId=271&fArticleI
d=2890867

http://www.disa.ukzn.ac.za:8080/DC/
BSAug85.0036.4843.028.002.Aug1985.6/
BSAug85.0036.4843.028.002.Aug1985.6.pdf

http://www.doj.gov.za/trc/decisions/1999/99_benzien.html

http://www.doj.gov.za/trc/media/1997/9705/s970519d.htm

http://www.justice.gov.za/trc/media/1996/9610/s961025c.htm

http://www.justice.gov.za/trc/special/children/nkomo.htm

http://news.bbc.co.uk/onthisday/hi/dates/stories/september/16/
newsid_2519000/2519297.stm

http://news.bbc.co.uk/onthisday/hi/dates/stories/september/16/
newsid_2519000/2519297.stm

http://sahistory.org.za/pages/people/bios/webster-d.htm

http://www.tac.org.za/Documents/Speeches/
ashleykrielmemlect_2004.doc

http://en.wikipedia.org/wiki/Moorgate_tube_crash

http://70.84.171.10/~etools/newsbrief/1993/news9309.28

INDEX

Ables, Sergeant 105, 106
Abrahams, Cyril
  128–132
Adams, Gavin 104
African National
  Congress (ANC) 100,
  101, 122, 125, 134, 266
Afrikaner Weerstands-
  beweging (AWB) 54
Agliotti, Glen 233,
  236, 238
Ahrensen, Noel 4
Ahrensen (née Klatzow),
  René [aunt] 3, 4
Alice in Wonderland 13, 14
Allen, David 168, 171
Allan, Jack 22–23
Ames, Frances 103
ANC *see* African
  National Congress
Ancer, Bernard 73
Anglo American fire 82
Anglo American
  scholarship 126
Anstey, Len 81
April, Hilton 261–262
Armscor 151, 168, 169,
  170, 171, 172, 189

arson 48–49, 51–54, 54,
  67, 252 *see also* fire
athletics, drugs in 252
Attwell, Kevin 41,
  42, 148
AWB *see* Afrikaner
  Weerstandsbeweging

Baker, Sally 186
Barclays Bank 128, 132
Barker, Anthony and
  Maggie 15
Barnaby, Frank 169
Barnard, Barry 88, 89
Barnard, Ferdi 138
Bartholomew, Bruce
  222, 223, 224
Basson, Gawie 140
Basson, Wouter 138
Bateman, Chris 87, 95
Bellagarda, Joe 179
Bellagarda, Yvonne 179
Benzien, Jeffrey 105–107,
  109, 110, 111, 112
Berman, Julian 7
Bester, Theresa 74, 76
Bester, Willem 192
Bierce, Ambrose 248

Biko, Steve 83, 88, 100,
  102, 103, 124, 163
Birkett, Norman viii
Bizos, George ix, 99, 121
Blackburn, Molly 121
Black Sash 121
Blake, William 11, 12
Blatchford, James Bruno
  [grandfather] 5, 6
Blatchford, (née Langs-
  ford) [grandmother] 5
Blunt, Anthony 4
Bodziak, William 224
Boraine, Alex 124
Botes, Pieter 100
Botha, Emarie 75
Botha, Marius 219
Botha, P.W. 135, 188, 195
Bourhill, Eddie 187–188
Bower (née Blatchford),
  Bertha [aunt] 6
British Scientific
  Workers Union 4
Browde, Jules 53
Buccaneer Shoes factory
  fire 74, 76
Bucwa, Kwanele Moses
  115

Budlender, Geoff 84, 85, 86, 126
Burger, Staal 138
Burgoynes 55
'Burning Car' case viii
Burt, Henry 152, 154, 155
Burton, Denis 56–57
Business Day 62

Cairncross, John 4
Calata, Fort 119, 121
Cameron, Bruce 242
Cameron, Jean 13, 14
Cantril, Richard 32
Cape Argus 90, 163
Cape Times 86, 87, 289
Carolus, Cheryl 105
Carroll, Lewis 13
Carte Blanche 62, 208
Cavallier, Tony 185
CCB *see* Civil Cooperation Bureau
Celliers, Fanie 167
Chandler, Norman 168, 169
Charles Johnson Memorial Hospital 15
Chaskalson, Arthur 85, 86, 276
Cheadle Thompson & Haysom 80, 82, 97, 98
Christie's 129
CIGNA 50, 51
Civil Cooperation Bureau (CCB) 99
Claasen, Jonathan 114
Cliffe Dekker Hofmeyr 42
Coca-Cola 261–262
Coetzee, Dirk 95, 96, 97, 98, 138
Coetzee, Leon 241, 244
Collison, Michael 66–69

Corbett, Michael 101
Corry, Janet 45
COSATU (Congress of South African Trade Unions) 82
Council for Scientific and Industrial Research *see* CSIR
Cradock Four 119–122, 139, 141
Crick, Francis 21
CSIR (Council for Scientific and Industrial Research) 67, 72, 74, 140
Currie, Donald 8–9

DCA *see* Directorate of Civil Aviation
Deal, Jimmy 183
De Kock, Eugene 95, 97, 116
De Lisle, Michael 10–11
De Melker, Daisy 213
Dempers, J.J. 163
Deneys Reitz 52, 142
De Villiers, Leon 15, 15–16
De Villiers (Sanlam) 247, 248
De Villiers, Thea 16
De Witt Morgan 241
Dick, Gavin 185
Di Maio, Vince 202–203
Directorate of Civil Aviation (DCA) 171, 187
Dixon, Roger 221
Doubel, Alf 7
Downes, Roy 171
Drummond, Chris 159
Du Plessis, Barend 121
Du Plessis, Professor

25–26, 27
Du Preez, Max 96, 122
Du Preez, 'Pat' 206, 207, 208
Du Toit, Waal 98
Dynamic Wealth 241–246

Edmonds, Bob 22
Edmonds, Daphne 24
Edwards, Graham 211
Edwards, Susan 50, 51
Elim church fire 139, 141
Eloff, Frikkie 242, 244, 245, 246
Engelbrecht, Krappies 99, 123
Evans, Peter 71, 73

Fagan, Harry 22
Findlay & Tait 88
fire 47–48
    investigation 14, 47, 48, 49, 50, 51, 52, 54, 55, 56
    see also arson
Fischer, Bram 4
footprinting 222, 223–224
Forbes, Alan 35
Friedman, Maggie 136, 137
Froneman, Mark 142

Gardiner, Hugh 71, 72, 73
Gauntlett, Jeremy 88
Gencor 77–78, 80
George, Peter 235
Gevers, Dr 11, 12, 13, 14, 19
Gill, Dorothy 33, 34, 36, 41

Gluckman, Jonathan vii, 83, 87–88
Goldstone, Richard 99
Goniwe, Matthew 119, 120, 121
Gordon (née Klatzow), Gladys [aunt] 3, 4
Gordon, Okkie 161
Greeff, Joshua 274, 275
Green, John 38
Gugulethu Seven 86–91, 95, 99, 108, 110, 273
Gunn, Shirley 134

Hardy, Athol 184
Hare, John 171, 172
Heher, Jonathan 132
Harms Commission of Inquiry 138, 144
Harms, Louis 138, 144, 145
Hart, Gina 186
Hattingh, Christiaan Pieter 185
Hattingh, Flip 116
Hawtrey, Arthur 29, 30
Heath, Marius 237
Heath, Willem 228, 237, 238
Helderberg disaster ix, 165–196
Hermanson, Sister Faith 23
Heyns, Anton 266
Hippert, Jimmy 193
Hlophe, John 274, 275
Hoffmann, Magistrate 92, 110
Hoffman, Paul 155
Hogan, Barbara 136
Holmes, Warrant Officer 211

horse racing 34–35, 252
Human, Justice 154

Israel, Syd 6

Jacoob, Zac 124
Jansen, Leendert 175
Jansen, Paul 104
Jenkins, Trevor 103
Jockey Club 34–36
Joffe, Mr 64–66
Johnson, Charles 233

Kassner, Grant 42
Kebble, Brett 228–239
Kebble, Roger 229
Kennedy, Robert F. 274
Khotso House 134, 135
Kingsmead School for Girls 24
King, William 75, 76
Kinross mining disaster 77–82
Kirby, Robert 170, 196, 264
Kirk, Paul 191
Klatzow, Cathryn [daughter] 51
Klatzow, Cyril [father] 3, 4, 6, 7, 15, 21, 36, 39
Klatzow, David
 background 3–6
 childhood 6–16
 education 8–24
 academic life
   career 24–33
   back-biting 32
   competition 28, 32
   research funding 32
 handyman, life as a 30–31, 36
 meeting and marrying Geraldine 24

divorce from Geraldine 30
 meeting and marrying Shelona 50–51
 forensic career, start of 33, 34
 marriage and raising children 51
 on the apartheid era ix, x, xi, 30, 84, 119, 124, 144, 149, 273
 cases arising from apartheid-era oppression 86, 88, 96, 99, 100, 104, 105, 113, 114, 121, 122, 123, 136, 152, 180
 philosophy on science 2–3, 149
Klatzow, James [son] 51, 125
Klatzow, Jonas and Leah [grandparents] 3
Klatzow, Leonard [uncle] 3, 4
Klatzow, Peter [brother] 6, 8, 9, 10
Klatzow, Shelona [wife] 50–51, 125, 136, 137
Klatzow (née Blatchford), Winifred Mabel [mother] 3, 5, 6, 7, 8, 10, 11, 16, 18, 19, 21, 23
Knobel, Deon 92, 108, 109
Kobrin, Janet 210–212
Kobrin matter 210–212
Kobrin, Raymond 210–212
Koch, Alfred 235, 236
Kossuth, Reg 37
Krebs, Maria 206–208
Krebs, Ralf 206–208

Kriegler, Johann 101, 132
Kriel, Ashley 103, 104–112, 141, 157, 273
Kritzinger, Klippies 98
Kruger, Jeremy 139, 141
Kruger, T.C.B. (Theuns) 171, 175

Landy, Charles 52
Lang, Dr 102, 103
Langa, Pius 276
Lategan, Jan 193
Lawyers for Human Rights 140
Lecante, Willem 241, 242
Legal Aid 250
Legal Resources Centre vii, ix, 84, 86, 143
Le Grange, Louis 87
Lemmer, J.M. 87
Lewis, Vic 51
lock-picking 59–61
Look, Flippie 171, 172
Loots, Beau 19
Lotz, Inge 1, 2, 163, 216–227
Louw, Leonard 246, 247, 248

Machel, Samora 166
Maclean, Donald 4
MADD see Mothers Against Drunken Driving
Magmoed, Shaun 114
Mail & Guardian 170, 196, 264, 290
Major, Tibor 129, 130, 131, 132
Malan, Dok 192

Malan, Magnus 188
Mamasela, Joe 96
Mandrax 145–149, 149, 253
Margo, Cecil ix, 166
Margo Commission of Inquiry 172, 195
Maritime & General Insurance Co. v Sky Unit Engineering 51–53
Maritz, Frans 225
Marquess of Queensberry 64
Matodzi Resources Limited 234
Matthee, Mervyn 255–256
Mbeki, Thabo 267
MCC see Medicines Control Council
McIntosh, Jimmy 53–54
McLaughlin and Lazar 23
Medicines Control Council (MCC) 146
Mellett, Leon 87
mercury, red 169
Meyer, Lucas 185
Mhlauli, Sicelo 119, 120
Miggels, Isaac 161, 162, 163
Miller, Andrew Kenneth 186
Minnaar, Andrew 233, 234, 235
Miranda, Michael 114
Mitchell, Mickey 183
Mitton, Jimmy 179, 186
MK see Umkhonto we Sizwe
Mkhize, Saul 85–86
Mkhonto, Sparrow 119, 120

Mlangeni, Bheki 97
Mostert, Floris 137
Mostert, Pietman 92, 108, 236
Mothers Against Drunken Driving (MADD) 42
Mtimkulu, Siphiwo 103
Munitoria Building 54–55
Mxenge, Griffiths 96
Myburgh, Bert 26, 27, 28

National Party (NP) 95, 117, 150, 151, 154, 267
National Prosecuting Authority (NPA) 191
National Union of Mineworkers 79
Nassif, Clinton 230, 233, 236, 237
Ndita, Tandaswa 275
Neaves, John 52
Neethling, Lothar 42, 91, 98, 100, 124, 145, 148, 149, 175, 277
Nel, Jurie 92, 108, 161
Nelson, Horatio 5
Newton, Dr 55
Nicholas, H.C. viii
Nienaber, Constable 85
Nofemela, Butana Almond 96, 145
Noseweek 247, 275
NPA see National Prosecuting Authority
NP see National Party
Ntsele, Dominic 234

Omar, Dullah 194
Orr, Wendy 102–103

Paarl Print factory fire 75–76
Padi and Faith (murder victims) 82
Pahad, Essop 234
Pahl, Basil 72
Pauw, Jacques 95, 97
Paver, Vera 24–25
Perón, Eva 169
Personal Finance 290
Philby, Kim 4
Piet Retief massacre 122–125
Plewman, Chris 82
poisoning 213–215
police
  apartheid-era attitudes 8–9
  Ashley Kriel case 103, 105–111
  atrocities 91
  attitudes 57
  Cradock Four case 120–164
  Elim Church fire 139–142
  fire investigation 42, 74, 75, 76
  forensics 42, 100, 102, 145, 146, 148, 149, 175, 273
  Gugulethu Seven case 86–91
  Henry Burt case 152–156
  incompetence 142–143, 212, 216
  Inge Lotz case 1, 2, 216–227
  Kebble case 228, 230, 233
  Khotso House case 134–135

Mkhize case 85
Oribi Hotel surveillance 138
Piet Retief massacre 122–125
politicisation 277
procedure 210
riot control 30
security police 103, 191
Trojan Horse Massacre 113–118
Webster case 135–138
wrongful shooting 82
polygraph test 61–62
Pretorius, Christo 219
Pretorius, Torie 191, 193, 194

Queensberry rules 64
Quincy 270, 271

Ramaphosa, Cyril 79, 80
Rasethaba, Sello 234
Ras, Leonie 229, 230, 233
Regina Mundi church, Soweto 150, 151
Reitz, Deneys 50
Reynolds, Peter 171
Rushton, Gordon 88

SAA (South African Airways) 165, 166, 167, 168, 170, 171, 172, 180, 181, 183, 185, 188, 192, 193, 194, 195, 196
SAASCO *see* South African Air Safety Council
Sabbagh, Danny 235
SABC *see* South African Broadcasting Corporation

SABS (South African Bureau of Standards) 98
SACC *see* South African Council of Churches
Sachs, Albie 100
SADF *see* South African Defence Force
SAFEX Rules 245
SAIA *see* South African Insurance Assurance
SAMJ (*South African Medical Journal*) 28, 265, 266
SANBS *see* South African National Blood Service
Sandberg, Piet 55, 56
sangoma case 250–251
Sanlam 240, 241, 246
SAPS *see* South African Police Service
Schoeman, Bennie 218
Schroeder, Hein 167
Schultz, Mikey 238
Schutz, Peter 210
Schwär, Theo 92, 108
Scope magazine 208
Scottish Mutual International 241
Scott, Ray 179
Seady, Helen 82
Selebi, Jackie 236, 237, 238
Sewnarain, Jerry 31
Shapiro, Hillel 33, 37, 38
Shipman, Harold 158
Simpson, O.J. 226
Skeat, Peter 235, 236
Sky Unit Engineering 51–53
Sleight, A.W. 169
Smit, Koos 27, 28

Smith, Lionel Shelsley 92, 108, 203
Sneeuberger (locksmith) 59
Snelgar, Tony 171
Son, Die 290
Sonnenberg, Cecelia 4
South African Air Safety Council (SAASCO) 187
South African Airways *see* SAA
South African Broadcasting Corporation (SABC) 92
South African Bureau of Standards *see* SABS
South African Council of Churches (SACC) 134, 135
South African Council for Natural Scientific Professions 76
South African Defence Force (SADF) 113
South African Insurance Assurance (SAIA) 62
South African Medical Journal see SAMJ
South African National Blood Service (SANBS) 28, 29, 265
South African Police Service (SAPS) 65, 227 *see also* police
Southeard, Greg 171
Southwood, Brian 172
Spruyt, Louis 11
Stamps, early Japanese 128, 129
Stern, Michael 8, 9, 10
Sterns 128
Strauss, Johann 73

Stroud, Maureen 38
Strydom, Johan 241, 242, 243, 244
Suzman, Helen 126
Swart, Blackie 185

Taljaard, Piet 193
Tambo, Oliver 8
Taylor, Jeremy 10
Taylor, Rob 9
Thatcher, Margaret 169
Thring, Wilfred 275
Tobias, Philip 103
Traverso, Jeanette 156, 276
Trojan Horse Massacre 113–118
Truth and Reconciliation Commission (TRC) 92, 195–196, 273
Tutu, Bishop Desmond 124
Tshabalala-Msimang, Manto 265
Tucker, Dr 102, 103
Twigge, Lieutenant 146
Tyson, Peter 32

Umkhonto we Sizwe (MK) 105, 122
United Nations (UN) 147, 290
University
of Cape Town (UCT) 92
of Durban-Westville 29, 31
of Fort Hare 120
of KwaZulu-Natal 29
of Manchester 136
of Natal 29
of the Orange Free State 4

of Oxford 4
of Pretoria 210
of Stellenbosch 116, 117, 161, 217
of the Witwatersrand (Wits) 2, 16, 17, 26, 27, 52
Uys, Dawie 165, 168, 170, 171, 176, 190, 191, 192, 193, 196
Uys, Dirk 274, 275
Uys, Johanna 191, 192, 193, 194

Van der Spuy, Johan 90
Van der Veer, Gert 170
Van der Vijver, Christhénus 275
Van der Vyver, Frederik Barend (Fred) 1, 216–227
Van der Walt, Stephen 75
Van Eeden, Eugene 246, 248
Van Heerden, Captain 172, 174
Van Niekerk, Dr 41
Van Nieuwenhuizen, Solly 42, 43, 126
Van Vuuren, Wynand 55–56
Van Zyl, Deon 225
Van Zyl, Renée 187
Veenendal, Leonard 100
Venter, Superintendent 192
Verhoef, Gordon 200
Verhoef, Jamie 200–203
Vermooten, Justice 208
Viljoen, Henri 254, 276
Viljoen, Tony 172–174
Virtue, Louis 146

Vlakplaas 94–103, 122, 145, 152
Vlok, Adriaan 87, 95, 135
Von Wesel, Nick 42, 43
Vorster, Vossie 185
Vos, Gerard 28–29
Vrye Weekblad 97, 99, 100, 101, 122, 124

Watson, James D. 21
Weatherby, Geraldine 24, 30

Weaver, Tony 87, 89, 91, 95
    trial 90
Webber Wentzel Bowens 171
websites 290
Webster, David 122, 135–137, 138, 141
Weekend Star 168, 170, 171, 172
Welch, John 194
Welz, Martin 275
Wentzel case 240–246

Whale, Mark 194
Wiggins Teape 131
Witbank Kombi Murder 142
Witdoeke 86
Wolmarans, Wollie 137, 203

Young, Anthony 76
Yule, Mr 10

Zapiro 277
Zumph, Dr 214